...hwitters Theo van Doesburg Claude...

...ander Rodchenko Karel Teige Josef Schmidt Georgii Stenberg

...eveld Max Burchartz Walter Gropius László Moholy-Nagy

...arie Čermínová Sybold van Ravesteyn Theo van Doesburg

Josef Šíma Nikolai Prusakov Grigori Ilyich Cyril Bouda

...tunato Depero Otto Baumberger César Domela Gustav Klutsis

...ema Donald Brun Georg Trump Willem Hendrik Gispen

...n (Hans) Arp Walter Cyliax A. M. Cassandre Man Ray

...wski Solomon Telingater Paul Urban Max Bill Jacob Jongert

...mberger František Muzika Pizzi & Pizio Xanti Schawinsky

...něk Rossmann Hans Aeschbach Hermann Eidenbenz

**The Enduring
Legacy of Weimar**
Graphic Design &
New Typography
1919–1933

Alston W. Purvis Cees W. de Jong

The Enduring Legacy of Weimar
Graphic Design & New Typography 1919-1933

Prestel
Munich · London · New York

"It was an age of miracles,
it was an age of art,
it was an age of excess ..."

F. Scott Fitzgerald, *The Crackup*

Contents

10
Cees W. de Jong
The Future

14
Alston W. Purvis
Weimar: An Overview

20
The Impact of Futurism

24
German Dada, Collage, and Photomontage

34
The Bauhaus

48
The Russian Influence

56
Independent Designers in the Netherlands

64
Jan Tschichold and New Typography

70
Weimar's End and its Enduring Legacy

74
Cees W. de Jong & Alston W. Purvis
Evident and Alive Today

382
Cees W. de Jong
Sans-serif Typefaces

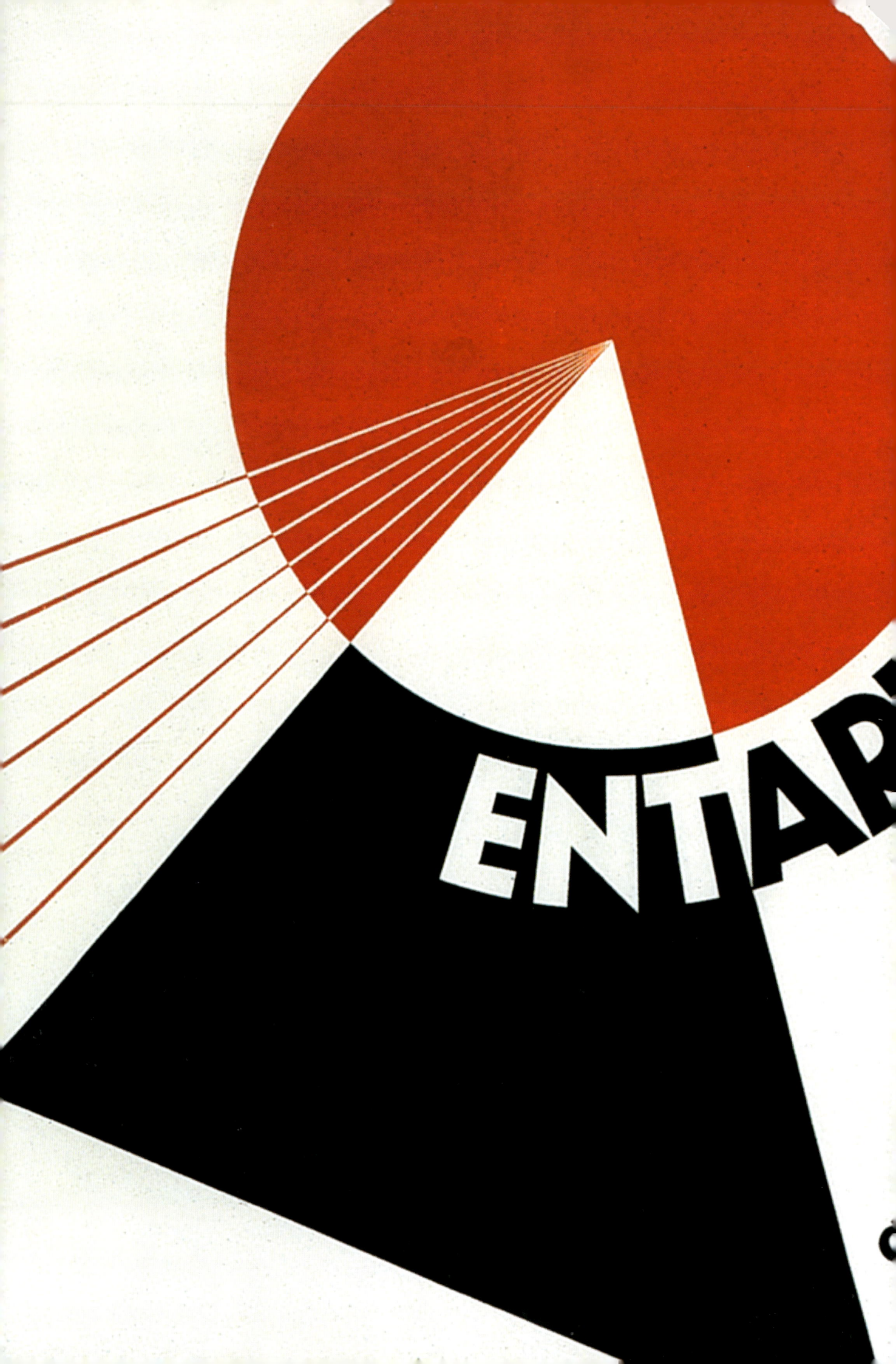

Previous page, a detail of: Hans Vitus Vierthaler (1910-1942), poster for *Entartete Kunst*, the Nazi exhibition of modern art in Munich, in 1936.

The Future

A small group of international artists devoted themselves to visual experiments in a wide variety of printed matter and design. This often politically motivated avant-garde group—Futurists, Dadaists, Constructivists, and others—emphatically rejected traditional aesthetic views.

During the Weimar Republic, the political posters of various movements and parties attracted great interest. You could not escape the large, colorful posters. The Nazi Party drew up precise guidelines for these. Texts had to be short and striking, and red, "the color of the revolution," had to dominate. The Fraktur font, part of the group of Gothic block letters, was often used for the typography. A continuous repetition of fixed themes was also prescribed. After the party seized power in 1933, this propaganda was fully put into the service of the *Reichsministerium für Volksaufklärung und Propaganda* (Reich Ministry of Public Enlightenment and Propaganda), led by Joseph Goebbels.

Special attention is given to the unusual development of the work of Suprematist and later Constructivist artist El Lissitzky (1890-1941). His style was imitated by Hans Vitus Vierthaler (1910-1942) when Vierthaler created the poster for *Entartete Kunst*, the Nazi exhibition of modern art in Munich in 1936. The graphic design of Vierthaler's exhibition poster features a black triangle that penetrates a red circle; the triangle's tip turns into a white wedge. The typography is sans serif. To advertise this exhibition, condemning modern, progressive, avant-garde art, Vierthaler borrowed the style of El Lissitzky.

Why did Vierthaler design this poster in this way? What were the guidelines of the Reich Ministry? And what concept played a part in this exhibition about "*entartete Kunst*" (degenerate art) that led them to create a poster in the Constructivist style?

For the cover of this publication, I did not borrow the style of Jean Arp and Walter Cyliax, using elements from the exhibition poster for Kunsthaus Zürich's *Abstrakte und surrealistische Malerei und Plastik*, 1929. Rather, I made a tribute to these artists. The circle as an element was used by several artists such as El Lissitzky, Jean Arp, Walter Cyliax, and Jan Tschichold. This new cover was designed with black, white, and red colors and a modern font, Avenir Next.

The font used for this book is Avenir Next (2004), designed by Adrian Frutiger (1928–2015). It is an adaptation of Frutiger's original 1988 design for Linotype in Bad Homburg, produced in collaboration with Akira Kobayashi (born in 1960). Avenir Next is a more humanist approach to the geometric-style sans serifs that emerged after the late 1920s such as Futura, designed in 1927 by Paul Renner (1878–1956) for the Bauer Type Foundry in Frankfurt am Main.

Accessible. The images in this publication are presented by artist and are all arranged in chronological order. You can find the development of the visual experiments in a wide variety of printed matter and design from 1919 to 1933.

As always, it was a pleasure to work together again with Alston W. Purvis, Professor of Visual Arts at Boston University's College of Fine Arts. Our collaboration has worked well for many years. And special thanks are extended to Martijn Le Coultre, IADBB.

This new aesthetic approach, which was created in a turbulent Europe between 1919 and 1933, has become a part of our global life. Perhaps motivated avant-garde designers can now find new ways to inspire us all for the future.

Cees W. de Jong

bauh

dess

Previous page, a detail of: Franz Ehrlich, poster for Bauhaus, Dessau, im Gewerbemuseum Basel, 1929.

Weimar: An Overview

The Weimar Republic is an informal name for Germany from the beginning of 1919 to January 30, 1933. The name has its basis in the city of Weimar, where the Republic's first constitutional assembly was held. However, the official designation of the country continued to be the *Deutsches Reich*, as it had been since 1871. In English-speaking countries, it was still known only as Germany.

The Weimar Republic, although culturally one of the most exciting periods in European history, was compelled to compromise from its beginning, and during its 15 years of existence it was beleaguered by continual problems including hyperinflation, war reparations, internal strife, political innocence, and extremism from both the Left and the Right. Unaccustomed to establishing political parties, the country was divided among almost 125, usually very weak, factions, making it very difficult to choose a president. In fact, there were only two: Friedrich Ebert (1871–1925), trained as a saddle-maker, and Paul Ludwig Hans Anton von Beneckendorff und von Hindenburg (1837–1934), a former general. In spite of the fact, however, that it was a political failure, the Weimar Republic was able to survive until the end of January 1933, and for a while it proved to be a period of artistic renewal, especially in the field of graphic design. In the preface to his 1980 book *Weimar: A Cultural History*, Walter Laqueur rightly referred to Weimar as "the first truly modern culture."

There are many important individuals in graphic design associated with the Weimar period. Within the Dada movement, these include Wieland Herzfelde (1896–1988), his brother John Heartfield (1891–1968), the painter George Grosz (1893–1959), Raoul Hausmann (1886–1977), Erwin Blumenfeld (1897–1969), Kurt Schwitters (1887–1948), and Hannah Höch (1889–1978). The Bauhaus included its founder and leading figure Walter Gropius (1883–1969), Lyonel Feininger (1871–1956), Johannes Itten (1888–1967), Wassily Kandinsky (1866–1944), Paul Klee (1879–1940), Gerhard Marcks (1889–1981), Oskar Schlemmer (1988–1943), and László Moholy-Nagy (1895–1946). Of monumental importance was Jan Tschichold (1902–1974), the driving force in the New Typography.

As Germany's largest city, Berlin was the only logical choice for the capital of the Weimar Republic. The previous Berlin had been imposing, but the new Berlin was the place for the determined, the spirited, and the artistic. As Peter Gay wrote in his book *Weimar Culture: The Outsider as Insider*, "It enchanted most, frightened some, but no one was left apathetic."

By the time German representatives had signed an armistice to end First World War combat on November 11, 1918, numerous political factions had already appeared on the scene. The most extreme was the Spartacus League headed by Karl Liebknecht (1871–1919) and Rosa Luxemburg (1871–1919), whose goal was to create a communist state. Two months after the armistice, on January 6, 1919, the Spartacists initiated an effort to depose Chancellor Friedrich Ebert and the interim government. Ebert used the Reichswehr (the professional army) and the Berlin Freikorps, a private militia consisting mainly of former soldiers, to quickly thwart the revolt. Liebknecht and Luxemburg were captured by Freikorps officers and brutally murdered.

A National Assembly was elected on January 19, 1919. To avoid the endless Berlin street battles, it met in Weimar, thus resulting in the Republic's unofficial name. The Assembly elected Ebert, of the Social Democratic Party (SPD), the Republic's first *Reichspräsident*. He signed the new German constitution on August 11, 1919, creating a parliamentary republic. The Treaty of Versailles, which officially ended the First World War, was signed that same summer, on June 28, 1919; it took effect on January 10, 1920. The French, guided by Prime Minister Clemenceau, were out for reprisal and wanted to make certain that Germany would never again endanger France. The treaty limited the size of the Reichswehr to 100,000 soldiers, restricted the navy to 36 ships, and allowed no air force whatsoever, thus leaving the country with almost no fighting abilities. Although theoretically in service of the Republic, the army was led predominantly by largely aristocratic conservatives sympathetic to the Right. For Germany, the harshest term was Article 231, the War Guilt Clause, which stated that Germany had to accept the blame for starting the war.

The treaty also forbade Germany from joining the League of Nations, thus branding Germany as a pariah among other countries, especially in Europe. Naturally, the Treaty of Versailles was insufferable to most Germans, whatever their political stance, left or right.

The Treaty of Versailles subjected Germans to exceedingly severe conditions. Germany was forced to cede 13% of its territory and 48% of its iron production, and more than 6 million citizens found themselves living in other countries. Inflation began to increase at a disturbing rate, as the government steadily printed more currency to pay these debts.

By 1923, Germany maintained it could no longer pay the reparations required by the Versailles Treaty and defaulted on some payments. French and Belgian troops occupied the Ruhr Valley, Germany's most productive industrial area, in January 1923 after Germany again failed to pay reparations on schedule to those countries. The occupation engendered passive resistance as well as industrial sabotage. Workers in the Ruhr Valley went on strike, and when a number of them were shot by French troops, their funerals sparked massive demonstrations against the invaders. This all served to unite Germans in their loathing of the French and Belgians.

As striking workers in the Ruhr Valley were still being paid by the government, additional currency was continually printed, resulting in hyperinflation. Million-mark banknotes were soon replaced by thousand-million-mark notes as the official exchange rate rose from 320,000 marks to the dollar on November 2, 1923 to around 4.2 billion marks to the dollar on November 20. By that time, more than two hundred factories were soon producing paper just to cover the escalating banknote production. Many people saw their savings vanish, and those with normal incomes became destitute overnight.

The Treaty of Versailles added to the humiliation of Germany's defeat in the war. The German cabinet had first rejected the terms of the settlement, but the public was unaware that the Allies had informed their leaders that a rejection of the conditions would result in a renewal of hostilities and an invasion of Germany. Criticism of the government escalated and the theory that the politicians had stabbed the army in the back became widespread.

Adolf Hitler constantly criticized the Republic for accepting the terms of the Treaty of Versailles. On the night of November 8, 1923, he and former German Army commander Erich von Ludendorff (1865-1937), along with 600 Nazis, took over a political meeting being held in the Bürgerbräukeller, a huge Munich beer hall. They declared the Weimar government deposed and stated that they would seize Munich. While marching through the center of town the next day, they were met by police. Gunfire ensued, with 16 Nazis and four police officers being killed. The Nazis fled, and Hitler disappeared in the confusion. However, he was arrested two days later and accused of treason. His one-month trial began in February 1924 and gave him widespread notoriety with much of the population in Germany. He dismissed the charge of treason outright and insisted he was only attempting to oppose what he considered the pathetic and corrupt Weimar government. He ranted against the Treaty of Versailles and used the trial to cleverly promote his political ideas. He was found guilty of treason and sentenced on April 1. While in jail, Hitler dictated his book *Mein Kampf* (*My Struggle*), which elaborated his future plans. He ended up serving only nine months of his five-year sentence before being released on December 20, 1924.

The German Communist Party, the KPD, on the other hand, slowly recovered from the 1919 Spartacist Uprising and the murders of Liebknecht and Luxemburg. In 1923, KPD party representative Ernst Thälmann abandoned any hopes of a revolution, and beginning in 1924, the KPD simply contested elections like any other political party.

In the meantime, Gustav Stresemann (1878–1929), chancellor since the summer of 1923, stabilized the inflation crisis first by introducing a new currency, the Rentenmark, which gradually restored the confidence of the German people in their money.

Stresemann persuaded the French, British and Americans to change the reparation conditions through the Dawes Plan, named after the US vice-president and banker Charles Dawes (1865–1951), who had played a major role in negotiating the agreement. Principal aspects were a reduction in the reparation payment schedule, the withdrawal of French and Belgian troops from the Ruhr Valley, and loans from the United States to help bring about an economic recovery. Stresemann's policy succeeded, to some extent due to a change of the French government, but mainly due to the international loans through which a stable German economy would be able to pay reparations and at the same time be attractive to American investors. The actual degree of the recovery has, however, been a matter of dispute, particularly due to the overdependence on American banks.

Under Stresemann's leadership, the Republic was able to successfully thwart attacks from both the Right and the Left. From 1924 until the Wall Street crash in October 1929, there was at least a semblance of political stability. Even though no party had a majority in the Reichstag (parliament), the Social Democrats always received the most votes up until 1930, and there was more support for parties that endorsed the Weimar Republic than for extremists such as the Nazis.

This stability was mainly the accomplishment of two men, Stresemann and von Hindenburg. Stresemann's diplomatic accomplishments outside Germany made him a popular political figure. Von Hindenburg, a war leader, was elected president in 1925, perhaps indicating that the conservatives had more or less decided to come to terms with the Republic. However, the Republic was constantly under attack from both the Left and Right. The Left accused the Social Democrats of betraying the workers, and the Right was against democracy of any kind. Yet during the next five years, the government managed to survive.

Previous page, a detail of: Fortunato Depero, cover for *Secolo XX*, 1928.

The Impact of Futurism

Futurism began when Italian poet Filippo Marinetti (1876–1944) published his Manifesto of Futurism in the Paris newspaper *Le Figaro* on February 20, 1909. This launched Futurism as a movement in which the arts confronted a new industrial society:

"We intend to sing the love of danger, the habit of energy and fearlessness. Courage, audacity, and revolt will be essential elements of our poetry.... We affirm that the world's magnificence has been enriched by a new beauty: the beauty of speed ... a roaring car that seems to ride on grapeshot is more beautiful than the *Victory of Samothrace*.... Except in struggle, there is no more beauty. No work without an aggressive character can be a masterpiece."

The manifesto endorsed war, the new machine age, speed, and modern life in general. It stunned society by declaring, "We will destroy museums, libraries, and fight against moralism, feminism, and all utilitarian cowardice."

Marinetti and his supporters produced a passion-laden poetry that defied appropriate syntax and grammar.

In January 1913, Giovanni Papini (1881–1956) began the journal *Lacerba* in Florence, and typography was challenged on every front. The June 1913 issue published Marinetti's announcement a revolt against classical typography. Harmony was rejected as it conflicted with "the leaps and bursts of style running through the page." On a page, three or four colors and many typefaces could increase the expressive impact of words. A new form of typography, called *parole in libertá* or "words in freedom," came into being.

Noise and speed were expressed in Futurist poetry. Marinetti urged poets to liberate themselves from grammar and explore new ways of expression. Since Gutenberg, most graphic design had been bound to a horizontal and vertical structure, but Futurist poets rejected such constraints outright and animated their pages with dynamic, nonlinear compositions.

In 1897 the French Symbolist poet Stéphane Mallarmé (1842–1898) published the poem "Un coup de dés" ("A Throw of the Dice"), where instead of using words in a linear sequence, he placed them in various places on the page to evoke ideas. Another French poet, Guillaume Apollinaire (1880–1918), published a book of poems entitled *Calligrammes* in 1918 in which letterforms form figures or pictographs. In these poems he explored the potential fusion of poetry and painting, introducing the concept of simultaneity to the time- and sequence-bound typography of the printed page.

Among the artists who used Futurist concepts in graphics and design, Fortunato Depero (1892–1960) produced a dynamic body of work in posters, typographic works, and advertising. In 1927 Depero published his *Depero futurista,* a collection of his typographic experiments, advertisements, and other works. From September 1928 until October 1930, Depero worked in New York and designed covers for the magazines *Vanity Fair, Movie Makers,* and *Sparks,* as well as print advertising. Futurism became a major influence on other art movements, and its violent, revolutionary techniques were adopted by the Dadaists, Constructivists, and De Stijl.

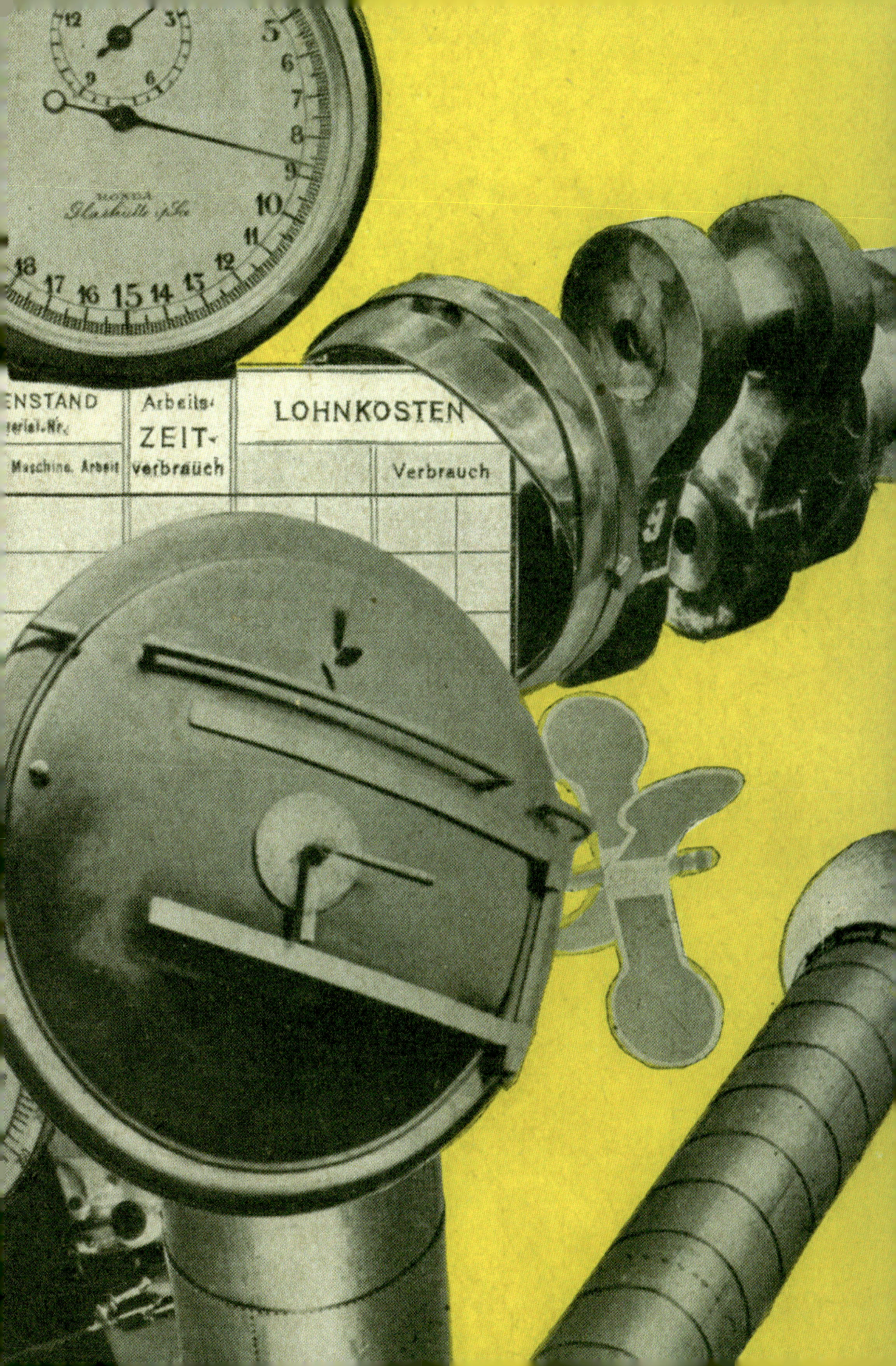

Previous page, a detail of: John Heartfield, cover for *Das deutsche Wirtschaftswunder*, c. 1926.

German Dada, Collage, and Photomontage

Dadaism first appeared in Zurich during World War I, when mainly German artists reacted against the war and its disastrous effect on European culture. Hans Arp (1887–1966), the poet Hugo Ball (1886–1927), and Richard Huelsenbeck (1892–1974) had emigrated from Germany to Switzerland when the war broke out. They were largely influenced by the Futurist Marinetti but without his nationalist philosophy and enthusiasm for war.

Reacting to the devastation of World War I, Dadaists promoted anti-art with a scathing approach. They were devoted to shock, dissent, and nonsense; discarding all social mores, they pursued total liberty. Dada began as a group after Ball launched the Cabaret Voltaire in Zurich as a meeting site for independent and original poets, painters, and musicians. Among Dada's principal members was a young and volatile Paris-based Rumanian poet, Tristan Tzara (1896–1963), who became editor of the periodical *Dada* in July 1917. Together with Ball, Arp, and Huelsenbeck, Tzara began to exploit sound, absurd, and accidental poetry. He created numerous Dada manifestos and participated in most Dada periodicals and events. Fortuitous placement and illogical titles typified his graphics.

Dadaism first appeared in Germany during World War I, with Berlin as its initial starting point. Those close to Wieland Herzfelde's (1896-1988) Malik publishing house, among others his brother John Heartfield (1891-1968), George Grosz (1893-1959), Raoul Hausmann (1886-1977), and Hannah Höch (1889-1978), were captivated by Richard Huelsenbeck's concepts brought from the Cabaret Voltaire in Zurich. What was mainly an aesthetic outrage in Zurich became in Berlin a movement of politically inclined artists. On February 15, 1919, a newspaper called *Jedermann sein eigner Fussball* (*Everyman His Own Football*) appeared in Berlin. Issued by Herzfelde's publishing house, Malik, it satirized with scathing humor everything the Dadaists despised. It attacked those who had begun the war, the church, the military, the aristocracy, and the bourgeois arts establishment in general. The typography was perplexing, with lines set in various angles in different typefaces as seen in future Dada magazine designs.

The Cabaret Voltaire functioned like other art institutions, and the bourgeois culture in Zurich was never really affected. In Berlin, though, it was a different story. Intellectuals connected with Malik united to start the Club Dada, but there were no art programs as such. The basic goal of the Berlin Dadaists was to destroy the art establishment in general. They did not have galleries, and used whatever became available. Just as armed battles occurred in the streets, Berlin Dadaists took their cultural revolution there as well and directed their efforts against Weimar politics. In no way did they want to begin a new artistic school, but instead they were against all styles and schools.

The bimonthly illustrated magazine *Die Pleite*, which began after *Jedermann sein eigner Fussball* had been prohibited, became an outlet for the Dadaists who had become members of the Communist Party or agreed with its politics. Herzfelde, Heartfield, and Grosz became adept political journalists, and Grosz's illustrations provided the paper with a sharp vision. Grosz was quite prolific in 1922-1923, producing *Ecce Homo,* his major collection of satires, and illustrating some twenty-one books. The Malik publishing house managed to survive during the currency crisis, and Herzfelde moved the company to new quarters with a separate gallery to display Grosz's work. Malik then became a main publisher of Russian and other left-wing writing, and Herzfelde and Grosz were again prosecuted, this time for the supposed indecency of *Ecce Homo*.

By far the master of radical bitterness in Berlin was Grosz. He denounced what he considered the acquiescence of Weimar politics with its meaningless rhetoric and assurances for brighter prospects to a generation half destroyed in World War I. Grosz often used prostitutes in his illustrations and attacked them with an ethical venom that had seldom been evidenced in art for centuries. For Grosz, everything and everybody in Germany was up for sale. Raised in a military milieu, Grosz volunteered at the beginning of the war for a squadron that was sent to the Western Front. Having become sick with brain fever and dysentery, he was soon discharged but was recruited again in the winter of 1917. On January 4 he was sent to a hospital, then transferred to an asylum.

After three months he was discharged, unrepentant as ever and with his detestation of the regime only solidified. Grosz was intimately connected with Herzfelde and Heartfield. He attacked what he considered an immoral culture and encouraged a social order devoid of any class distinctions. His illustrations possess the angry strength of profound political beliefs regarding what he considered a corrupt and decadent environment.

German Dadaists furthered a radical typographic method in an attack on what they considered bourgeois values. Through discarding all traditions in art and design, they produced leaflets and newspapers that promoted communist dogmas using unconventional type and images. Displaying a total repudiation of what Dadaists saw as obsolete design, the movement had an indirect effect on what would later become known as the New Typography. They wanted to promote a fresh art, or more specifically an anti-art. To Dadaists, life was simultaneously a jumble of discordant sounds, colors, and rhythms. Dada soon moved from Zurich to other cities throughout Europe. The Dadaists proclaimed that they were not interested in creating art but that they instead wanted to ridicule and libel a civilization gone mad. However, in spite of themselves, several Dadaists created important visual art and significantly affected the field of graphic design. Dada artists maintained that they conceived the medium of photomontage, a method of deploying parts of recovered photographs taken from magazines and newspapers to produce clashing combinations and new connotations. Raoul Hausmann (1886-1977), Hannah Höch (1889-1978), and Erwin Blumenfeld (1897-1969) were doing exceptional work in this medium by 1918 and considered photomontage the most effective approach to expressing the contemporary world, employing the mystery of dreams and photographic directness and realism. Blumenfeld was born in Berlin and immigrated to the United States in 1941. There he became a successful fashion photographer, producing work for *Harper's Bazaar*, *Life* magazine, and *Vogue*.

The great expressive artist of Dada was Kurt Schwitters (1887-1948) from Hannover, who created works of art from scraps of paper and objects found on the street. He created an apolitical derivative of Dada that he called Merz, invented from the word *Kommerz* (commerce) in one of his early collages. By 1919, these Merz pictures became magnificent arrangements employing ephemera, trash, and other found ingredients to contrast colors, shapes, and textures. His complex compositions used the Dada components of nonsense, surprise, and chance together with a keen design sensibility. When he attempted to become part of the Dada movement as "an artist who nails his pictures together," he was rejected for appearing too bourgeois. Rather than having a bohemian appearance, he looked more like a banker. Schwitters both wrote and designed poetry that contrasted logic with nonsense. His definition of poetry was basically a combination of letters, syllables, words, and sentences. By the early 1920s, Constructivism became an additional inspiration for Schwitters after he'd met Russian Constructivist El Lissitzky (1890-1941) and the founder of the De Stijl movement, Theo van Doesburg (1883-1931), the latter inviting him to the Netherlands to endorse Dada.

There, together with artist and art historian Kate Steinitz (1889-1975), Schwitters and van Doesburg produced the booklet *Die Scheuche: Märchen* (*The Scarecrow: A Fairy Tale*), in which type was transformed into playful figures. From 1923 until 1932, Schwitters published twenty-four issues of his journal *Merz*, with the eleventh issue being devoted to advertising typography. During this period, Schwitters ran a successful graphic design business with Pelikan, a manufacturer of office equipment, ink and other supplies. In addition, the city of Hannover hired him as a typography consultant for a number of years. When the political situation in Germany worsened during the early 1930s, Schwitters began staying in Norway and moved to Oslo in 1937. After Germany invaded Norway in 1940, he fled to the United Kingdom, where he remained until his death. Ironically, during his later years he reverted to traditional painting, mainly landscapes.

Differing with the artistic endeavors of Schwitters, the Berlin Dadaist brothers John Heartfield (1891-1968) and Wieland Herzfelde (1896-1988), along with the painter Grosz, maintained strong political beliefs and devoted most of their art to inciting public awareness and advancing changes in existing society. John Heartfield was the English name assumed by Helmut Herzfelde in dissent against German bellicosity and the army in which he had served from 1914 to 1916. The most forceful political exploitation of photomontage is seen in the work of Heartfield who, during the late 1920s and early 1930s, raised it to a fever pitch of provocative intensity. No artist has ever attained this force. Through photomontage, Heartfield was able to accomplish what could not be achieved through painting. Only the direct realism and accuracy of photography made this work credible. His commanding political use of photomontage elevated it to a provocative level. An original affiliate of the Berlin Dada group in 1919, Heartfield utilized the abrasive quality of photomontage as a propaganda tool. He uncompromisingly attacked the Weimar Republic and the growing Nazi Party in book jackets, magazine covers, and illustrations for the *Arbeiter Illustrierte Zeitung* (*AIZ: Workers' Illustrated Newspaper*), along with a few posters. The *AIZ* was the main communist newspaper in Germany. First published in 1930, it ceased to exist in 1938 due to Nazi pressure. Heartfield's montages are among the most crucial in the development of the medium. He did not take his own photographs or retouch existing photographs, but instead used prints obtained from magazines and newspapers and infrequently commissioned images from professional photographers. After stormtroopers occupied his apartment studio in 1933, Heartfield fled to Prague, where he continued his visual assault. In 1938, after learning that he was on a Nazi hit list, he managed to get to London. In 1950, he moved to Leipzig, then in East Germany, where he worked as a designer of theater sets and posters. Before his death in 1968, he designed photomontages protesting the Vietnam War and promoting world peace. *Unfortunately Still Timely* was the title of a retrospective of his work.

The most successful aesthetic user of photomontage in Berlin was clearly Hannah Höch; she worked on a small scale and, unlike Heartfield, never created for reproduction purposes. Her photomontages display a tense, pungent vision, as she cuts into the images and not only around them. Höch was fully cognizant of the latent eroticism of machinery and often used images such as ball and cogs as parts of her themes. In spite of the use of contrasting images, her montages are consistently unified on a single plane. Höch found much creative inspiration in the newspapers and magazines of the time. From the type and images, she further developed the medium of photomontage in which discordant elements were combined to form new and often shocking messages. She was one of the most captivating artists in Berlin until she moved to the Netherlands in 1926. A close friend of Kurt Schwitters, Raoul Hausmann, and Bauhaus designer László Moholy-Nagy, Höch was an innovator of photomontage in Germany, but unlike John Heartfield, who used the medium as a political tool, Höch made it an expressive part of Dadaism.

Wieland Herzfelde, Heartfield's younger brother, worked as a poet, critic, and publisher and briefly edited the periodical *Neue Jugend* (*New Youth*). After being imprisoned in 1914 for distributing communist writing, Wieland began the Malik publishing venture, a leading avant-garde publisher of Dada, leftist political propaganda, and radical writing.

Dada was foremost an energetic force that persisted in inspiring invention and revolt. It began as dissent against warfare, and its caustic and attention-seeking actions became even more radical after World War I. In 1921 and 1922, dissent began to appear among its adherents, and the movement began to fragment. French writer and poet André Breton (1896–1966), earlier involved with the Dadaists, claimed that Dada had lost its bearings, necessitating another route entirely. Without a cohesive path, and with many of its followers gradually moving toward Surrealism, the Dada movement was finished by the end of 1922. However, Schwitters and Heartfield persisted in creating their best work up until the early 1930s. Dada's denunciation of convention made it enhance the visual language initiated by Futurism and produced a typographic revolution. The 1920s witnessed a cultural renaissance in Germany, with cabarets and jazz bars becoming widespread. Art and architecture reflected the new concepts of the day. This period was one of the most exciting in European art and culture, as prewar censorship had been eliminated. In the 1920s, Berlin rivaled Paris as Europe's cultural center, with major advances in painting, architecture, writing, and drama. Artists in Berlin were inspired by progressive cultural movements, such as Impressionism and Cubism in Paris, and much of the new architecture was geometrical in style. However, many conservatives increasing felt that artists were destroying German traditions and were un-German.

Most Weimar artists attempted to depict daily life, as they felt that art should reflect contemporary society. This approach was called *Neue Sachlichkeit* (New Objectivity). As seen in the work of painters such as Grosz, Dada took on a political stance in Germany, quite unlike the anarchist approach in Zurich. Reappearing themes in Berlin Dada were the ubiquitous crippled war veterans who could be seen on almost every street corner in Berlin.

Many young artists also saw the Weimar Republic itself as merely a product of the war, displaying only a semblance of democracy while remaining connected to the old Prussian regime.

In 1921, Raoul Hausmann produced what is probably the best-known of all Dada sculptures, *The Spirit of Our Times*. It exemplifies Hausmann's view that the average German "has no more aptitudes than those which circumstance has pasted on the inside of his cranium: his mind stays vacant."

As Robert Hughes commented in *The Shock of the New*, Weimar Dada "was also visibly and determinedly part of a social whole, and that ambition to work as exemplary public speech, to interpret and comment on and shape the fabric of the time instead of just decorating it, is what makes the culture of Weimar Germany so much more interesting than Paris in the twenties. For a time, Berlin was the leader of modernist culture. Paris Dada is mere froth and capering beside its German equivalent; there is no French architect of the period (except for Le Corbusier, a student of Peter Behrens, who built very little on the twenties) whose achievements in theory and building can be compared with the work of Walter Gropius, Mies van der Rohe, Bruno Taut, or Hans Meyer; no experiment in learning compared to the Bauhaus; no French theater equal in vitality to the work of Brecht and Piscator, and few French films outside the work of Jean Renoir and Vigo's masterpiece *Zéro de conduit* can stand beside the cinema of Lang or Lubitsch."

In 1927, the over-praised director Fritz Lang produced the tasteless film *Metropolis*, a badly conceived and basically reactionary invention. *Metropolis* is shown as a city of the future, where dominated workers struggle in underground factories, while the elite relaxes on large estates with fountains and wandering pet peacocks.

In Berlin, Dada began in a city that existed in a semi-breakdown, both artistically and politically, and the anxiety and hedonism there in the 1920s approximated frenzy. The Spartacists confronted both the army and the Freikorps in street clashes, while the Dadaists calmly conducted a creative and intellectual revolt. Dada was bizarre, but certainly not a prank. Instead, it was indicative of the anguish developed during World War I and the subsequent misery. Supposedly, the name Dada, a colloquial French term a hobby horse, was found by chance in a Larousse French-German dictionary while attempting to find a name for a singer in the Cabaret Voltaire. The origin of the name, though, is debatable. Most Dadaists did not concur regarding its source, typical of the movement's inherent anarchy. The initial exhibition of Dadaist work opened in May 1919, but drew little notice compared to the big International Dada Fair in June 1920. In the latter exhibit, a large banner with the slogan "Dada fights together with the revolutionary proletariat" spanned the exhibition rooms. The image of an army officer with a pig's head hung from the ceiling. Collages and photomontages depicting the muddle of urban life were intermingled with drawings from Grosz's portfolio *Gott mit uns* (*God with Us*).

The fair engendered some intense public reactions, as well as legal problems from the government for what it considered as slandering the military. This large Berlin Dada Fair brought together various German Dada factions. Of the approximately 175 items displayed, more than half were by Grosz, Hausmann, Heartfield, Höch and Herzfelde. The most noticeable Dadaist absence from the fair was Huelsenbeck, who seems to have ended up on bad terms with Hausmann and subsequently rejected Dada to complete his medical studies. The fair was not a great success. Visitors were not all that stunned, and most regarded it as inconsequential. The KPD's daily *Die Rote Fahne* even instructed workers to reject Dada's assaults on their "cultural heritage." To make matters worse, the police, upset by Grosz's biting work, raided the gallery and the Malik Verlag offices, and shortly afterward Grosz and Herzfelde were again accused of insulting the military.

French painter Marcel Duchamp (1887-1968) was soon connected with the Dada movement and most likely became its most famous visual artist. Cubism had initially inspired his motifs of geometric flat surfaces, whereas Futurism moved him to express time and movement. Duchamp became Dada's most eloquent spokesman; to him, both art and life were disciplines of arbitrary possibilities and deliberate selection. This attitude of total liberty permitted Duchamp to produce ready-made sculptures, for example a bicycle wheel mounted on a wooden stool, and display found objects, such as a urinal, as artistic creations. Many in France were incensed when Duchamp painted a mustache on a reproduction of the *Mona Lisa*. However, this was not intended to be an assault on the *Mona Lisa* as a work of art. According to Duchamp, it was simply a criticism aimed at institutions and communities that had lost touch with the actual humanism of the Renaissance.

Expressionism
Expressionism developed as a movement in Germany before the beginning of World War I. Colors, drawings, and proportions were frequently embellished or distorted, and symbolism was a fundamental component. Lines and colors were explicit, and value distinctions were amplified. Tangible effects were achieved through dense paint, open brushwork, and outline drawing. In addition, woodcuts, lithographs, and posters were often important means of expression. Rebelling against predictable artistic approaches and social norms, expressionists had a sense of shared calamity. Most German expressionists rejected the military, the educational system, and governments in general. Instead they felt an empathy for the indigent and for social outcasts, both of whom were regularly illustrated in their work. Idealism inspired their faith in an art in support of a different social structure.

German Expressionism constituted two initial factions: Die Brücke (The Bridge), which began in Dresden in 1905, and Der Blaue Reiter (The Blue Rider), which originated in Munich in 1911. Expressionists purposely followed original approaches to art and life. The Bridge artists converted their themes to convey their own emotions; on the contrary, Blue Rider considered art to be entities without subjects that expressed emotions.

The Bridge's paintings and woodcuts were typified by weighty, fresh lines, often aggressive statements denoting hostility and suffering. German expressionism also involved the theater, film, and literature, as in books such as Franz Kafka's *Metamorphosis* and *The Trial*. Although not tied to any one faction, excellent examples of the expressionist concern for humanity are seen in the drawings, prints, sculptures, and posters of Käthe Schmidt Kollwitz (1867-1945). The wife of a doctor who ran a hospital in a working-class district of Berlin, Kollwitz witnessed firsthand the wretched conditions of the poorer classes and chronicled their predicament with expressive strength. Sympathy for the suffering of women and children is often evident in her poster designs.

Early affiliates of the Blue Rider included Russian émigré Wassily Kandinsky (1866-1944) and Swiss artist Paul Klee (1879-1940). Not so interested in addressing the suffering of society, they instead sought a spiritual truth beyond the physical world and dealt with pure form and color. Kandinsky was the principal advocate of painting that could reveal the spiritual side of life through color, lines, and form. His book *Concerning the Spiritual in Art* (1910) presented the case for non-objective painting that could express emotions without subjects. He compared color and abstraction to music with its ability to express feelings. Inspired by children's and primitive art, Klee attained a subjective strength in his work. His *Pedagogical Sketchbook* (1925) defined the basics of art and its relations and spatial properties. Concepts regarding color and form as pursued by Kandinsky and Klee developed into significant fundamentals for design by their instruction at the Bauhaus.

Klee, like Kandinsky, was devoted to a kind of painting with its roots in German metaphysics. The confirmation of Klee's fixation with metaphysics was an extraordinary book, *The Thinking Eye*, produced during his Bauhaus teaching years. It was one of the most comprehensive guides on the design discipline ever written.

Dadaists promoted an anarchic typographic idiom as a symbol of the destruction of bourgeois values and a mirror of the crises within the Weimar Republic, which after World War I was struggling to bring democracy to a nation that had long lived under monarchs and the military. Through disruption of the status quo in art and design, Dadaists sought to change in culture what they were incapable of changing in the government. Thus they took to the streets with leaflets and newspapers that advocated communist ideology and incorporated unconventional type and images to agitate the masses. Whether Dada really had an effect on mainstream advertising is debatable, but the movement did represent a renunciation of previous design approaches.

Previous page, a detail of: Herbert Bayer, exhibition poster for *Europäisches Kunstgewerbe, Leipig*, 1927.

The Bauhaus

"It is obvious," wrote Aldous Huxley in 1928, "that the machine is here to stay. Whole armies of William Morrises and Tolstoys could not now expel it.... Let us then exploit [it] to create beauty—a modern beauty, while we are about it." Concepts from all advanced art and design movements were investigated, shared, and used to confront questions of functional design and industrial manufacture at a design school originally launched in Weimar, Germany. Das Staatliche Bauhaus, known as the Bauhaus (1919–1933), arose. There, modern furniture, architecture, product design, and graphics were molded by the efforts of its faculty and students and a progressive design approach.

Shortly before the beginning of World War I in 1914, Belgian painter-designer-architect Henri van de Velde (1863–1957), who had served as director of the Weimar Arts and Crafts School, left his post to return to his native Belgium. Architect Walter Gropius (1883–1969), then thirty-one years old, was one of three likely replacements van de Velde recommended to the grand duke of Saxe-Weimar. Since the school was closed during the war years, it was not until after the war that Gropius was named director of the new school that combined the applied-arts-focused Weimar Arts and Crafts

School with a fine arts institute, the Weimar Art Academy. Gropius was already well-known when the Republic began, but he reached the apex of his prominence in the Bauhaus, which will forever be associated with his name.

Gropius received authorization from the new Socialist government in Thuringia to name the new school Das Staatliche Bauhaus (The State Home for Building).

He selected a designation recalling the medieval *Bauhütte*, in which both craftsmen and artists worked together. As he stated in the first Proclamation of the Weimar Bauhaus in 1919, in this school, artists would no longer work separated from society.

On March 20, 1919, Gropius officially opened the Bauhaus in Weimar. As with many postwar movements, Gropius sought a unity of art and craft. Graphic design was a decisive force, and formal design principles were stressed. The Bauhaus helped to engender a revolution in typography and inspired new typefaces such Paul Renner's (1878-1956) Futura in 1927.

Many of the graphic design advances during the 1920s resulted from the Bauhaus, but these typographic innovations were usually known only to an exclusive audience. In its early years, Bauhaus aims were at the same time creative and instructive. In addition to Gropius, the masters were: Lyonel Feininger (1871-1956) (until 1925), Johannes Itten (1888-1967) (until 1923), Vassily Kandinsky (until 1933), Paul Klee (until 1931), Gerhard Marcks (1889-1981) (until 1925), Adolf Meyer (1881-1929) (until 1925), and Georg Muche (1895-1987) (until 1927). They were joined in 1923 by Oskar Schlemmer (1988-1943) (until 1929) and László Moholy-Nagy (1895-1946) (until 1928).

Supporting the shared foundations of fine and applied arts, Gropius sought a new congruence of art and technology. He felt that an aesthetically taught designer could "breathe a spirit into the lifeless creations of automaton."

The Bauhaus was an inevitable result of the German dedication to design in industry that had its roots earlier in the century. The Deutscher Werkbund (German Craftsmen's Association) attempted to raise the level of design and public awareness, bringing together architects, artists, community and manufacturing representatives, teachers, and reviewers. The reason that the Werkbund wanted to bring together artists, craftsmen and manufacturing was to improve the practical and visual aspects of mass production, primarily regarding less expensive consumer goods.

Beginning in 1907, Gropius worked for three years as an assistant at Peter Behrens's architectural office. Behrens's encouragement of objectivity greatly inspired the young Gropius, as did the influence of van de Velde. During the 1890s, van de Velde had contended that the engineer was to be the next architect; he supported rational design with the latest tools and resources such as reinforced concrete, steel, aluminum, and linoleum.

The Bauhaus years in Weimar
The early Bauhaus years in Weimar (1919-1924) were visionary, and they received much impetus from modern art movements such as Constructivism. Workshops were taught by both artists and craftsmen. They were established according to medieval guidelines – those of master, journeyman, and apprentice – and no division was seen between the fine and applied arts. The Bauhaus years in Weimar, 1919-1925, can be seen as the school's period of preparation. The artists first hired by Gropius held to no formal artistic creeds, nor were they all equally enthusiastic about the workshop program.

Progressive and basically dissimilar concepts regarding form, color, and space were combined into the Bauhaus philosophy when Klee was recruited in 1920 and Kandinsky in 1922. Klee combined modern European art with that of non-Western civilizations and that of children. Kandinsky's belief in the independence of color and shape resulted in the liberation of his painting from any form of realism.

Predictably, some conflicts arose among the faculty. Johannes Itten, a painter, teacher, and brilliant color theorist whom Gropius had brought from Vienna to teach the vital *Vorkurs* (preliminary course), was at the center of Bauhaus instruction. Itten was devoted to aesthetics and far less interested in applied arts than Gropius. His objectives were to unleash the students' creative gifts, to enlarge their understanding of materials, to convey basic design principles relating to all the visual arts, and to encourage the detailed analysis of old master paintings. In 1923, Itten resigned from the Bauhaus due to differences regarding the manner in which the *Vorkurs* was being taught, because the Bauhaus had begun to place more emphasis on rational design for the machine age. Gropius began to find Itten's spirituality in conflict with this philosophy.

After Itten left the Bauhaus, the preliminary course was taught by two other masters: a former student named Josef Albers, and László Moholy-Nagy. However, the real problem was not on the inside; it was hostility from the right wing, the fear that traditional craftsmen had of the progressive Bauhaus work, and dislike of the bohemian brashness of Bauhaus students. Gropius forbade any political pursuits, and this helped to some extent. However, in 1925 the Bauhaus moved from Weimar to the more welcoming city of Dessau. There, Gropius was able to design and build his famous Bauhaus buildings, Klee and Kandinsky continued to paint, and Breuer constructed his magnificent furniture.

Josef Albers (1888-1976) attended Itten's *Vorkurs* in 1920, and in 1923 Gropius asked him to join the Bauhaus faculty. Early in the spring of 1919, Bauhaus teacher Lyonel Feininger (1871-1956) became influenced by De Stijl in the Netherlands and made certain that those in the Bauhaus were aware of its importance. In the latter half of the 1920s, van Doesburg was in touch with the Bauhaus and moved to Weimar the next year. He wanted to teach there, but Gropius found him too rigid with his implacable insistence on rigorous geometry. Gropius remained against forcing any particular vision on students. In spite of the fact that he was not a faculty member, van Doesburg had a decided influence on the school because his house was used as a gathering place for Bauhaus students and a few faculty members. He remained in Weimar until 1923, giving lectures on De Stijl, and Bauhaus furniture design and typography were particularly affected by De Stijl philosophy. Van Doesburg had been residing in Weimar since mid-1923. As a result, the *De Stijl* magazine became somewhat detached from its Dutch roots and became a more international publication.

Ongoing disagreements between the Bauhaus and the Thuringian government authorities led the latter to insist that the Bauhaus stage an exhibition to display its achievements and prove its worth. When the exhibition opened in 1923, it received close to 15,000 visitors, and the international commendation was far beyond what had been anticipated. By that time there was a stronger emphasis on the applied arts, causing Gropius to introduce a new slogan, "art and technology: a new unity," and another Bauhaus symbol was designed to denote this transformation. Joost Schmidt (1893–1948), then a student, designed the poster for this exhibition.

During the same year, 1923, Gropius invited Hungarian László Moholy-Nagy (1895–1946) to teach the preliminary course. A tireless innovator, he first studied law before moving on to painting, photography, film, sculpture, and graphic design. New materials such as acrylics and plastic, procedures such as photomontages and photograms, in addition to the use of transparencies, all played a part in his experiments. Youthful and eloquent, Moholy-Nagy had a distinct effect on Bauhaus teaching, and he became the chief assistant to Gropius. Moholy-Nagy was deeply influenced by the idealism of the Russian avant-garde at the beginning of the Bolshevik Revolution and the social task of his time.

Gropius and Moholy-Nagy served as co-editors of *Staatliches Bauhaus in Weimar, 1919–1923*, the catalogue for the 1923 exhibit. The cover was designed by Herbert Bayer (1900–1985), still a student at the time, while the pages were designed by Moholy-Nagy. Moholy-Nagy provided an important Bauhaus declaration regarding typography, explaining it as "a tool of communication. It must be communication in its most intense form. The emphasis must be on absolute clarity."

Moholy-Nagy's fervor for typography and photography resulted in the amalgamation of the two art forms. He envisioned graphic design, particularly in the form of the poster, as moving toward the "typophoto." His 1926 *Pneumatik* poster is a clear example of this. He recognized the strong importance of photography in poster design which, through enlargements, distortion, double exposures, and montage, is immediately recognizable.

Moholy-Nagy used the camera mainly as a design tool. Customary photographs were replaced by unusual compositions through the manipulation of light and shadows to organize the page area. Standard vantage points were replaced by extreme close-ups, distant views, and skewing. Texture, repetition, and lighting variations all contributed to the effect. However, Moholy-Nagy's increasing work in photography began to irritate the Bauhaus painters when he proclaimed what he called the inevitable triumph of photography over painting.

In 1922, Moholy-Nagy began to work with photograms, a technique using objects and light on photographic paper. Over the course of the following year, photomontage also became part of his design portfolio. He found the photogram to be the core of photography, as it permitted one to use photography without a camera.

The Bauhaus intended to create a design language that the public could understand, but many in Germany did not recognize the value of its detached objectivity. Most German graphic designers of the period simply followed the then dominant styles or whatever their clients demanded. However, certain aspects of the New Typography such as asymmetry and sans-serif type were often used along with traditional illustration and lettering.

In the beginning, there was still an emphasis on craft, as Gropius saw this as a way to overcome the "class difference" between artists and craftsmen. He first consigned each department to two masters: a technical instructor and an aesthetic teacher of form. The departments included weaving, pottery, bookbinding, carpentry, metalwork, mural painting, and stage design. According to Gropius, the Bauhaus was created "not to propagate any style, system, dogma, formula, or vogue, but to exert a revitalizing influence on design." Ideally, it was to prepare young artists and artisans to approach industrialization and its effect on society and culture. Also, Bauhaus typography inevitably engendered radical changes in advertising design.

By 1923 the Bauhaus had a clear objective: the total design of the commonplace environment. This included everything from family houses to large estates, as well as furniture and ordinary utensils.

Herbert Bayer was commissioned to design one- and two-million-mark banknotes for Thuringia. Under Moholy-Nagy's guidance, the first Bauhaus books were published using Constructivist typography. Marcel Breuer, while still a student, designed some De Stijl-based chairs. In the 1923 exhibition, which was partially in the Provincial Museum, there were progressive architectural works, including Mies van der Rohe's design for a thirty-story glass skyscraper.

According to Gropius, the Bauhaus did not promote any styles, systems, dogmas, formulas, or vogues but simply exerted a stimulating influence on design. It existed to prepare a generation of artists and artisans to confront the demands of industrialization and its impact on society and culture. It is evident that Bauhaus typography and graphic design courses were factors in how radical advertising was created.

A three-phase, five-year program under the supervision of both artists and craftsmen would expose students to the theoretical and the practical progressing from basic design theories to workshop apprenticeships and finally to actual architectural projects that would ideally bridge the gap between the fine and applied arts. The curriculum at the Bauhaus was now intended to make Gropius's dream an actuality. After finishing the basic course, each student was taught in a workshop by two masters, who provided a command of materials, aesthetics, content and form. The ambience of the Bauhaus was creative and adaptable; typography, furniture design, lamp design, carpet design, pottery, bookbinding, and dance were all approached with total liberty. The Bauhaus was at the same time a school and a collective business. Gropius and the other masters did not create disciples. Instead, it was a place where students inspired the masters and teachers inspired their students.

Funding for the Bauhaus was sparse and indigence, particularly among students, was ubiquitous. In 1923, when the Bauhaus staged its first exhibition, there were no funds for cleaning the building, and the masters' wives offered their help with this task. Gropius's curriculum would form the core of the Bauhaus program for fourteen years, but the experimental nature of the school, the conflicts inevitable among highly-motivated individuals, and the external political pressures were unavoidable factors.

A five-year program under the direction of both artists and craftsmen would expose students to theoretical and applied arts as well as to aesthetic and the utilitarian approaches. Bauhaus graduates progressed from basic design theory to workshop apprenticeships, where they would be involved with actual architectural projects, bringing together the fine and applied arts. The untried structure of the school, the unavoidable disagreements among highly inspired artists, and the external political pressures brought about a continuous process of modification.

At the end of 1919, many involved with the local right wing began to accuse the Bauhaus of having "Spartacist-Jewish leanings" and of accepting Jews and foreigners instead of true Germans. Feininger had been born in the US, Klee was Swiss, and Itten an Austrian, and the students included Marcel Breuer, a Hungarian.

In spite of an improvement in the school's direction, its fortunes declined. After the KPD (the German Communist Party) entered the Thuringian government in October 1923, the army moved in and the government collapsed.

Gropius avoided any connection with political parties, left or right, but his apartment was raided by troops, and the subsequent elections brought in a right-wing government dominated by nationalists and parties that considered the Bauhaus a menace.

By 1924, it was clear that the lack of harmony among the faculty and the dearth of funds were obstructing the Bauhaus's essential objective, the fusion of art and technology. To add to the school's difficulties, the new right-wing provincial government began to take away its funding. In December the school's budget was reduced to an unfeasible amount, and by April 1925 the school had to either close or move. Clearly, continuing in Weimar was impossible under such conditions. The Council of Masters decided to shut down the Weimar Bauhaus on April 1, 1925, after which the Bauhaus moved to the city of Dessau. There a progressive mayor not only backed Gropius but also arranged for new school buildings to be designed by him.

The Bauhaus had attempted to establish a universal design language that the masses could understand, but not all Germans responded to its imperturbable objectivity, absence of humor, and what they considered "the human touch." Most German graphic designers were not tied to doctrines, but simply understood and established current trends. A client's wishes and the designer's partiality, however, made certain that attributes of the New Typography such as asymmetry and sans-serif typefaces were often combined with old-style illustration and lettering, producing a hybrid style.

The Bauhaus at Dessau
Conflicts between the Bauhaus and the government in Weimar had been present from the onset. These only deepened after another, more traditionalist administration was elected and attempted to enforce intolerable restrictions on the school. On December 26, 1924, Gropius and the faculty all signed a letter of resignation, effective April 1, 1925. Two weeks later, the students also sent a letter to the government stating that they would depart with the masters. Gropius and Fritz Hesse, the mayor of Dessau, agreed to move the Bauhaus to this medium-sized industrial city between Weimar and Berlin, and the Bauhaus reopened in the fall of 1925. A new building compound was designed by Gropius and put into use on December 4, 1926 after taking about a year to construct, and the courses were restructured. The new classrooms and workshops could accommodate up to 80 students trained as architects and designers. Contracts were concluded with local manufacturers to allow furniture and utensils developed at the Bauhaus to be produced. Few such undertakings had been possible during the Weimar period, but in Dessau the situation changed by 1926.

When the new glass and concrete buildings were inaugurated, there was a more united faculty and a revised curriculum. The pottery, bookbinding, and stained glass workshops were disbanded, and the printing workshop began to emphasize typography and advertising.

A department of architecture was founded under the direction of Hannes Meyer (1889–1951), a Swiss architect inspired by Le Corbusier with strong communist leanings. László Moholy-Nagy, who had taken over the preliminary course in 1923, now influenced workshops headed by Bauhaus graduates Marcel Breuer, Josef Albers, and Herbert Bayer.

There were salary reductions, and beginning with only 63 students, the school initially used provisional spaces in the local museum and the arts and crafts school, the latter temporarily coming under Gropius's supervision due to the resignation of its director.

It was at Dessau that the Bauhaus idea of "art and technology: a new unity" was developed. There was a shift of focus from idealism to actual building, and less emphasis on craft and painting. An important development was the formation of a school company to handle the sale of Bauhaus designs and products.

The move to Dessau also engendered a policy change. The results of the restructuring were soon evident as the Bauhaus introduced such classics as Breuer's tubular steel chair. Constructivist typography by Moholy-Nagy and Bayer using single-case sans-serif type and photomontage transformed advertising layout and book design. Gropius's Bauhaus buildings and other architectural projects he designed with his Dessau students provided concrete form to Bauhaus architectural ideas.

The new curriculum in 1926–1927 was as follows:
Basic course: Moholy-Nagy and Albers
Cabinet-making: Breuer
Metal workshop: Moholy-Nagy
Weaving: Muche, succeeded by Stölzl
Sculpture: Schmidt
Theater: Schlemmer
Wall painting: Scheper
Advertising and typography: Bayer, Schmidt

During the Dessau period, the uniqueness and values of the Bauhaus were fully realized. The De Stijl and Constructivist foundations remained clear, but the Bauhaus did not simply emulate them. Instead, it established its own rules to solve design questions. The Bauhaus Corporation, a business association, was established to manage the sale of samples studios' products to manufacturers. Many Bauhaus concepts began to affect life in the 20th century. These included furniture designs and numerous other products, practical architecture, environmental design, and especially typography. The masters were now referred to as professors, and the previous master-journeyman-trainee arrangement was discarded. In 1926, the Bauhaus was retitled Hochschule für Gestaltung (College of Design), and the important *bauhaus* journal was introduced.

This journal and the series of fourteen *Bauhausbücher* (Bauhaus books) in turn developed into significant mediums for circulating progressive concepts regarding design philosophy and its use in architecture and design. Kandinsky, Klee, Gropius, Mondrian, Moholy-Nagy, and van Doesburg were either editors or authors of books in this series. Moholy-Nagy designed twelve of the books and eight of the covers. Modern architecture was implied on book number 14's cover by using a photograph of typography printed on glass with its shadow over a red surface.

Moholy-Nagy's design for Arthur Müller Lehning's Amsterdam-based avant-garde periodical *i10* displays De Stijl typographic concepts with traces of Constructivism and Merz. The printer was initially bothered by the disregard of typographic norms, but ultimately he began to grasp and appreciate the design.

Five former students received appointments as professors. These included Josef Albers (1888–1976), who taught an introductory course examining the constructive aspects of substances; Marcel Breuer (1902–1981), the director of the furniture workshop, who conceived tubular-steel furniture; and Herbert Bayer, who became a professor at the recently introduced typographic and graphic design studio. Clearly, Bayer's intense interest in typography was well-established before the Bauhaus moved to Dessau.

In addition to getting printing assignments from Dessau companies to help with the Bauhaus finances, Bayer's workshop came up with noteworthy typographic developments in a Constructivist style. Sans-serif fonts were almost always used, and Bayer designed a universal lowercase typeface that reduced the alphabet to simple and rational shapes. Bayer rejected the use of capital letters, stating that the capital and lowercase alphabets are discordant in design, with two entirely dissimilar signs voicing one sound—a fundamental break with the extensive use of capital letters in German texts. Bayer often used flush-left, ragged-right typesetting without justification. Radical differences in type size and weight were employed for graphic hierarchy. Bars, rules, and points were utilized to organize the page area, unite varied rudiments, guide the eye across a page, and emphasize central components. Basic shapes and the use of black ink with one unmixed color were favored. A grid structure and a clear arrangement of type sizes, rules, and images gave the designs a sense of harmony. Energetic organization using clear horizontals, verticals and at times diagonals characterize Bayer's Bauhaus design.

This is evident in Bayer's poster for Kandinsky's 60th birthday exhibition. A graphic hierarchy was established with horizontal and vertical orientations, and the entire design was moved diagonally to attain an active but still stable architectural arrangement. With the text organized in a seven-column grid, Bayer's 1927 poster for an exhibition of European arts and crafts continues with an architectural structure in its design.

The final Bauhaus chapter began in 1928 when Gropius left to resume his architecture practice and Meyer succeeded him as director. Meyer intensified the stress on architecture, changed the furniture and metal workshops into an interior design department, and introduced a city planning course and a photography workshop taught by Walter Peterhans. During the same year, both Bayer and Moholy-Nagy departed for Berlin, where they worked principally in graphic design and typography. The former Bauhaus student Joost Schmidt took the place of Bayer as master of the typographic and graphic design workshop. He rejected the strict Constructivist outlook and added a larger number of typefaces to the workshop's inventory.

By 1930, disagreements with the civic powers, to a large extent over his leftist views, resulted in Meyer having to resign. Ludwig Mies van der Rohe (1886–1969), a renowned Berlin architect, followed him as director. Mies changed the curriculum to some extent, giving further importance to architecture. The curriculum also began to be more theoretical, causing a deterioration of the laboratory structure. On a positive note, the school began to receive some private financial funding through the sale of design patents in addition to fabric and wallpaper patterns. This source of income became even more significant when, due to the rise of Nazism, the city of Dessau decided to close the Bauhaus.

By 1931, the Nazi Party controlled the Dessau city council, and in 1932 it voided the Bauhaus faculty contracts. Mies van der Rohe attempted to save the Bauhaus by conducting classes privately in an empty telephone factory, but after eight months the Nazis ultimately closed that as well. So in spite of his pledge to maintain the political neutrality of the school, Nazi provocation made its survival unsustainable. The Gestapo insisted on the elimination of all "cultural Bolsheviks" from the faculty in favor of having them replaced by Nazi supporters. The faculty ultimately voted to disband the Bauhaus, and it came to an end on August 10, 1933. The Bauhaus had existed for fourteen years, spreading the concept of Functionalism in many areas and bringing about fundamental changes in design.

The increasing threat of Nazi oppression forced many of the Bauhaus faculty members to join the exodus of intellectuals, musicians, and artists to the United States. In 1937, Moholy-Nagy founded the New Bauhaus (now the Institute of Design) in Chicago. In the following year, Herbert Bayer began his new design career in America. Josef Albers first taught at Black Mountain College in North Carolina before being appointed director of the art school at Yale University in 1950. This immigration significantly affected the development of American design following World War II.

Kandinsky moved to Neuilly-sur-Seine, near Paris, and Feininger went to New York. After three years in London, Gropius, too, moved to the United States in 1937, where he was appointed a professor at the Harvard Graduate School of Design and head of the Architecture School. In addition, he opened an architectural studio with Breuer, who was also a Harvard professor.

Mies became head of the architecture school at the Armour Institute of Technology in Chicago, later called the Illinois Institute of Technology. Also in Chicago, when Moholy-Nagy tried to resurrect the Bauhaus in 1937 with the brief appearance of the New Bauhaus, he was joined by György Kepes, a fellow Hungarian and author of the literary milestone *Language of Vision*, published in 1944.

The three periods of the Bauhaus consisting of bold experiments in the beginning, confidence at its midpoint, and doubt at its conclusion reflect the history of the Weimar Republic itself. From November 1918 to 1924, the Republic experienced a revolution, a civil war, the French occupation, political assassinations, and enormous inflation, but was a time of artistic exploration. Between 1924 and 1929, there was relative economic stability, a reduction in political savagery, a restored status among other countries, and overall prosperity. Finally, between 1929 and 1933, it was a time of growing unemployment, government by decree, and an upsurge in violence; in addition, the new media and films industries produced mainly right-wing propaganda, while the leading designers, architects, and writers were pushed to the side. The achievements and influences of the Bauhaus went far beyond its fourteen-year existence and produced a progressive design movement that spanned architecture, industrial design, graphic design and all forms of visual communications.

The Russian Constructivists and affiliates of De Stijl in the Netherlands also experimented with progressive architecture and design. What distinguished the Bauhaus from these other groups was Gropius's commitment to stylistic diversity. Because of the presence of artists as varied as Kandinsky, Klee, Feininger, and Schlemmer, an atmosphere of broad-mindedness and rationality characterized the Bauhaus throughout.

Previous page, a detail of: Stenberg Brothers, Georgii & Vladimir Stenberg, movie poster for *The Eleventh Year of the Revolution*, 1928.

The Russian Influence

Of all the trends in Soviet art, Constructivism was closest to the Leninist ideal. Any traces of mysticism were now replaced by an assertion of the material. Art would now be accessible to everyone and not limited to an isolated few. Previous divisions between artists and artisans, architects and engineers would be erased in an overall view of art as a productive medium.

Russia was torn apart by the turmoil of World War I and then by the revolution at the end of the second decade of the twentieth century. Czar Nicholas II (1868–1918) was deposed and killed along with his entire immediate family. Russia was then engulfed by civil war, and the Bolshevik Red Army had won by 1920. Throughout this time of political turbulence, a fleeting renaissance of pioneering art in the Soviet Union had a wide impact on twentieth-century graphic design. Beginning with Marinetti's lecture series in the Soviet Union, Soviet artists produced original innovations for a decade. Typographic and design experimentation characterized their Futurist-influenced journals which published work by both visual and literary art groups. Poet Vladimir Vladimirovich Mayakovski's autobiographical production was printed in a discordant Futurist manner designed by David and Vladimir Burliuk. This became a prototype for others, including Ilja Zdanevich.

In 1917, soon after the Russian Revolution, the Bolsheviks introduced an information sector, the Soviet Telegraph Agency (ROSTA). Two years later, ROSTA posters began to support the Red Army in the civil war. Candid drawings depicted historic and public events in designs aimed mainly at semiliterate people. Typical images showed expensively clothed industrialists being chastised for their wicked ways. Produced on single pages in a comic-strip format, they were generally termed "ROSTA windows." Distributed between the fall of 1919 and January 1922, they were placed in storefronts and public places, where they would be readily seen. Originally, they were all made by hand as separate entities, but by the spring of 1920, they began to be produced using stencils, so that hundreds could be made in a single day. Vladimir Mayakovsky was closely involved with the ROSTA windows, and although he did not select the subjects, they were taken from his writing or endorsed by him. Nearly a third of the ROSTA designs were his own creations.

Kazimir Malevich (1878–1935) initiated a painting approach using basic forms and pure color that he named Suprematism. His innovative geometric method was entirely nonobjective and rejected any imagery. To him, the core of art was the perceptual result of shape and color. To illuminate this, probably in 1913, he produced a painting with only a black square on a white background, declaring that the feeling this provoked was the essence of art. In such works as the 1915 *Suprematist Composition* and the cover of *Pervyi tsikl lektsii* (*First Circle of Lectures*), Malevich produced structures with only the rudiments of color and form.

The new Soviet art was clearly augmented by the revolution, as art was then viewed as a social need. After the 1917 revolution, artists devoted their efforts to supporting the Bolsheviks, but in 1920 a theoretical divide gradually developed regarding the artist's role in Soviet society. Many artists, including Malevich and Kandinsky, argued that art must be a spiritual pursuit separate from social obligations. They disavowed partisan objectives, contending that the purpose of art was only to articulate forms in time and space. Led by Alexander Rodchenko (1891–1956), around twenty-five artists came up with a dissimilar view in 1921. They rejected "art for art's sake" in favor of industrial and functional design supporting the Soviet Union. These Constructivists, as they labeled themselves, maintained that artists must cease making impractical articles such as paintings and instead produce posters, asserting that only this medium would serve the community as a whole. Rodchenko soon abandoned painting in favor of graphic design and photojournalism.

Soviet Constructivism was mainly due to the painter, architect, architectural engineer, graphic designer, and photographer El (Lazar Markovich) Lissitzky (1890–1941), a visionary designer who significantly affected the history of graphic design.

At the age of nineteen, after being refused admission by the Petrograd Academy of Arts for being a Jew, Lissitzky pursued his architecture studies in Darmstadt, Germany. The structural nature of architecture formed the basis of his future creative work. At the start of World War I, he returned to Russia to work as an architect.

Marc Chagall, director of the progressive art school in Vitebsk, hired Lissitzky as a teacher in 1919. Malevich was also teaching there and soon became an important stimulus for Lissitzky who developed a painting style that he labeled *PROUNs* (an acronym for "projects for the establishment of a new art"). Different from the uniformity of Malevich, Lissitzky used three-dimensional forms that receded and protruded from the picture planes. He called them "an intersection between painting and architecture." PROUNs greatly influenced his work in graphic design as in his 1919 poster *Beat the Whites with the Red Wedge*. The "red" Bolsheviks are depicted as a red wedge cutting into a white circle signifying the "white" conservative armies of Alexander Kerensky.

Lissitzky saw the Russian Revolution as a fresh beginning. He felt that communism would introduce a new direction, that technology would supply the needs of the population, and that the artist/designer (he referred to himself as a "constructor") would create a union between art and industry. Refusing to acknowledge individual artistic creation, he placed an increasing emphasis on graphic design.

In 1921, Lissitzky was made director of the architectural department at the new VKhUTEMAS art school in Moscow. That same year, he traveled to Germany and the Netherlands, where he came into contact with De Stijl, Bauhaus, Dadaists, and kindred Constructivists. He also encountered Dutch architect Hendricus Theodorus Wijdeveld (1885-1987) and in 1922 designed a cover for the Dutch avant-garde magazine *Wendingen*, started by Wijdeveld in January 1918.

In the early 1920s, the Soviet government supported original art with an international periodical. Together with editor Ilya Ehrenburg (1891-1967), Lissitzky helped to produce the trilingual magazine *Veshch* (Russian)/ *Gegenstand* (German)/*Objet* (French). The title (meaning "object") was selected by the editors who found art to be the creation of new objects. Lissitzky designed the asymmetrical covers on an angle with most elements elevated in the composition. Lissitzky and Ehrenburg were cognizant of the fact that similar but separate art movements had occurred in Europe, and they saw *Veshch* as a focal point for inventive works from various countries.

Lissitzky's Berlin period permitted him to spread Constructivist ideas in Weimar during frequent Bauhaus visits and through editorials and lectures. His most significant joint venture was the design and writing of a double issue of *Merz* with Kurt Schwitters in 1924. The editors of *Broom*, an American avant-garde magazine printed in Italy devoted to radical writing and art, hired Lissitzky as a designer. One *Broom* cover is designed using graph paper, giving a predetermined structure to the design.

Advertisements were designed for the progressive Pelikan Ink Company, for which Lissitzky at times used drafting instruments to create the designs. In 1925 he predicted that Gutenberg's way of printing would soon be obsolete and would be replaced by photomechanical technology, opening new avenues for graphic designers.

Lissitzky did not just design the book, but instead said he constructed it. In 1923 *For the Voice*, also translated as *For Reading Out Loud*, thirteen poems by Vladimir Mayakovski, Lissitzky worked with basic components from a metal type case and set by a German with no understanding of Russian. One innovation was a right margin die-cut tab to help readers find poems; the meaning of each poem was interpreted abstractly.

A groundbreaking book project during the 1920s was *The Isms of Art 1914-1924*, edited by Lissitzky and Dadaist Hans Arp. Lissitzky's design produced a new graphic system for arranging images and text. A three-column horizontal grid for the title page and the three-column vertical grid for the text provided the forty-eight-page book with a solid structure. Asymmetry and a skillful use of empty space contributed to the design. Large numbers used as compositional components linked illustrations to captions. Sans-serif type and thick rules are initial aspects of his modernist approach.

Lissitzky often used photomontage for various designs. On a poster for a Soviet exhibition of architecture in Switzerland, both the female and the male images have the same importance, a strong message in a primarily male-dominated culture.

After returning to the Soviet Union in 1925, Lissitzky dedicated a great deal of energy to designs for the Soviet government, including numerous publications and architectural projects. After an eighteen-year struggle with tuberculosis, he died in December 1941. Through his control of modern technology and foresight, El Lissitzky developed a standard for future designers. Later, typographer Jan Tschichold wrote, "Lissitzky was one of the great pioneers…. His indirect influence was widespread and enduring. A generation that has never heard of him … stands upon his shoulders."

In a culture in which the poster had become a key source of mass communication, Rodchenko, initially a painter who moved on to graphic design and photography, was by far one of the most exceptional poster designers. The writer who collaborated with Rodchenko was the most important poet of Russian modernism, Mayakovsky. They shared a studio name which read "Advertisement Constructors, Mayakovsky-Rodchenko." The Soviet government eventually created an important administrative position for Rodchenko as director of the Museum Bureau. Afterwards, he quietly worked as a photographer and designer.

Like Lissitzky, Rodchenko was a devoted communist with an enormous creative energy and a temperament that led him to investigate new possibilities using typography, photomontage, and photography. An early fascination with geometry led to an exactness in his paintings. However, in 1921 Rodchenko rejected painting to devote his energies to graphic design. While in art school, Rodchenko met Varvara Stepanova (1894–1958), whom he eventually married. In painting, photography, writing, and theater design, she became a noteworthy member of the Soviet avant-garde.

In 1923, Rodchenko began to design a magazine entitled *Novy LEF* (*Left Front of the Arts*), edited by Mayakovski, which addressed all creative arts. Overprinting, exact registration, and photomontage were often used. The latter paralleled an increased use of montage in the growing Soviet film industry.

In 1924, Rodchenko's ten cover designs for the "Miss Mend" books by Jim Dollar (a pseudonym of Soviet author Marietta Shaginian) used a consistent composition in black and an additional color. The titles, numbers, second colors, and photomontages vary with each volume.

Georgii (1900–1933) and Vladimir Augustovich (1899–1982) Stenberg were talented brothers who collaborated on magnificent poster designs for the theater and more than three hundred movie posters from 1923 until Georgii's untimely death in 1933. Due to contemporary reproduction problems with photographs, they devised a projector to enlarge film images, allowing them to produce accurate drawings for their posters by altering, copying, and combining images that were placed next to flat areas of color. Their powerful posters were supported by compelling, clear-cut texts.

By far, the master of photomontage for Soviet propaganda was Gustav Klutsis (1895–1944), who called the medium "the art construction for socialism." With heroic and intrepid images, Klutsis used the poster to glorify Soviet achievements. His posters have often been compared to those of John Heartfield, whose work Klutsis had probably seen when it was shown in the Soviet Union during the 1930s. Although many of his posters praised Stalin, Klutsis's inflexible avant-garde style resulted in his arrest in 1938, and in 1944 he died in a Soviet labor camp.

Another Soviet artist who greatly affected Soviet modernism was Vladimir Vasilyevich Lebedev (1891–1967). A devoted Bolshevik, he first produced bold propaganda posters for the Soviet news agency, and these became the foundation for his illustrated children's books. Lebedev's ability to abbreviate shapes to basic geometry, employ primary colors, and clearly tell stories made him the initiator of the twentieth-century Soviet illustrated book. In books such as *Priklyucheniya chuchela* (*The Adventures of the Scarecrow*, 1922), *Azbuka* (*Alphabet Book*, 1925), *Morozhenoe* (*Ice Cream*, 1925), *Okhota* (*The Hunt*, 1925), *Tsirk* (*Circus*, 1925), *Vchera i segodnya* (*Yesterday and Today*, 1925), and *Bagazh* (*Baggage*, 1926), Lebedev developed a method by which he condensed figures to basic shapes against empty backgrounds broken only by bright colors and various textures.

Like many in France, Lebedev admired the natural approaches in children's art. "When I make illustrations for children," he said, "I attempt to remember my own childhood perceptions."

Through Marxist fables, Lebedev displayed the advantages of the Soviet Union as opposed to capitalist countries. But a good communist, he argued, "doesn't refute the need for a particular method in illustrations. And the more an artist displays one's personality, the more real the art will be, the profounder it will affect the viewer, the nearer it will convey the viewer to art." However, most in the Communist Party did not agree. During the Great Purges of the 1930s, Lebedev's books were censured for their "formalism," and he was forced to accept the style of social realism by reducing his work to triviality. He always regretted this compromise.

The Soviet government accepted progressive art for only a few years directly following the 1917 revolution. By 1922, it began to reproach avant-garde art for what the government considered its "capitalist cosmopolitanism" and in its place supported social realism, although Constructivism remained to some extent an inspiration to Soviet graphic and industrial designers. Soviet painters such as Malevich who did not emigrate drifted into poverty and obscurity. Rodchenko, who somehow managed to escape Stalin's purges, even began painting again and worked as a photojournalist. Many other artists simply disappeared in the gulag. Constructivism, though, continued to maintain its influence in the West and strongly persisted throughout the 1920s and in future years.

de papierkabel op de trekschijf.

Previous page, a detail of: Piet Zwart, N. V. brochure spread for *Nederlandse Kabelfabriek*, Delft Kabels, 1933.

Independent Designers in the Netherlands

The De Stijl movement in the Netherlands began during the late fall of 1917. Its founder and principal spokesman, Theo van Doesburg (born C. E. M. Küpper; 1883-1931), was joined by painters Piet Mondrian (1872-1944), Bart Anthony van der Leck (1876-1958), and Vilmos Huszár (1884-1931), architect Jacobus Johannes Pieter Oud (1890-1963), and others. Engrossed by abstract geometry, De Stijl artists pursued the universal principles of stability and harmony.

Mondrian had been living in Paris for a while in the prewar years, but had returned to the Netherlands shortly before the war began. He soon decided that the Cubist method of analyzing surface forms was incorrect and what he was attempting to accomplish could be achieved only without the visible world as a source. According to him, the artist must reduce forms to basic shapes: horizontal and vertical lines, the three primary colors, and black and white. In 1917, he joined forces with van Doesburg to produce the magazine *De Stijl*.

Mondrian constitutes the basis of the De Stijl philosophy and its visual forms. Inspired by van Gogh, Mondrian rejected traditional landscape painting in the style of The Hague school for an abstract approach.

Early in 1912, he moved to Paris and started to explore Cubism. He soon rejected any form of representation and brought Cubism to a pure, abstract conclusion. When the war started in August 1914, Mondrian was in the neutral Netherlands, where he remained until the war ended.

Dutch philosopher M. H. J. Schoenmakers (1875–1944) greatly affected Mondrian's philosophy. Schoenmakers considered horizontals and verticals to be the two basic counterparts determining world order together with the three primary colors red, yellow, and blue. Mondrian soon started to produce purely abstract paintings based this principle. He felt that the cubists had not recognized the inevitable consequence of their work, bringing abstract art to an absolute solution.

For a brief period, paintings and designs by Mondrian, van der Leck, and van Doesburg displayed a remarkable similarity. They all limited their palettes to the primary colors with the neutrals black, gray, and white, horizontal and vertical lines, and determined parts consisting of rectangles and squares.

In the Dutch language, the word *schoon* means both "pure" and "beautiful." De Stijl artists believed that beauty came from the clearness of the artistic conception and wanted to cleanse art by discarding all realism and subjectivity. In its place, the essence of their paintings would be a harmony and stability permeating the world. With his asymmetrical paintings, Mondrian attained this ideal, and his impact on modern graphic design remains profound.

A 1925 cover by van Doesburg and László Moholy-Nagy (1895–1946) for van Doesburg's book *Grundbegriffe der neuen gestaltenden Kunst* (*Principles of Modern Design*) shows the application of De Stijl principles to graphic design. Before De Stijl had begun as a movement, van der Leck had used geometric forms of pure color and produced graphic designs using flat colors and black bars for arranging the picture surface.

Van Doesburg published and edited the journal *De Stijl* from 1917 until his death in 1931, and this helped to spread the movement's ideas to a broader audience. Huszár designed the first logo for *De Stijl,* employing letters made from a grid of squares and rectangles, and he also created some of the first title pages. Later, in 1921, van Doesburg devised a new horizontal format that was used until the last issue in 1932, a year after van Doesburg's death. Mondrian stopped contributing to the journal in 1924, after van Doesburg formulated his theory of Elementarism, which contended that diagonals were more effective compositional elements than horizontals and verticals. This, alas, ended both their collaboration and their friendship.

In his designs for alphabets and posters, van Doesburg applied horizontal and vertical arrangements to both letterforms and layouts. All curved lines were eliminated and only sans-serif typefaces were favored.

The square was used as a constant element in his letterform design, but without curves and diagonals the uniqueness and legibility of letters were decreased. Layouts were designed using a grid, and color was included as an essential structural element. Red was preferred as a second color since, in addition to its ability to counter black, it implied revolution.

Van Doesburg understood the liberating quality of Dada and invited Kurt Schwitters to come to the Netherlands to help promote it. There they worked together on several typographic initiatives, and van Doesburg began to experiment with Dada typography and poetry which he published in *De Stijl* under the pseudonym I. K. Bonset. He viewed Dada and De Stijl as contradictory yet consistent movements: Dada would erase the past, and De Stijl would help to build a new society on the ruins of earlier civilization. As F. Scott Fitzgerald wrote in *The Crackup*, "the test of a first-rate intelligence is the ability to hold two opposed ideas in the mind at the same time, and still retain the ability to function." This certainly applied to van Doesburg. In 1922, van Doesburg organized an International Congress of Constructivists and Dadaists in Weimar. One of the constructivists present was El Lissitzky, who was commissioned by van Doesburg to design a 1922 issue of *De Stijl*.

A prime example of De Stijl architecture is seen in Gerrit Rietveld's (1888–1964) 1924 design for the Schroeder House in Utrecht. Its design was considered so radical that neighbors tossed rocks at it, and the Schroeder children were teased at school. The next year, Oud designed the Café de Unie in Rotterdam with an asymmetrical façade suggesting a De Stijl poster.

Van Doesburg was actually De Stijl itself, and it was predictable that the movement ended after his death in 1931 at the age of forty-seven. However, many were influenced by its visual concepts in future years, and its impact on graphic design is still evident today.

In 1918, Amsterdam architect H. P. Wijdeveld (1885–1987) introduced the avant-garde magazine *Wendingen*. Beginning as a monthly periodical on architecture, construction, and decoration, for thirteen years it addressed all artistic activities. For the magazine layouts, Wijdeveld built letters from basic typographic material and used the same approach on his *Wendingen* covers, stationery designs, and posters. In the design of his *Wendingen* pages, Wijdeveld used hard and weighty edges built from right angles, typographically related to the brick architecture of the Amsterdam school. This is abundantly apparent in his covers for the Frank Lloyd Wright issues of *Wendingen* and his 1929 poster publicizing an International Economics Exhibition at the Stedelijk Museum in Amsterdam. Wijdeveld designed only four *Wendingen* covers; the others were created by various architects, sculptors, painters, and designers. The 1922 cover by Lissitzky and the 1929 cover by Huszár are among the most striking.

Previous page, a detail of: Jan Tschichold, movie poster for Norma Talmadge in *Die Kameliendame*, Phoebus Palast, 1927.

Jan Tschichold and New Typography

Much of the original advances in graphic design during the early years of the twentieth century were related to modern art movements and the Bauhaus, but these developments were often observed by a limited few. The designer who actually used these new methods to solve ordinary design questions and elucidated them to an extensive number of printers, typesetters, and designers was Jan Tschichold (1902–1974). The son of a sign painter in Leipzig, Tschichold initially studied calligraphy at the Leipzig Academy and later became part of the design staff at Insel Verlag as a conservative calligrapher. In August 1923, Tschichold, at the age of twenty-one, visited the Bauhaus exhibition in Weimar and was intensely captivated. He quickly incorporated Bauhaus design ideas and those of the Russian Constructivists into his own work and soon became the preeminent advocate of *die neue Typographie* (the New Typography). For the October 1925 issue of *Typographische Mitteilungen* (*Typographic Impartations*), Tschichold produced a twenty-four-page supplement titled *Elementare Typographie*, which explained and included examples of asymmetrical typography for printers, typesetters, and graphic designers. It was printed in red and black and contained avant-garde designs together with Tschichold's own observations.

Most printing in Germany at this time continued to employ Textura typefaces and symmetrical page designs. Tschichold's twenty-four-page supplement was clearly a surprise and soon provoked an enduring enthusiasm for a new way of approaching typography.

His 1928 book, *Die neue Typographie: Ein Handbuch für zeitgemäss Schaffende* (*The New Typography: A Handbook for the Contemporary Designer*), actively endorsed these groundbreaking ideas. Repelled by what he considered the then prevalent "degenerate typefaces and arrangements," his goal was to engender a new beginning and introduce a typography to represent a contemporary graphic awareness and promote functional design. He stated that the ultimate objective of typography should be to convey communication using the briefest and most effectual means.

Tschichold's brochure promoting this book clearly shows his new approach to discarding decoration and replacing it with lucid typography. He stated that an active energy should be present in every design and that type should have movement instead of being static. Symmetrical arrangement was wrong as it emphasized form over text connotation. Tschichold was convinced that asymmetrical typography articulated the machine era. He professed that sans-serif types in an assortment of weights and proportions were the true contemporary typefaces. Their extensive variety of values and textures made possible an expressive result that was needed in progressive design. Tschichold's designs during this period were built on a fundamental horizontal and vertical grid arrangement. The use of rules and bars as well as boxes was frequently a part of the structure, and photography was always favored over illustration. His objective was to create designs based on the meanings of the words. His productive career established a norm for book design, ordinary printing, advertising, and posters.

Beginning in 1924, posters became one of his most important media. From 1926 until 1928, his thirty-one posters for the Phoebus-Palast movie theater in Munich would rival the Stenbergs in the Soviet Union as archetypes of film posters.

In March 1933, armed Nazis raided Tschichold's Munich apartment and arrested both him and his wife. Condemned as a "cultural Bolshevik" who generated "un-German" typography, he was denied a teaching position in Munich. After six weeks of "protective detention," Tschichold quickly left with his wife and four-year-old son for Basel, Switzerland, where he worked mainly as a book designer. In 1935 he published *Typographische Gestaltung* (*Typographic Design*), where he again expressed his opposition to conventional symmetrical typography. Unexpectedly, he soon rejected the New Typography and began to include roman, Egyptian, and even script typefaces in his designs. He considered the New Typography a response to the disorder in German typography in the 1920s, and he decided he had arrived at a point at which further development was no longer viable or needed.

In 1946 he wrote that the New Typography's "intolerant approach matches the German partiality for the absolute, and its aspiration to control." Tschichold now began to feel that graphic designers should work with a more humanist approach that made use of the wisdom and achievements of the past. He still believed that the New Typography was suitable for advertising and publications concerning modern painting, sculpture, and architecture. However, he considered it absurd for a book of poetry and found extensive texts in sans-serif typefaces "pure agony." Tschichold's disavowal of his earlier views invited a bitter attack from Swiss designer Max Bill (1908–1994), a former admirer who never forgave Tschichold for what he considered a professional betrayal.

With his employment from 1947 to 1949 as a designer for Penguin Books in London, Tschichold was instrumental in restoring traditional typography. He then decided that designers should exploit the entire heritage of design. Much of his later work used symmetry and serif typefaces, but he still supported independent ideas and creative freedom. Tschichold continued to design until his death in 1974. He recognized the significance of the New Typography and felt that its refinement and lucidity succeeded in energizing twentieth-century typography. His revival of classical typography also restored this approach in book design, and he left a permanent legacy in graphic design history.

Futura was designed by Paul Renner (1878–1956) between 1927 and 1930 for the Bauer type foundry in Germany. It had fifteen versions, including four italics and two display fonts, and became the most widely used sans-serif family. As a teacher and designer, Renner supported the belief that designers should not only preserve their inheritance but should also try to create new forms true to their own time. Even mystical medievalist Rudolf Koch designed a very popular geometric sans-serif typeface, Kabel, which, unlike Futura, was invigorated by surprising design refinements.

Previous page, a detail of: Herbert Matter, travel poster for *Engelberg*, Switzerland, 1934.

Weimar's End and its Enduring Legacy

The Nazi Party had been banned after Hitler's arrest but continued to function covertly. After leaving prison, Hitler began to assume power again. By 1926, he was the acknowledged head of the party, and under his leadership it thrived. In 1925, there had been only 27,000 members, but by the end of 1928 there were more than 100,000. Then the 1929 economic crisis helped the Nazi Party become one of the largest parties in Germany.

There were many Germans from all walks of life who detested the Nazis but neither did they have any abiding fondness for the Republic. Hesitant to accept what they saw as the questionable merits of democracy, they learned to live with the Republic and in a way saw it as an inevitability, even appreciating a few of its leaders such as Stresemann. However, they never came to like the Republic nor did they have any faith in its future.

By 1929, Germany had seen five years of relative success. However, the Wall Street crash in October 1929 brought about immense problems. Stresemann's untimely death on October 3, 1929 was catastrophic for the Republic to which he had given all his energies, and many felt he was the only one who could lead Germany through such turbulent times. He had committed his political party to the Republic and Germany to Europe, and with his exit these obligations would soon evaporate. Having their own problems, American banks were now forced to call in their loans. German exports quickly declined, and unemployment began to rise as many factories closed. By January 1932, the number of Germans who were out of work would exceed 6 million.

The new economic crisis created immense problems for the government. In March 1930, Heinrich Brüning of the (Catholic) Center Party was named chancellor, and since his party did not have a majority, he relied on President von Hindenburg to keep him in office. Afterward, the Reichstag met rarely, foreshadowing the demise of the Republic. In September 1930, Brüning called for general elections, hoping that his party would win a majority. However, the Nazis won 107 seats and became the second largest party after the Social Democrats. Brüning's draconian reduction in government spending made him highly unpopular among the unemployed and resulted in him being called the "hunger chancellor." When a number of German banks failed during the 1931 financial crisis, hopes of recovery were further diminished, and Brüning resigned in May 1932.

In an election on July 31, 1932, the Nazi Party won 230 seats, making it the largest party in the Reichstag. However, Franz von Papen of the Center Party, at that time chancellor, refused to resign and began to plot with President von Hindenburg to keep Hitler out of the government. However, von Hindenburg was already 78 when he first assumed the presidency in 1925 and could not control the upstart former corporal. Hitler insisted on becoming chancellor, but von Hindenburg still refused to appoint him despite the fact that his party was now the largest one. In the end, notwithstanding these reservations about the Nazi Party and Hitler's personality, von Hindenburg appointed Hitler as chancellor on January 30, 1933. When von Hindenburg died in 1934, Hitler became both chancellor and president.

The Escape from Fascism
Emigration reached its peak in the late 1930s, as many European cultural figures moved to America. This included numerous graphic designers. The skills they brought with them produced significant changes in the development of their field in the United States.

One of the most important émigré book designers was Georg Salter (1897–1967). Once he was no longer allowed to work in Germany because he was Jewish, Salter and his brother Stephan settled in New York in 1934. Between 1922 and 1934, Salter had already produced more than 350 book designs for thirty-three German publishers. More than two-thirds of Salter's output was book covers, which soon began to exemplify his work. His perceptive understanding of literature helped him to uniquely present the content of a book with a jacket.

As a result, his designs became decisive images for many important twentieth-century literary works. His cover design for Alfred Döblin's novel *Berlin Alexanderplatz* (1929) is a major triumph from his design career in Germany.

The arrival of fascism in Europe led to one of the largest international emigrations of intellectual and artistic geniuses in the history of the West. During the late 1930s, many of the important scientists, writers, architects, artists, and graphic designers left Europe for a new life in the United States. Among the artists were Ernst, Duchamp, and Mondrian. After the Nazis forced the Bauhaus to close in 1933, faculty, students, and alumni scattered throughout Europe, Great Britain, and the United States. Walter Gropius, Mies van der Rohe, and Marcel Breuer took functionalist architecture to the United States, and Herbert Bayer and László Moholy-Nagy brought original approaches in graphic design. Other European graphic designers who came to America and made significant contributions include Herbert Matter and Ladislav Sutnar.

Moholy-Nagy arrived in Chicago in 1937 and briefly established the New Bauhaus. Although it closed after just one year for financial reasons, Moholy-Nagy was then able to open the School of Design in 1939. The main financial support came from Moholy-Nagy himself and other faculty members, many of whom agreed to forgo their salaries if necessary.

Posters Bayer produced during and after World War II were surprisingly illustrative when compared to those in the Constructivist style created in the Bauhaus period. His 1939/40 cover for *PM* was one of his last designs before the transformation of his design style was apparent. Aware of a new American clientele, Bayer began to create realistic illustrations and then combine these with the fundamental structure he had initiated in Dessau.

Weimar's End and its Enduring Legacy
Beginning in 1929, the Weimar Republic endured a number of setbacks from which it would never recover, including Stresemann's death of a heart attack at age 51 in 1929, three years after receiving the Nobel Peace Prize. After the New York Stock Exchange crashed in October 1929, American loans ended and the "Golden Twenties" came to a sudden close.

The causes for the Weimar Republic's failure are a topic of ongoing dispute. From the start, moderates had shunned it and radicals on both the Left and Right hated it. It was often called a "democracy without democrats." The Weimar Republic probably experienced the most serious economic problems of any Western democracy. Hyperinflation and massive unemployment were of course chief reasons. The Weimar Republic was frail from its beginning, and the depression was overwhelming. As in many parts of the world, the 1930s in Europe presented a disheartening picture. The uncertain and worsening economic and political conditions erased the optimism and idealism of the 1920s, and as National Socialism became the dominant force in Germany, conditions became progressively more uncomfortable for the artistic avant-garde. No single cause can explain the downfall of the Weimar Republic. The most commonly asserted reasons are economic problems, institutional problems and certain individuals.

With the emigration of so many talented artists, designers, and architects to other countries, especially the United States, Weimar's legacy continued to endure. Its impact on graphic design is still very evident and alive today.

"The Weimar Republic created nothing. It liberated what was already there."

Professor Peter Gay in *Weimar Culture*

Evident and Alive Today

Filippo Marinetti Oskar Schlemmer Guillaume Apollinaire

El Lissitzky Theo van Doesburg Kurt Schwitters Herbert Bayer

Vladimir Stenberg Friedrich Kiesler Oskar Fischer H. Th.

Hendrik N. Werkman László Moholy-Nagy Jindřich Štýrsky

Käte Steinitz Kurt Schwitters John Heartfield Vít Obr

Wyndham Lewis Walter Käch Jan Tschichold Carl Otto Müller

Hans Leistikow Otakar Mrkvička Louis Heijmans Paul S

Karl Gossow Franz Ehrlich Jean Carlu Vilmos Huszár

Myron Chepovskyi Ladislav Sutnar Gerard Kiljan Anton Sta

Alfred Willimann Max Gebhard Herbert Matter Andreas K

Vojtěch Tittelbach Wim Brusse Walter Herdeg Antonín Pelc

chwitters   Theo van Doesburg   Claude Dalbanne   Piet Zwart

xander Rodchenko   Karel Teige   Joost Schmidt   Georgii Stenberg

eveld   Max Burchartz   Walter Gropius   László Moholy-Nagy

arie Čermínová   Sybold van Ravesteyn   Theo van Doesburg

Josef Šíma   Nikolai Prusakov   Grigori Ilyich   Cyril Bouda

unato Depero   Otto Baumberger   César Domela   Gustav Klutsis

ema   Donald Brun   Georg Trump   Willem Hendrik Gispen

(Hans) Arp   Walter Cyliax   A. M. Cassandre   Man Ray

ski   Solomon Telingater   Paul Urban   Max Bill   Jacob Jongert

mberger   František Muzika   Pizzi & Pizio   Xanti Schawinsky

něk Rossmann   Hans Aeschbach   Hermann Eidenbenz

1912

Filippo Marinetti
1876–1944

Filippo Marinetti, cover for *Zang Tumb Tumb,* 1912.
20.4 x 12.2 cm
Private collection

Filippo Marinetti, cover for *Les mots en liberté futuristes*, 1919
19.2 x 13 cm
Private collection

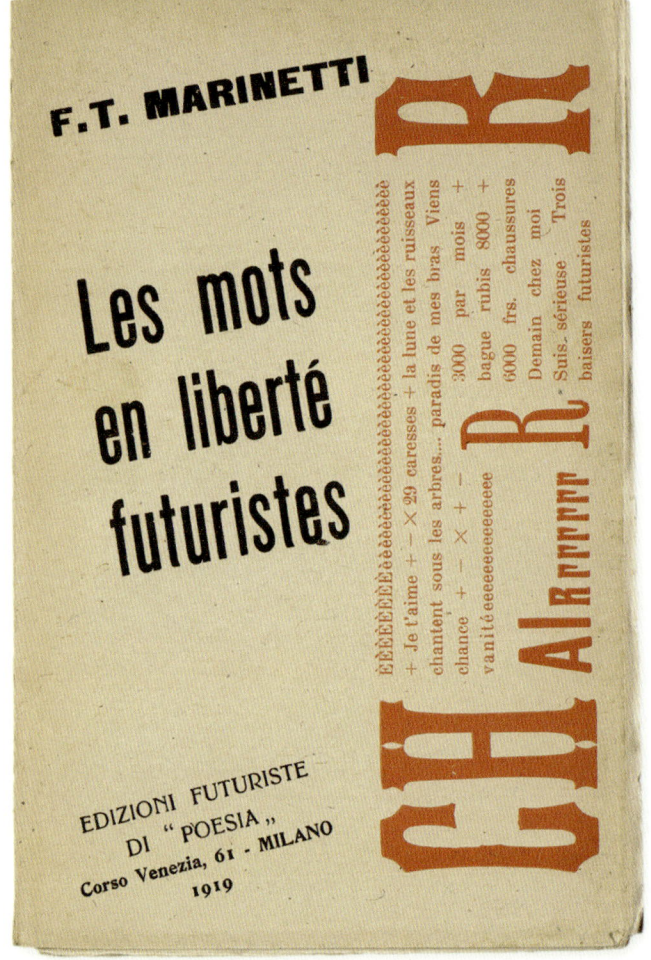

Filippo Marinetti, foldout from *Les mots en liberté futuristes*, Montagne + Vallate + Strade x Joffre, 1919.
34.6 x 24.6 cm
Private collection

Filippo Marinetti, "Une assemblée tumultueuse", foldout from *Les mots en liberté futuristes*, 1919.
33 x 26.4 cm
Private collection

Filippo Marinetti, foldout from *Les mots en liberté futuristes*, 1919.
23.5 x 33.8 cm
Private collection

Filippo Marinetti, cover and pages from *Parole in libertá futuriste*, 1932.
24 x 23 cm
Private collection

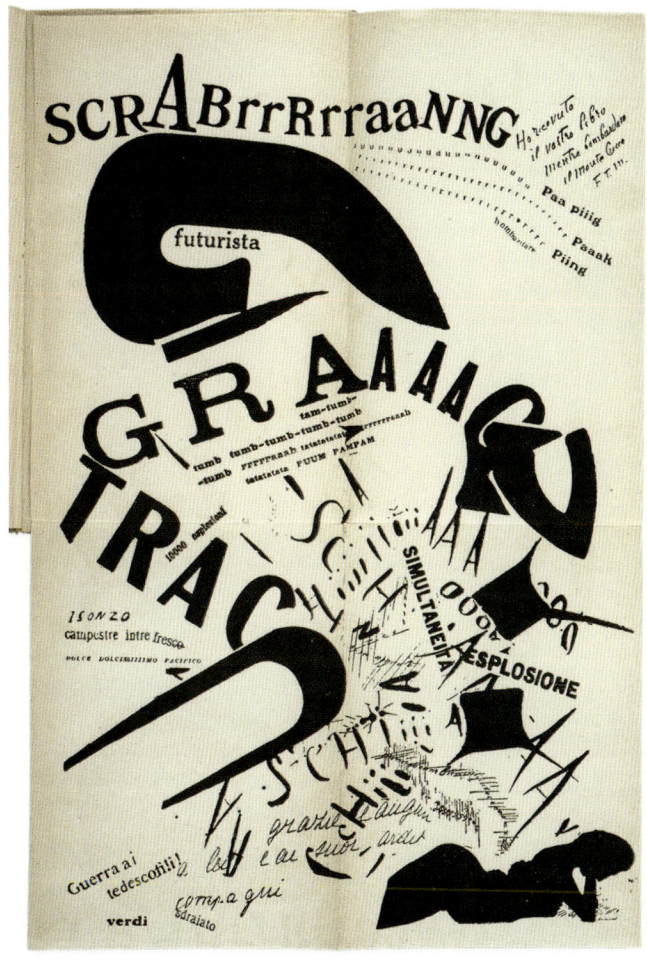

Oskar Schlemmer, poster for exhibition *Willy Baumeister, Oskar Schlemmer, Kunsthaus Schaller, Stuttgart*, 1918.
65 x 51 cm
Private collection
Courtesy www.iaddb.org

Oskar Schlemmer
1888-1943

KUNSTHAUS SCHALLER STUTTGART MARIENSTRASSE 14

AUSSTELLUNG: WILLY BAUMEISTER – OSKAR SCHLEMMER

1918

Guillaume Apollinaire
1880–1918

Guillaume Apollinaire, "Il pleut" from *Calligrammes*, 1918.
24.8 x 16.2 cm
Private collection

Guillaume Apollinaire, poem from *Calligrammes*, 1918.
24.8 x 16.2 cm
Private collection

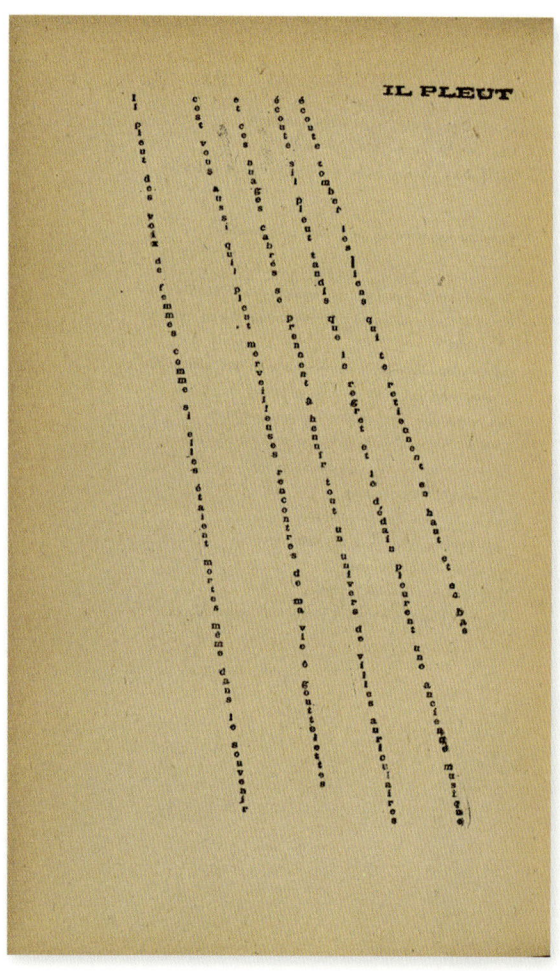

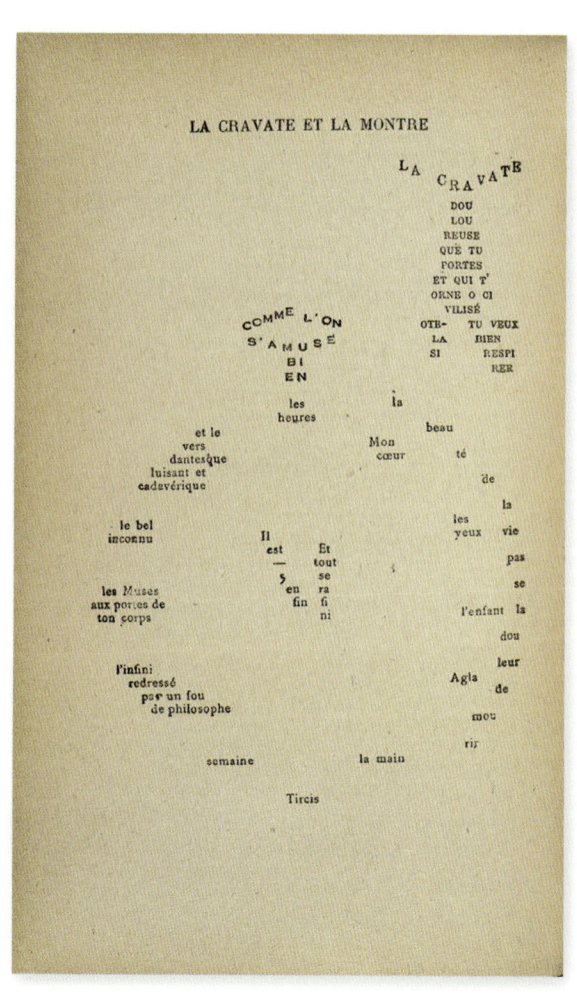

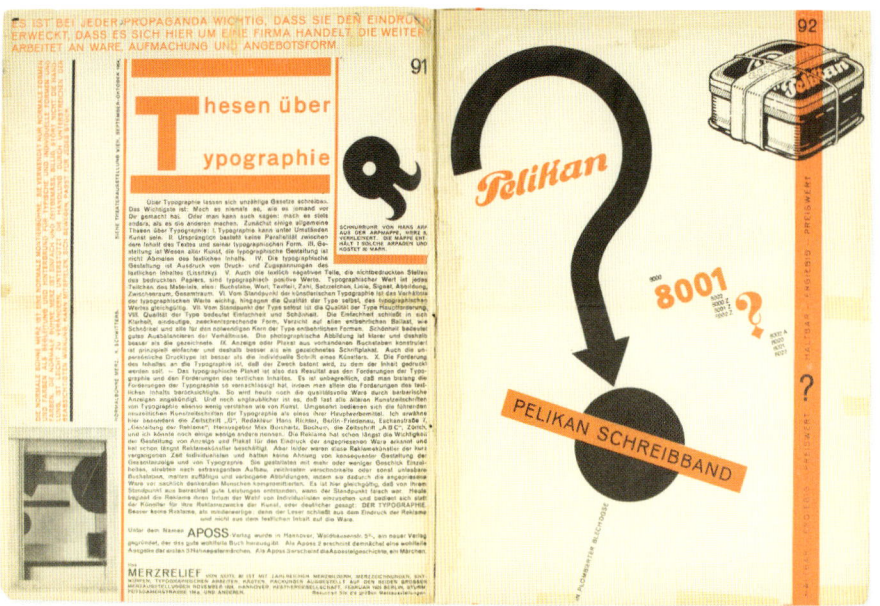

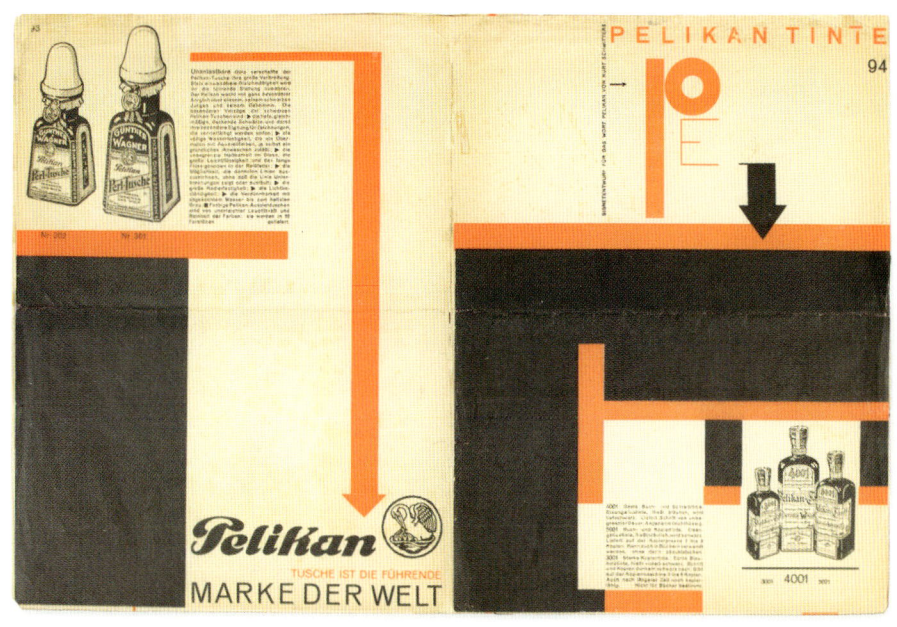

Kurt Schwitters, poster for
Plakat Ausstellung, 1928.
47.6 x 64.8 cm
Private collection
Courtesy www.iaddb.org

NSTVEREIN WIESBADEN

AKAT
SSTELLUNG

928 IM NEUEN MUSEUM

GEÖFFNET VON 10 BIS 13 UND VON 15 BIS 17 UHR
SONNTAGS VON 10 BIS 13 UHR · MONTAGS GESCHLOSSEN

Kurt Schwitters, poster for *Ausstellung Karlsruhe Dammerstock*, 1929.
84 x 59.4 cm
Private collection
Courtesy www.iaddb.org

1920

Theo van Doesburg
1883–1931

Theo van Doesburg, front and back cover for *De theorie van het syndicalisme*, 1920.
19.2 x 18.2 cm
Private collection

LITERATUUROVERZICHT SYNDICALISME INDUSTRIAL-UNIONISM

Syndicalisme & Socialisme. (In Italië door Arturo Labriola. In Duitschland door Robert Michels. In Rusland door Boris Kritschewsky. In Frankrijk door Hubert Lagardelle; opstellen over „Les Caractères du Syndicalisme français", door Victor Griffuelhes en over „Anarchisme et Syndicalisme", door Hubert Lagardelle.) Emile Pouget. La Confédération Générale du Travail, L'Organisation, la tactique (l'action directe) les résultats. Georges Sorel. La décomposition du marxisme. Victor Griffuelhes. l'Action Syndicaliste. Le Parti Socialiste et la Confédération du Travail. (Redevoeringen van Hubert Lagardelle, Jules Guesde en Edouard Vaillant op het soc. kongres te Nancy (1907).) Ed. Berth. Les nouveaux Aspects du Socialisme. M. T. Laurin. Les Instituteurs et le Syndicalisme. G. Sorel. La Révolution dreyfusienne. P. Delesalle. Les Bourses du Travail et la C. G. T. Chr. Cornelissen. Op weg naar een nieuwe Maatschappij. A. van Emmenes. Onafhankelijke en „moderne" vakorganisatie. L. Jouhaux. Le Syndicalisme et la C.G.T. (1920). (Een feitelijk overzicht). Victor Griffuelhes. Voyage révolutionaire. Fernand Pelloutier. Le Congrès Général du Parti Socialiste Français (1899), précédé d'une Lettre aux Anarchistes. Pouget et Pataud. Comment nous ferons la Révolution. Pouget. Le sabotage. Pouget. L'Organisation du surmenage. Sorel. Matériaux pour une théorie du prolétariat. Sorel. Réflexions sur la Violence. Fernand Pelloutier. La Vie Ouvrière. Kritsky. L'Evolution du Syndicalisme. Rudolf Rocker. Die Prinzipienerklärung des Syndikalismus. Rudolf Rocker. Zur Geschichte der parlamentarischen Tätigkeit in der modernen Arbeiterbewegung. Franz Barwich. Das Rätesystem von unten auf. Der kommunistische Aufbau des Syndikalismus im Gegensatz zum Partei-Kommunismus und Staatssozialismus. Karl Roche. Zwei Sozialisierungsfragen. Karl Roche. Organisierte direkte Aktion. Peter Kropotkin. Gesetz und Autorität. Peter Kropotkin. Der Wohlstand für Alle. John Graham Brooks. American Syndicalism: The I.W.W. W. W. Craik. Outlines of the History of the Working Class Movement. Brissenden. The I.W.W. Daniel de Leon. Die Prinzipien-Erklärung der I.W.W. Grover H. Terry and B. H. Williams. The Revolutionary I.W.W. F. Wolffheim. Betriebsorganisation oder Gewerkschaft? K. Schröder und F. Wensel. Wesen und Ziele der rev. Betriebsorg. Lenin. Der Radikalismus, eine Kinderkrankheit des Kommunismus. Al deze werken zijn verkrijgbaar bij de:

NIEUWE AMSTERDAMMER 2e CONST. HUYGENSSTRAAT 79 A'DAM

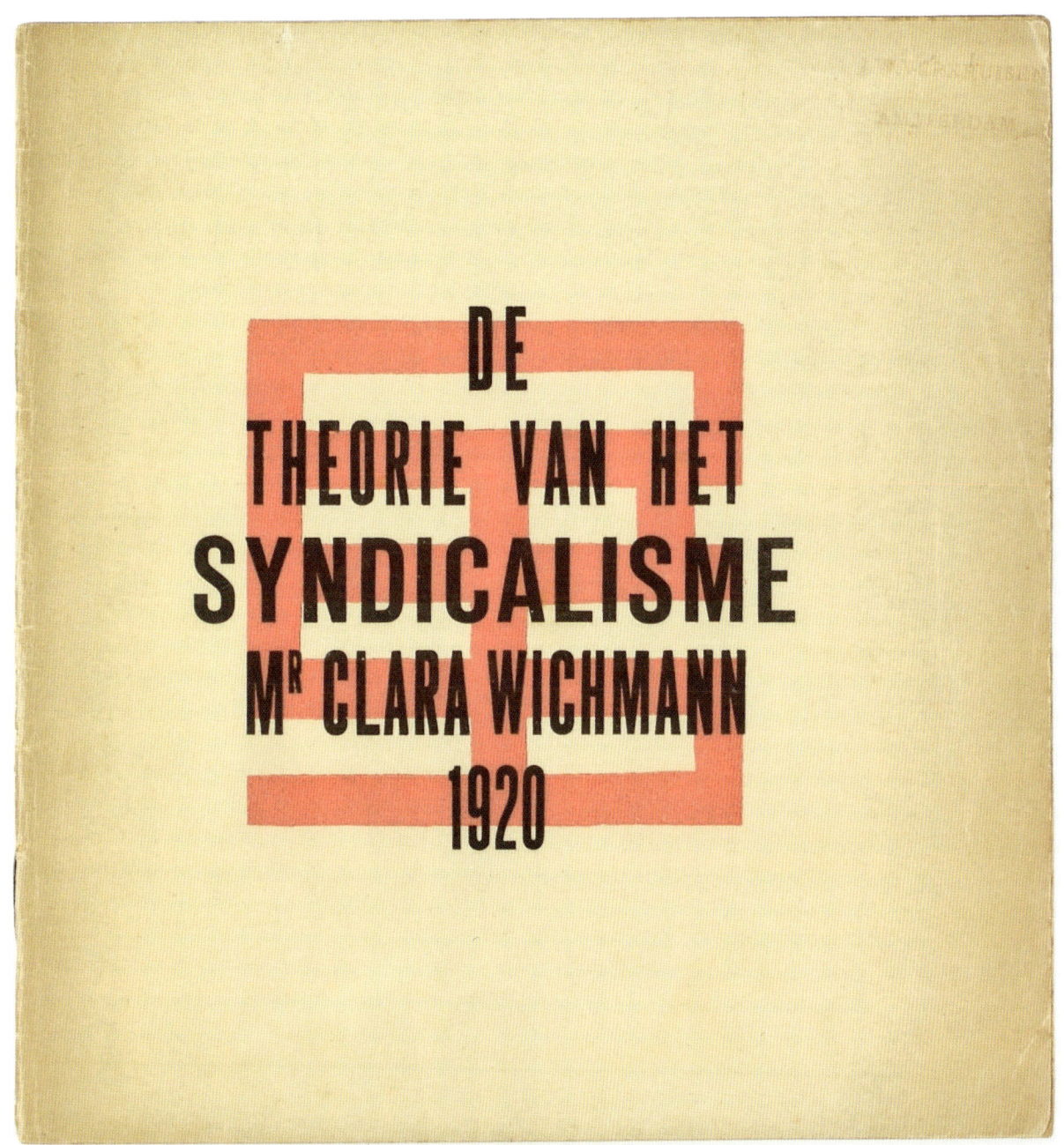

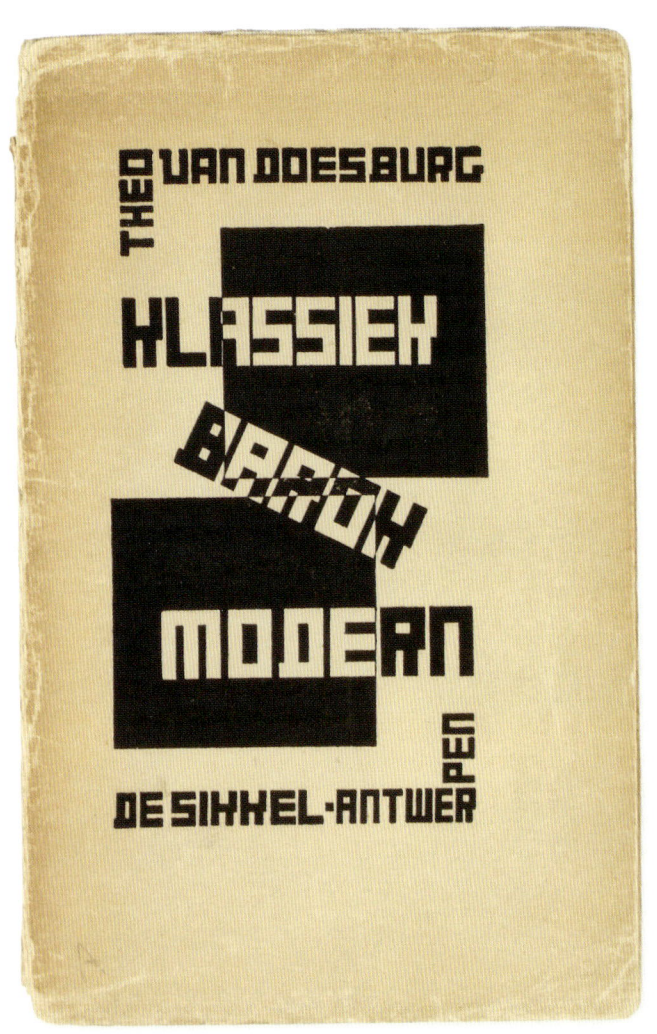
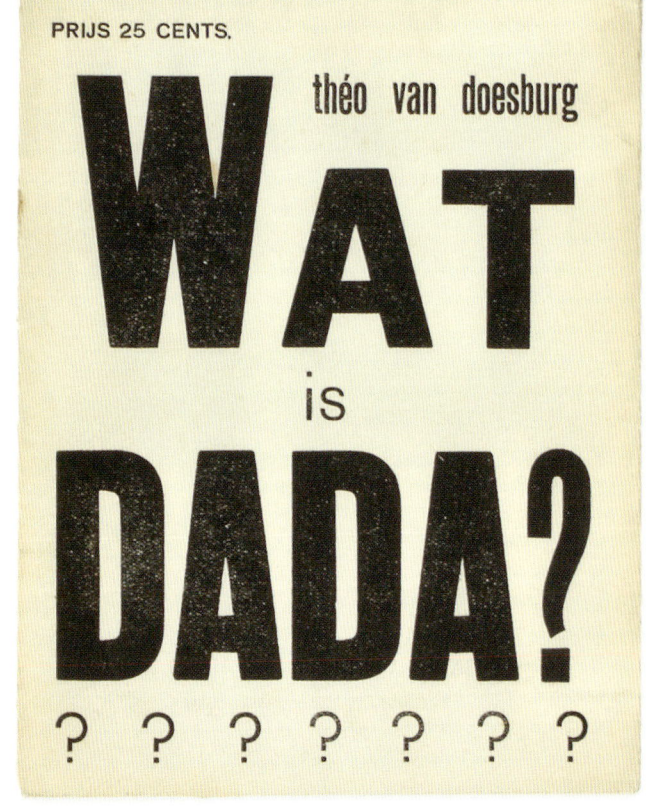

Theo van Doesburg, cover for *Klassiek, barok, modern*, De Sikkel Antwerpen, 1920.
22.5 x 14.5 cm
Private collection

Theo van Doesburg, cover for *Wat is Dada,* 1923.
15.7 x 12.2 cm
Private collection

Theo van Doesburg,
postcard for magazine
NB De Stijl, 1927.
10.5 x 15.8 cm
Private collection

Theo van Doesburg, cover,
NB De Stijl, 1927.
21.7 x 27.1 cm
Private collection

Theo van Doesburg,
front and back cover for
magazine *De Stijl*, 10 jaren
De Stijl 1921–27. 1927.
21.7 x 27.1 cm
Private collection

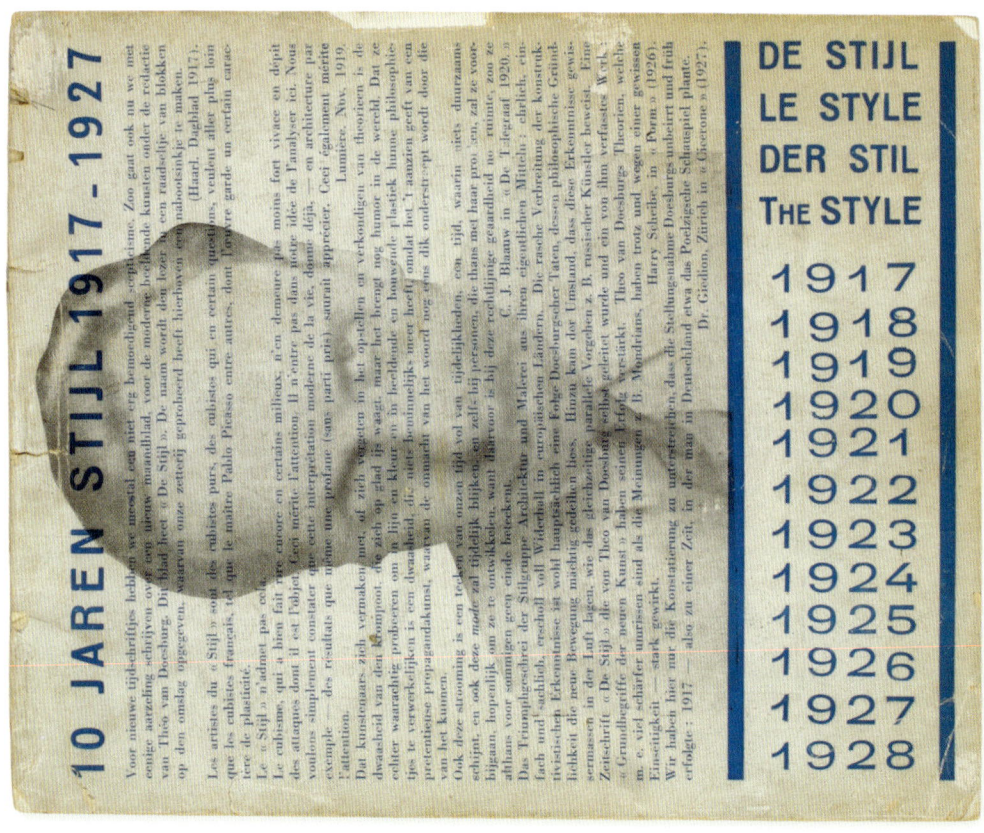

Theo van Doesburg, cover for *AC: Art Concret*, 1930.
18.5 x 13.8 cm
Private collection

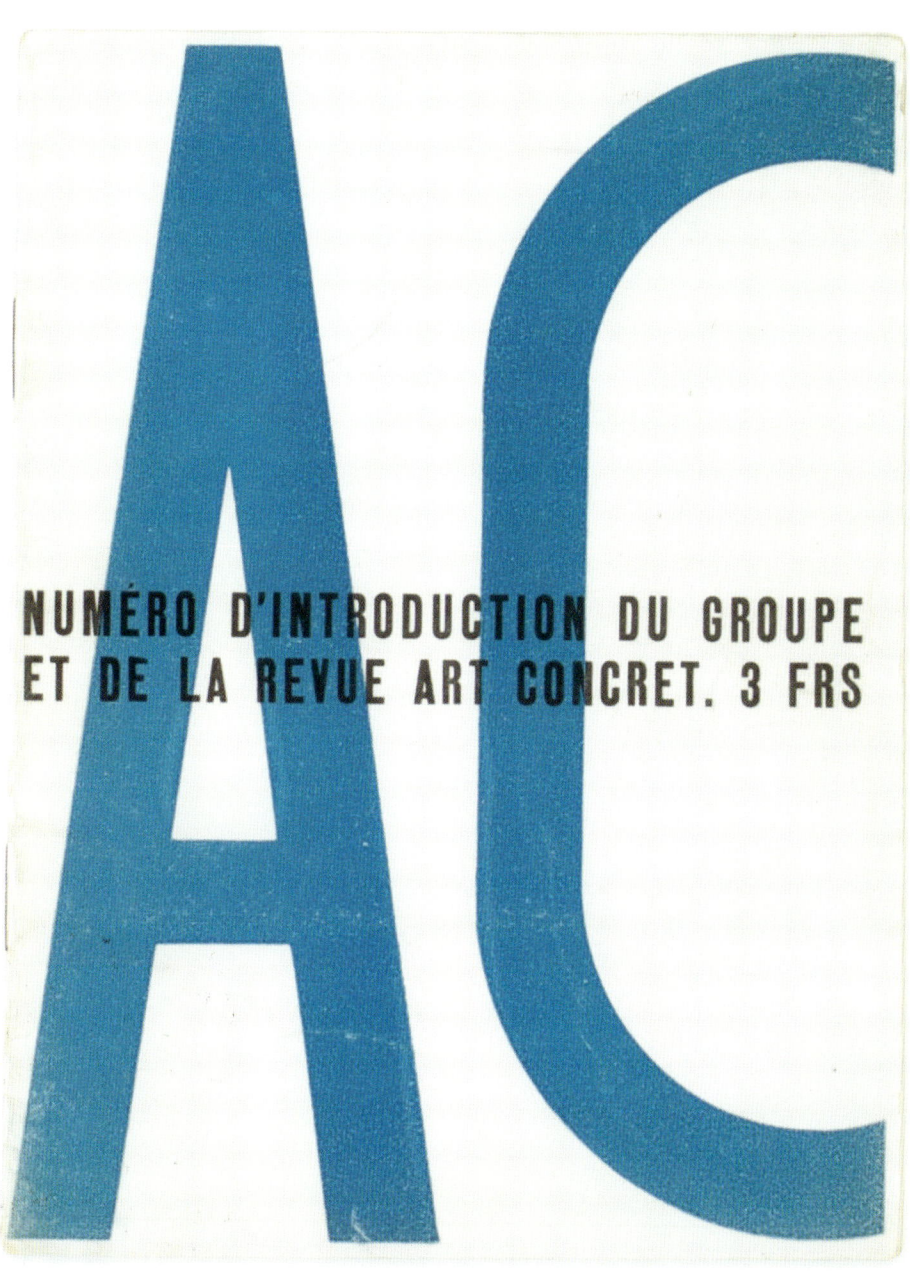

Claude Dalbanne
1877–1964

Claude Dalbanne, cover and spreads for *Bonjour cinéma*, 1921.
17.9 x 11.7 cm
Private collection

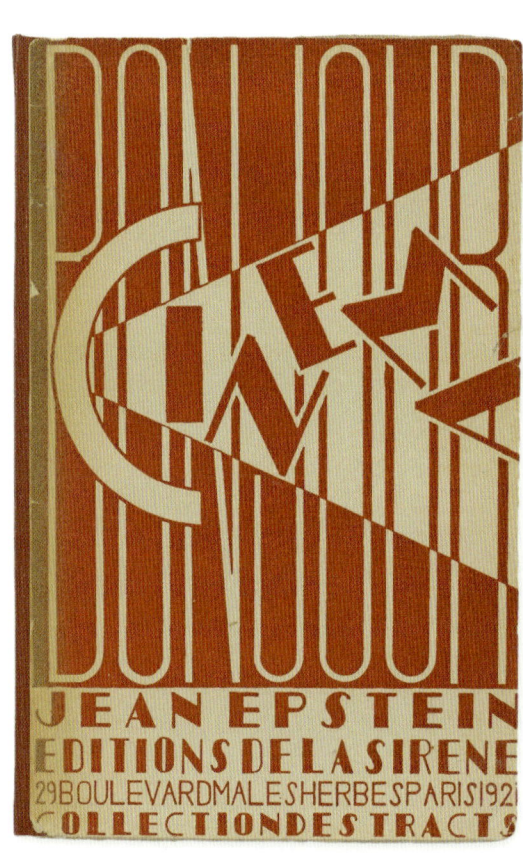

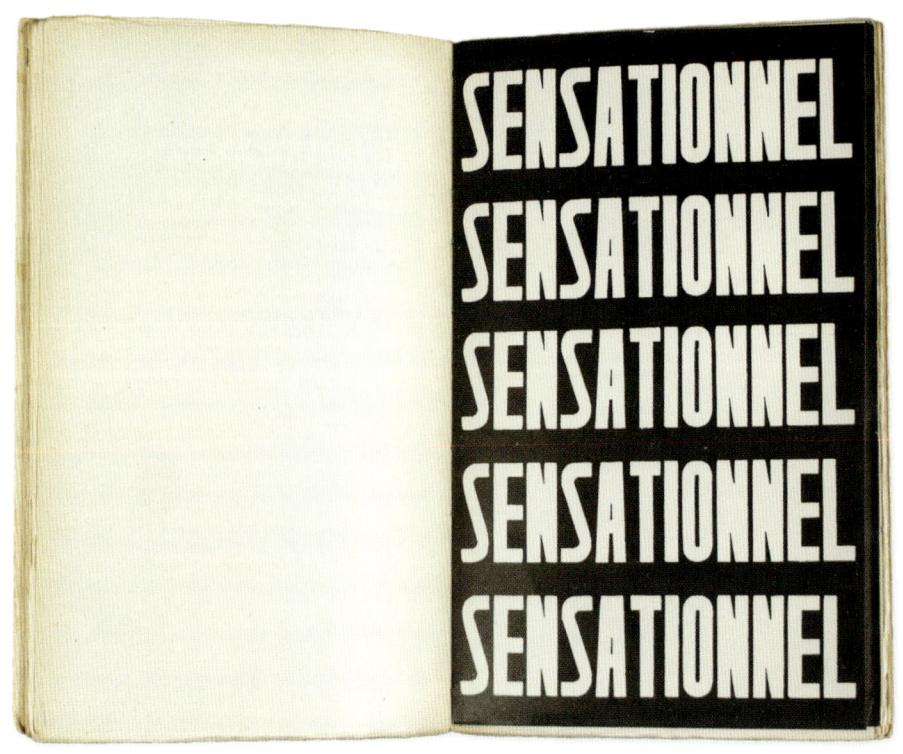

Alla Nazimova

la femme coupable
Avec un rire élastique
il bondit sur sa joie
et s'étonne de la musique
nègre d'un jazz-band
Il penche la tête de côté
en de lasses attitudes
ne manquez pas d'observer
la belle coupe de ses cheveux
Il est précis acrobatique
comme un ressort bien remonté
et
j'aime surtout
en marge du champ
quand il n'exprime rien
que lui-même.

Sessue Hayakawa

NAZI
NAZI
NAZIMOW

NAZIMOWA

TOURNE

OH

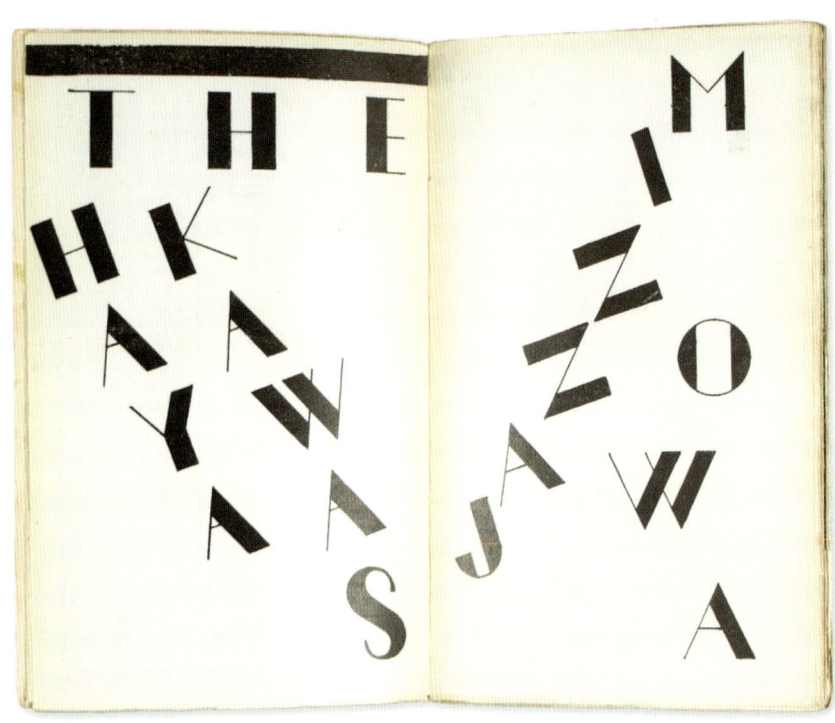

Claude Dalbanne, spreads
for *Bonjour cinéma*, 1921.
17.9 x 11.7 cm
Private collection

Claude Dalbanne, spread for *Bonjour cinéma*, 1921.
17.9 x 11.7 cm
Private collection

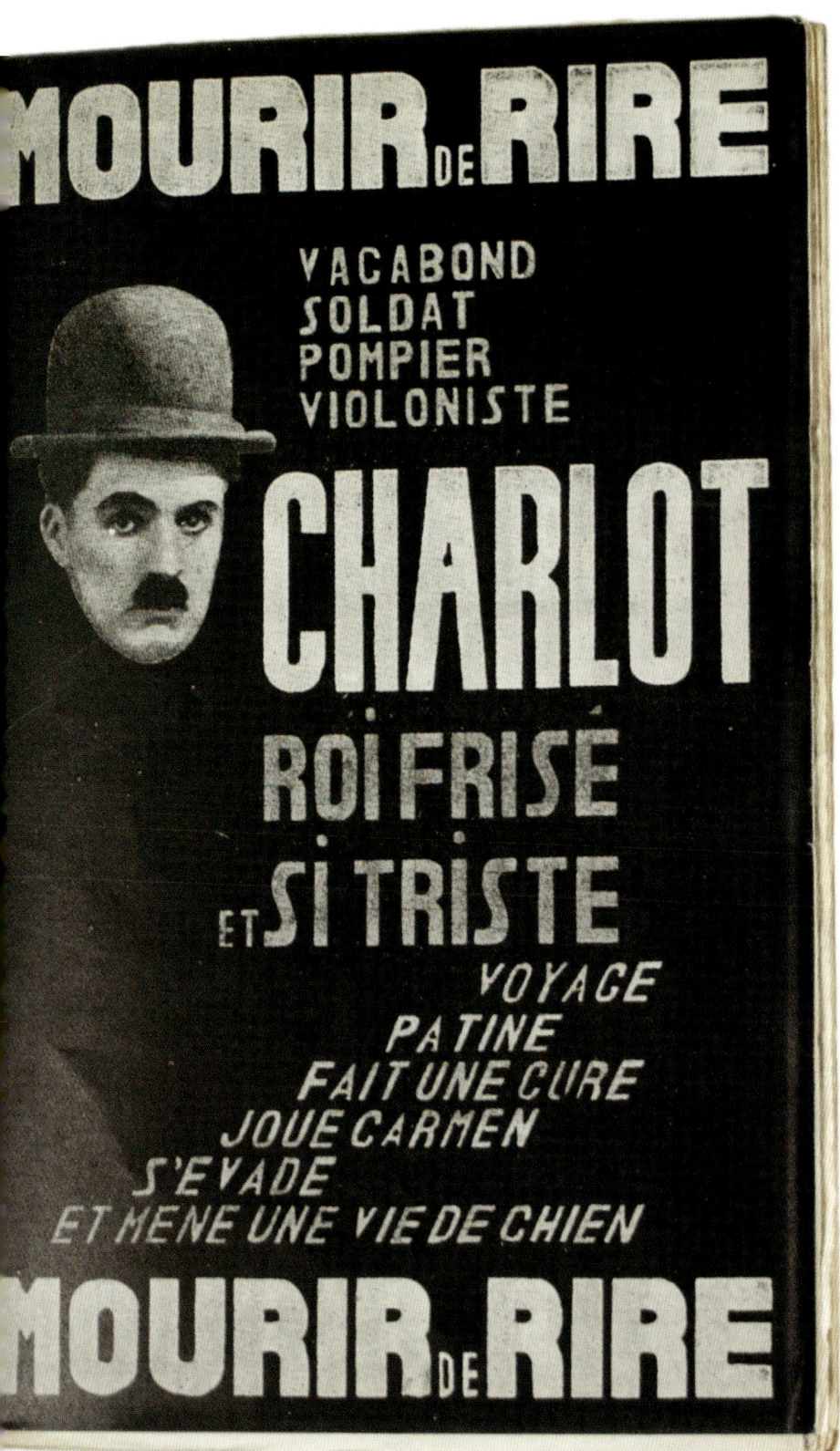

Piet Zwart, poster for *Laga Rubber-Vloeren* (rubber flooring company), c. 1922. 91 x 65 cm.
Private collection
Courtesy www.iaddb.org

Piet Zwart
1885-1977

Piet Zwart, cover and pages
of *Normalisatieboekje* for NKF,
Nederlandse Kabelfabriek,
Delft, 1923–1932.
18.2 x 10.9 cm
Private collection

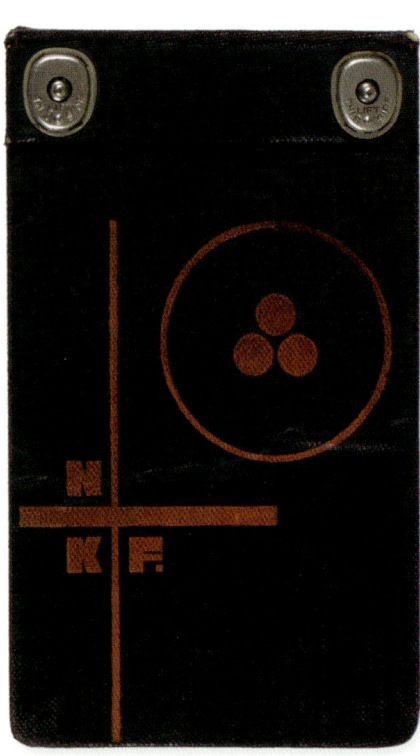

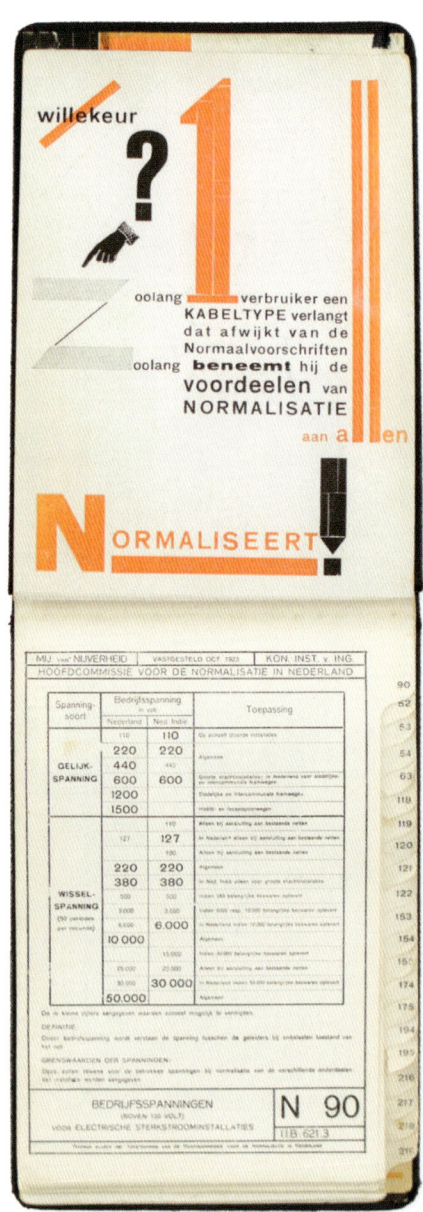

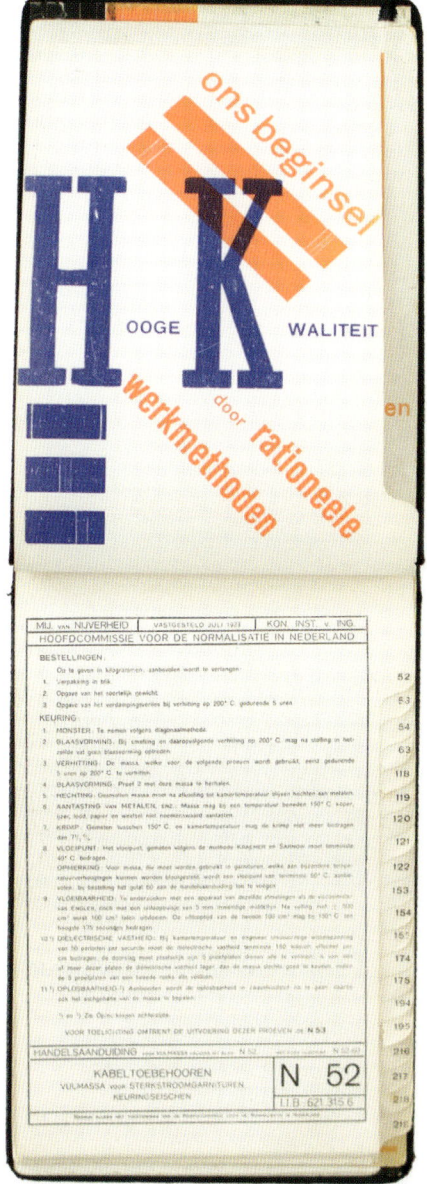
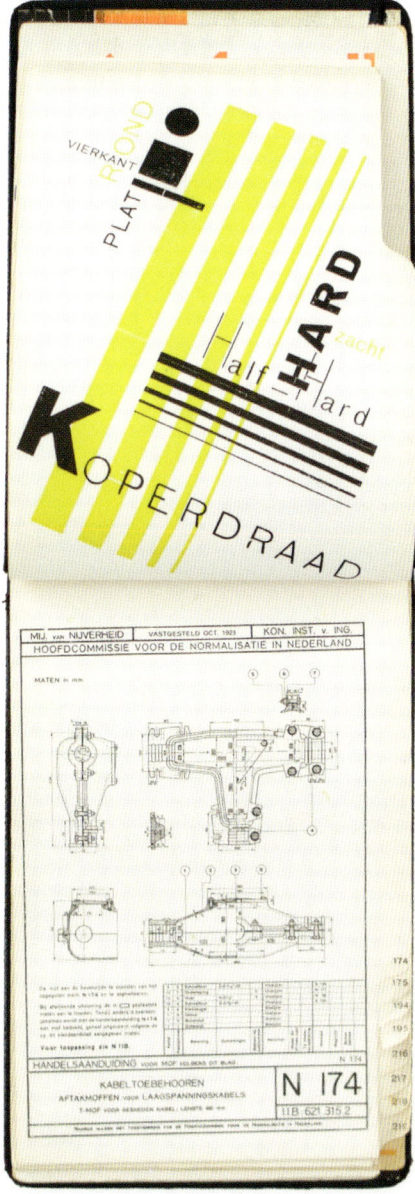
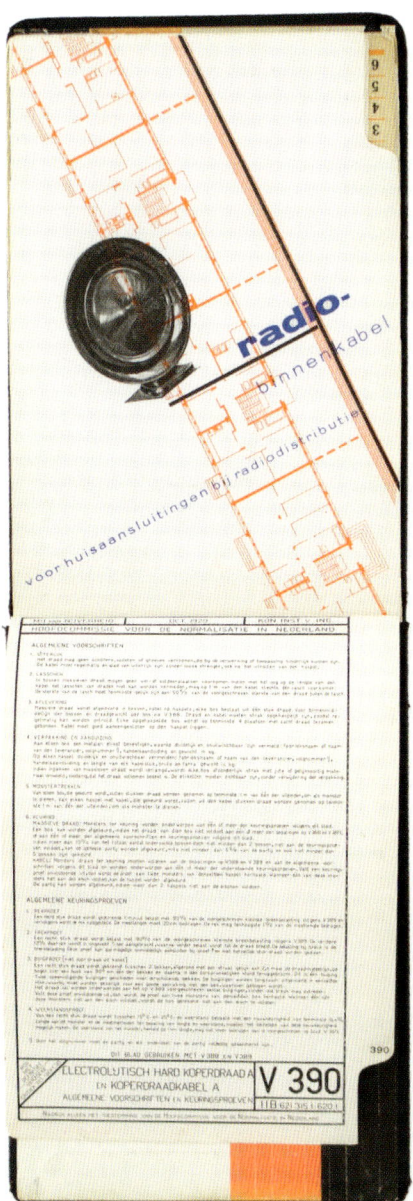

Piet Zwart, poster for *ITF Film,*
The Hague, 1928.
108 x 78 cm
Private collection
Courtesy www.iaddb.org

Piet Zwart, N.V. brochure cover for *Nederlandse Kabelfabriek*, Delft Kabels, 1933.
21.5 x 17.8 cm
Private collection

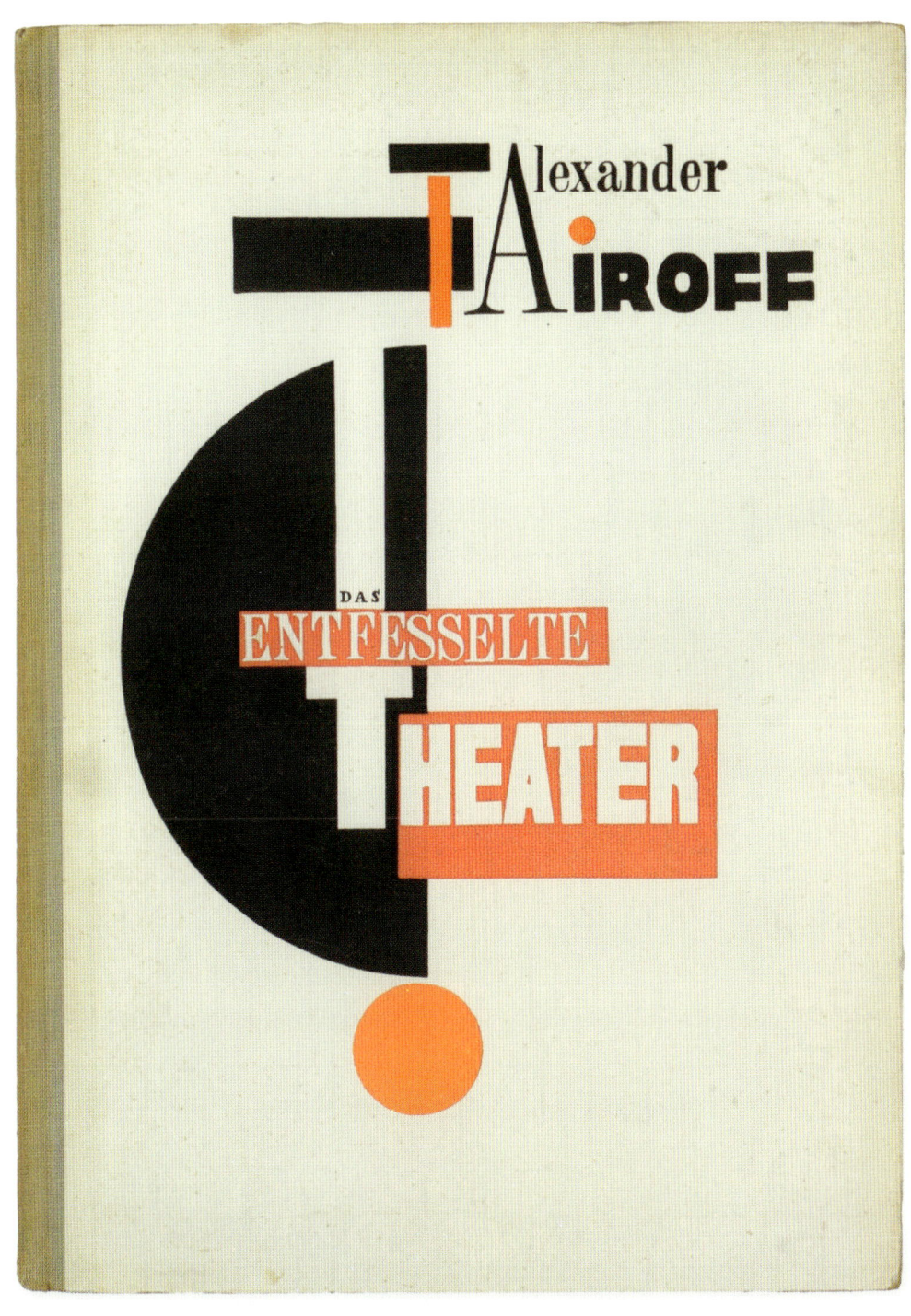

El Lissitzky, cover for *Das entfesselte Theater*, 1923.
24.9 x 17.8 cm
Private collection

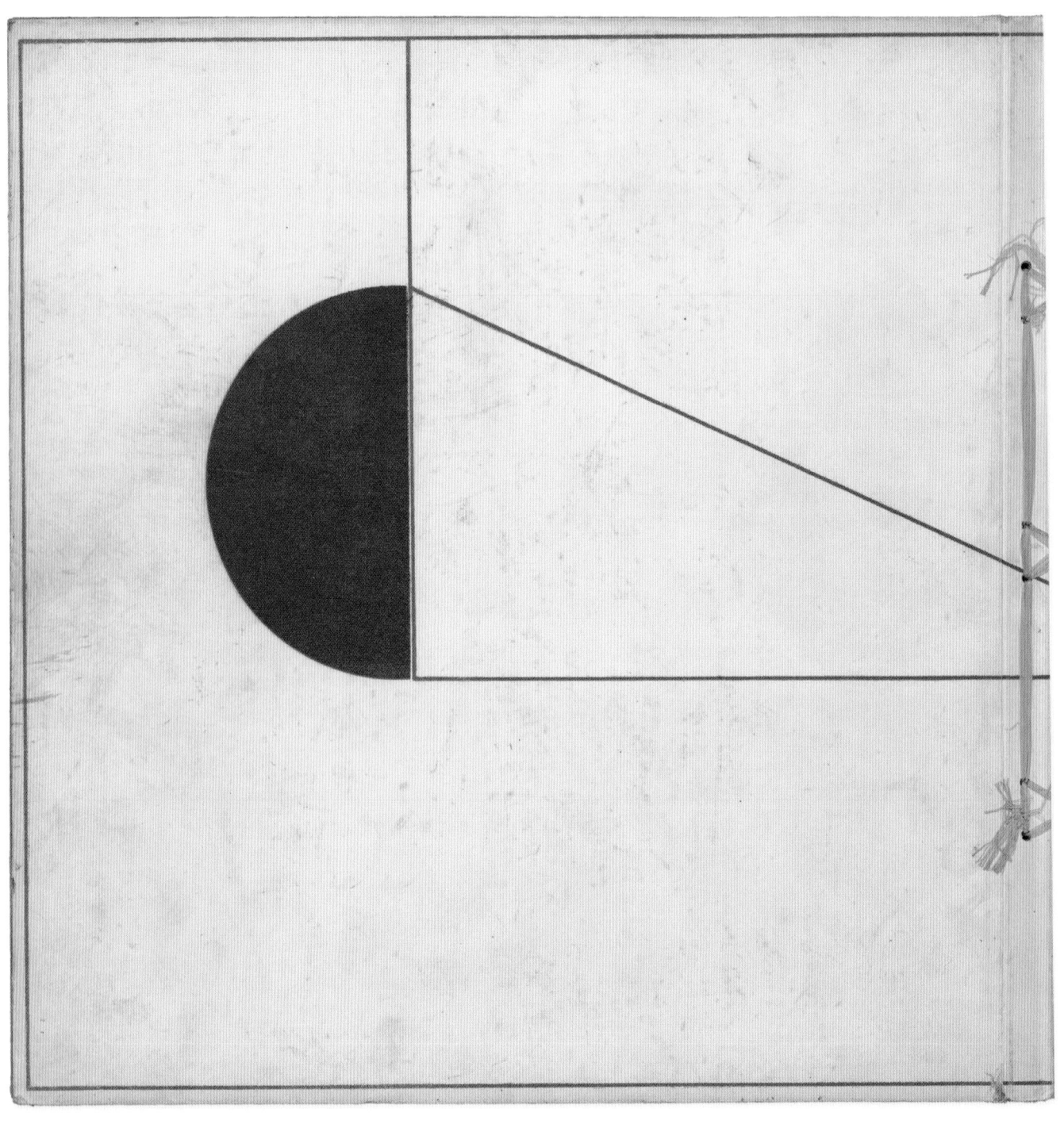

El Lissitzky, cover for magazine
Wendingen, 1922.
33 x 33 cm.
Private collection
Courtesy www.iaddb.org

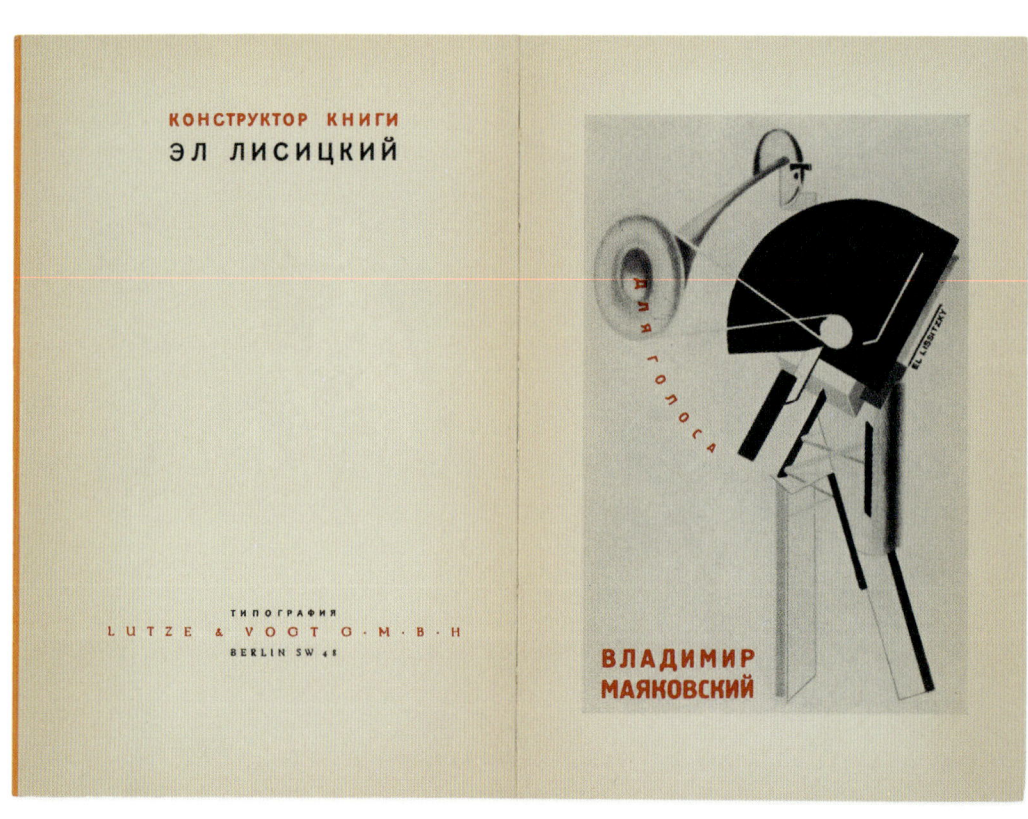

El Lissitzky, cover and spreads for *Dlja golosa* by Vladimir Mayakovsky, Berlin. RSFSR Gosudarstvennoe izdatel'stvo, 1923.
18.7 x 13 cm
Universiteit van Amsterdam, Bijzondere Collecties, Amsterdam

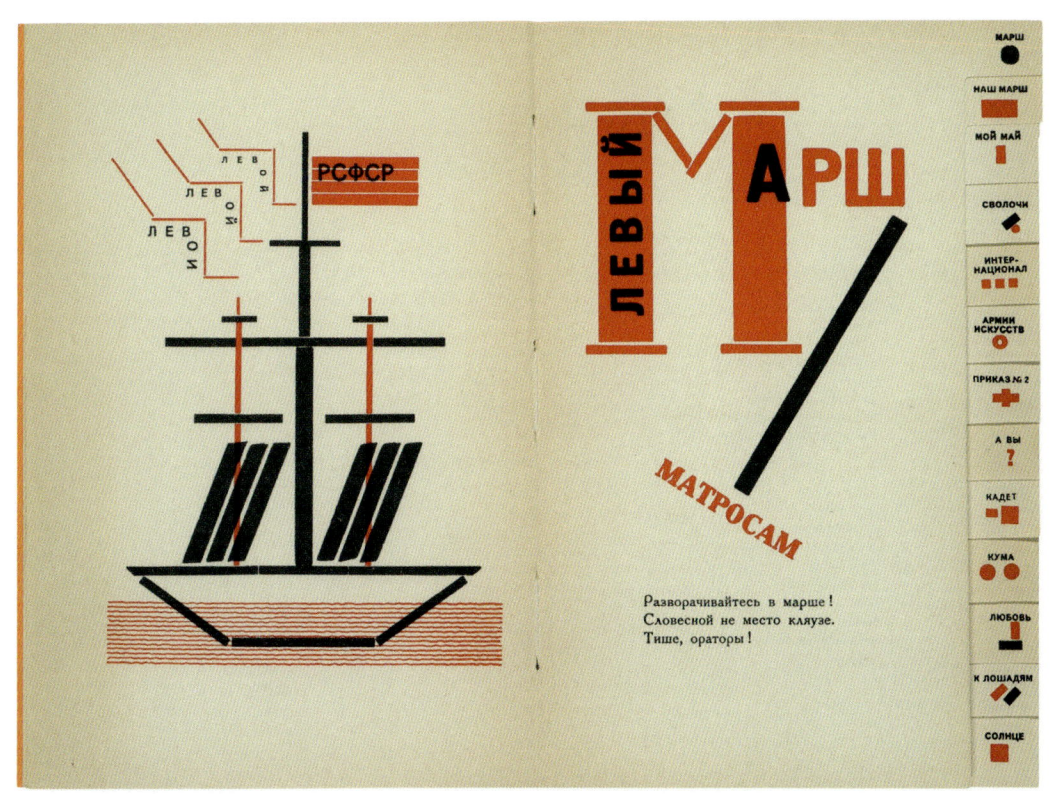

El Lissitzky, cover and spreads for *Pressa Köln*, 1928.
21.2 x 15.2 cm
Private collection

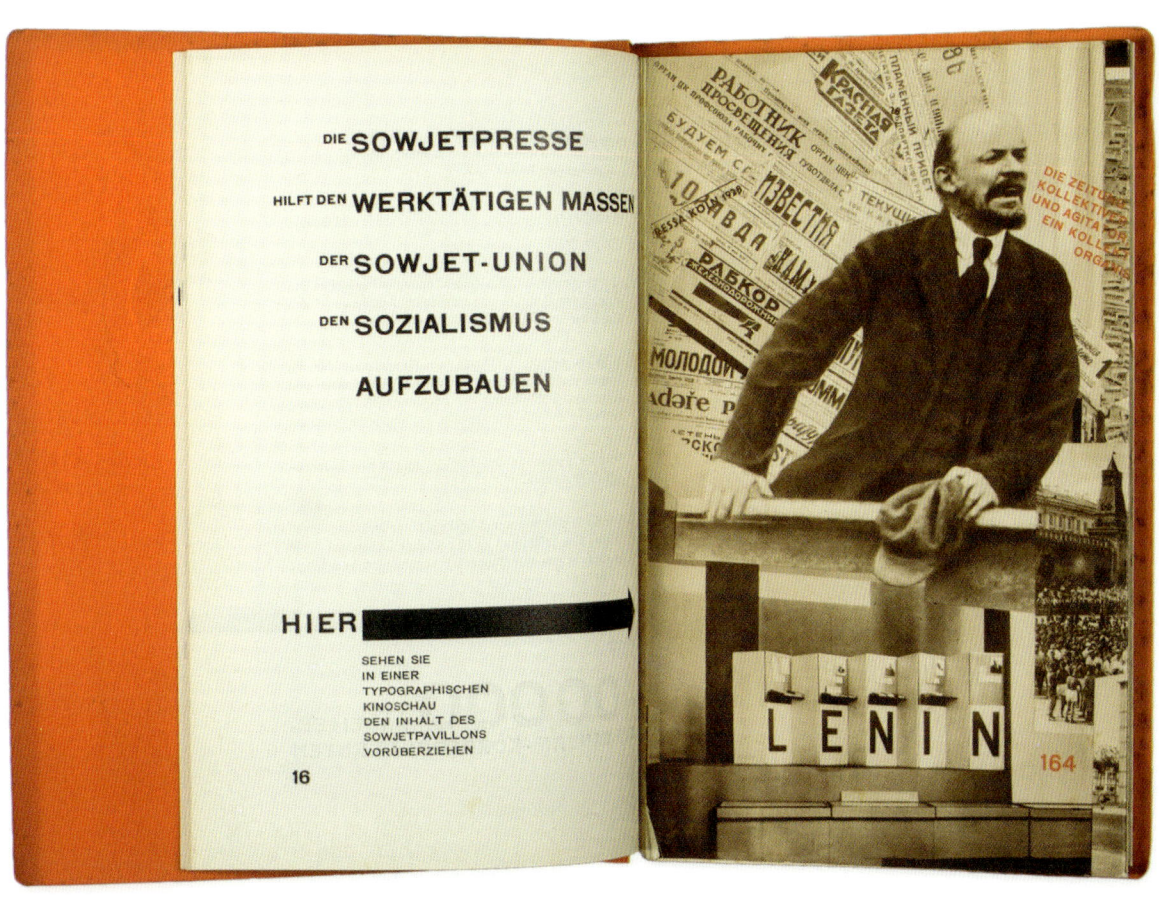

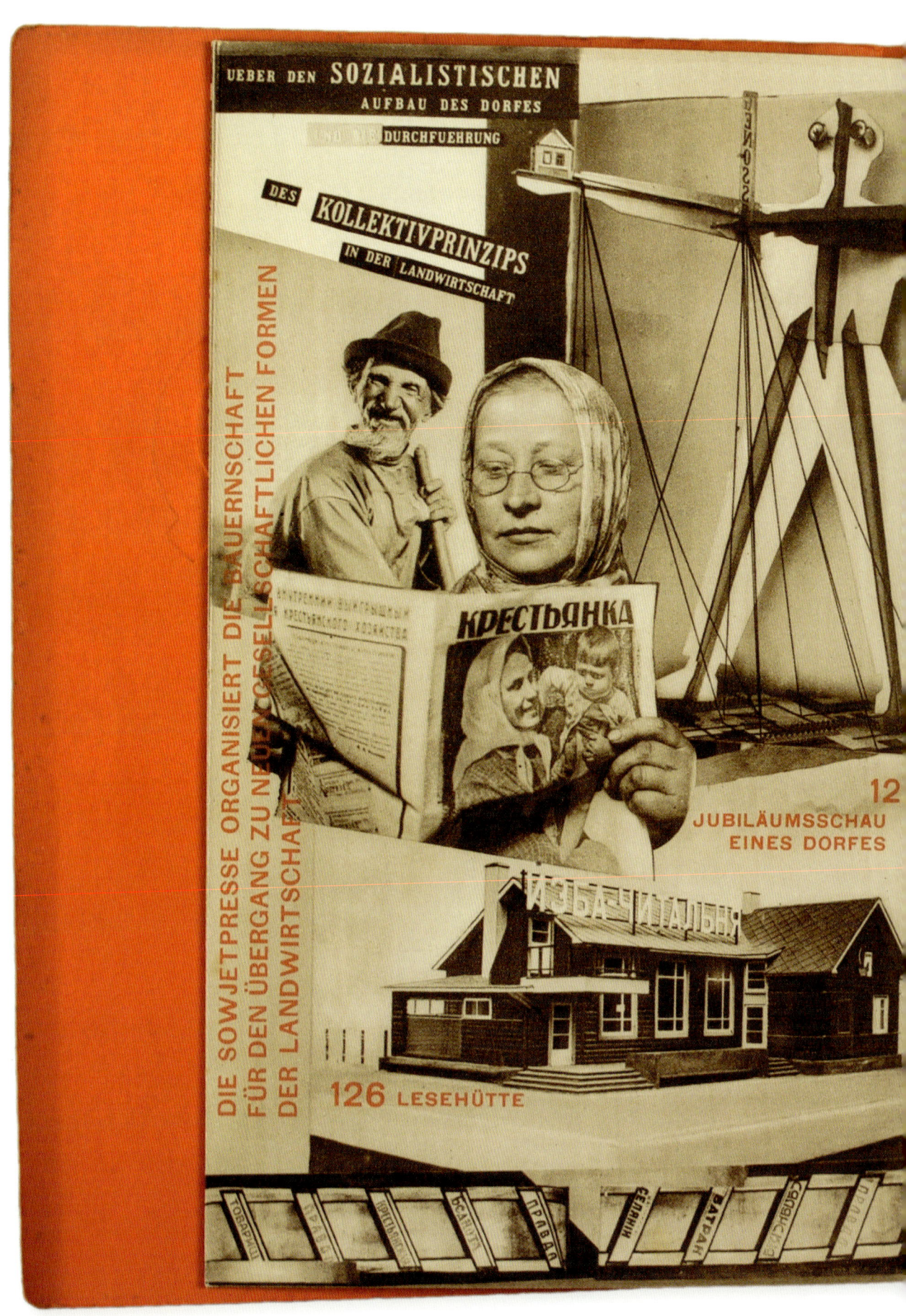

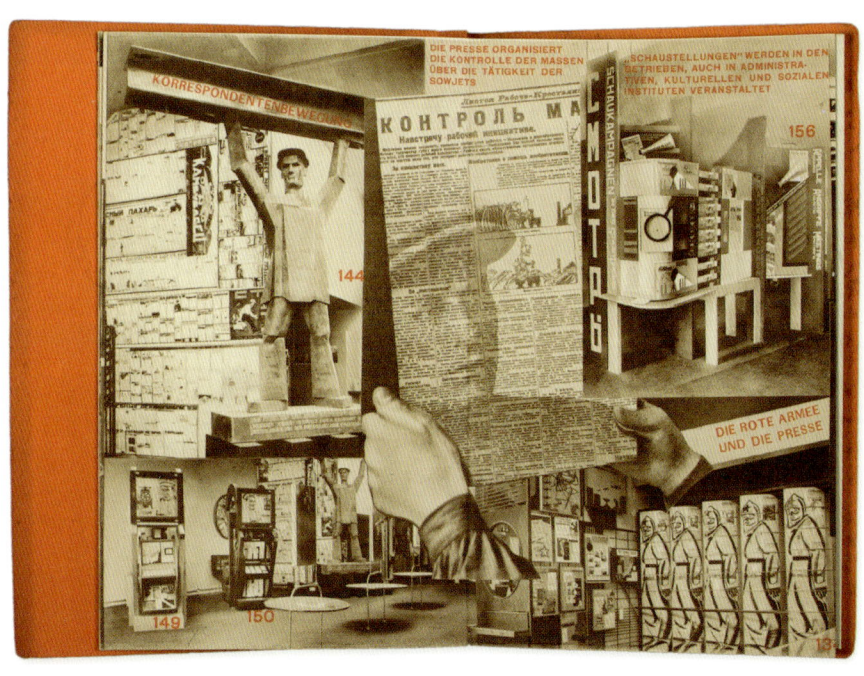

El Lissitzky, cover for
*Russische Ausstellung,
Kunstgewerbemuseum
Zürich*, 1929.
22.7 x 14.7 cm

El Lissitzky, cover and spread for *Amerika*, 1930.
28.8 x 22.6 cm
Private collection

El Lissitzky, cover and spread for *USSR im Bau*, no. 2, 1934.
41.8 x 29.7 cm
Private collection

El Lissitzky, cover and spread for *SSSR na stroike*, 1935.
41.8 x 29.7 cm
Private collection

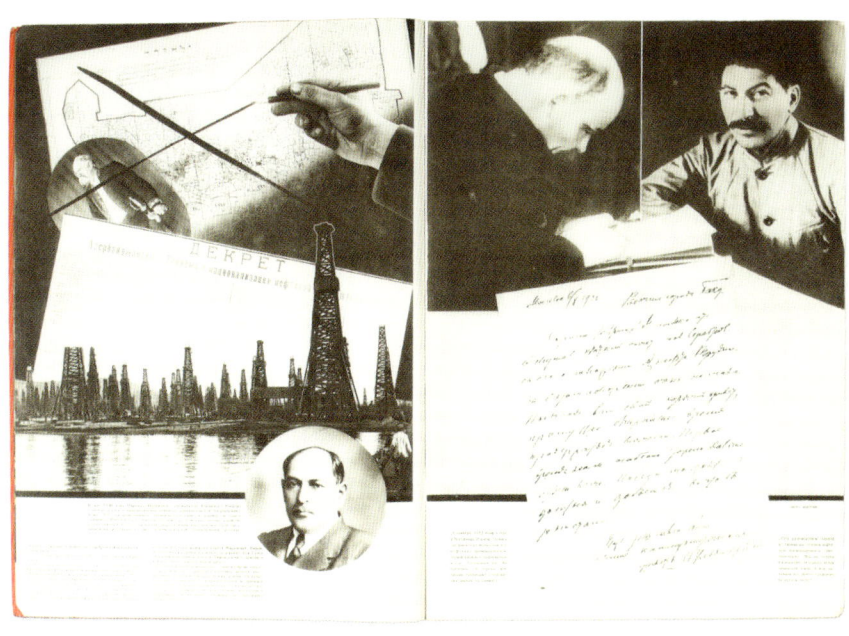
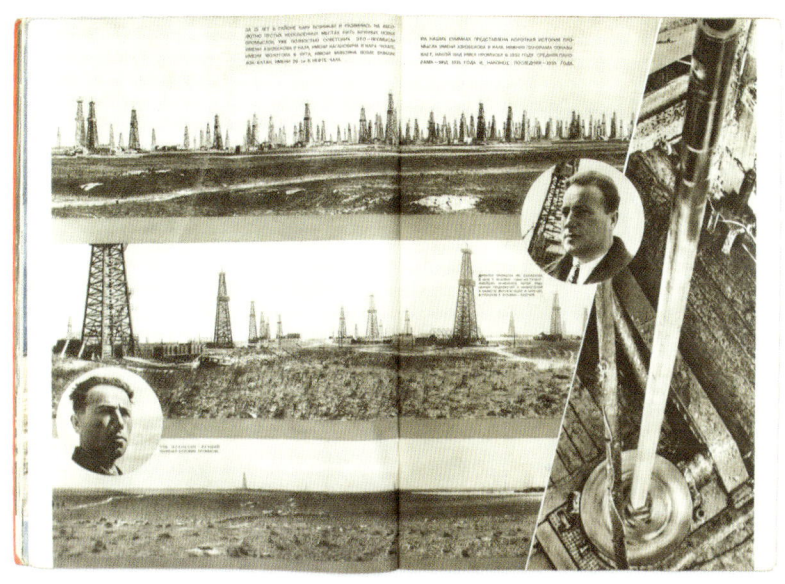
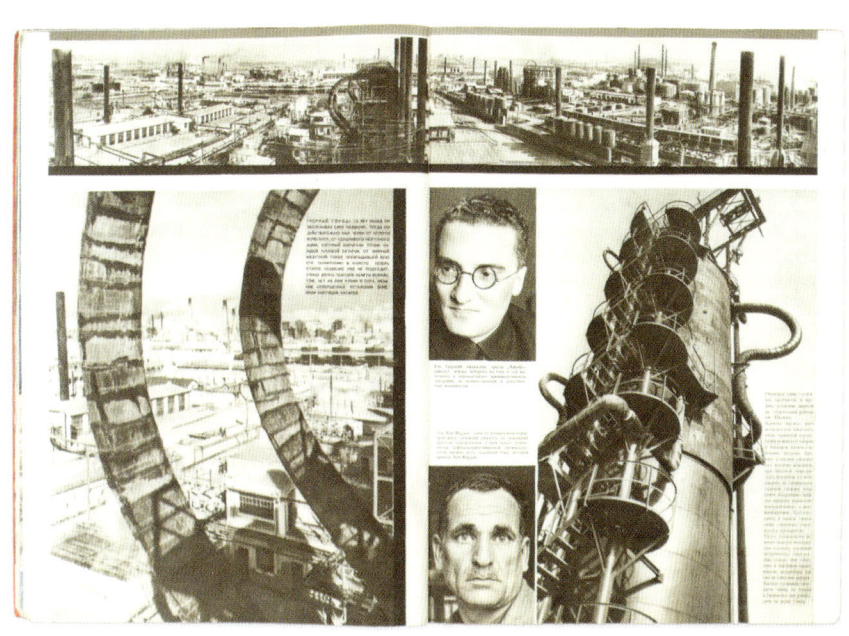

El Lissitzky, cover and spread for *URSS en construction 1917–1937*, 1937.
41.8 x 29.7 cm
Private collection

Theo van Doesburg and Kurt Schwitters, poster for *Kleine Dada Soirée*, 1922. 27.9 x 30.2 Private collection

Theo van Doesburg
1883–1931

Kurt Schwitters
1887–1948

1923

Herbert Bayer
1900–1985

Herbert Bayer, cover design,
*Staatliches Bauhaus in Weimar,
1919-1923*, 1923.
24.8 x 25.4 cm
Private collection

Herbert Bayer, emergency money Weimar, 1923.
7 x 14.1 cm
Private collection

Herbert Bayer, exhibition poster for *Europäisches Kunstgewerbe, Leipig*, 1927.
90 x 60 cm
Private collection
Courtesy www.iaddb.org

Herbert Bayer, cover of program booklet, *Werkbund annual convention in Breslau,* 1929.
10.5 x 14.8 cm
Private collection
Courtesy www.iaddb.org

Herbert Bayer, cover of program booklet, *Werkbund annual convention in Breslau,* 1929.
10.5 x 14.8 cm
Private collection
Courtesy www.iaddb.org

Herbert Bayer, poster for
Teutoburger Wald, 1931.
102.4 x 69.3 cm
Private collection
Courtesy www.iaddb.org

Herbert Bayer, brochure cover and spread, *Wohnbedarf*, 1933.
15 x 21.3 cm
Private collection

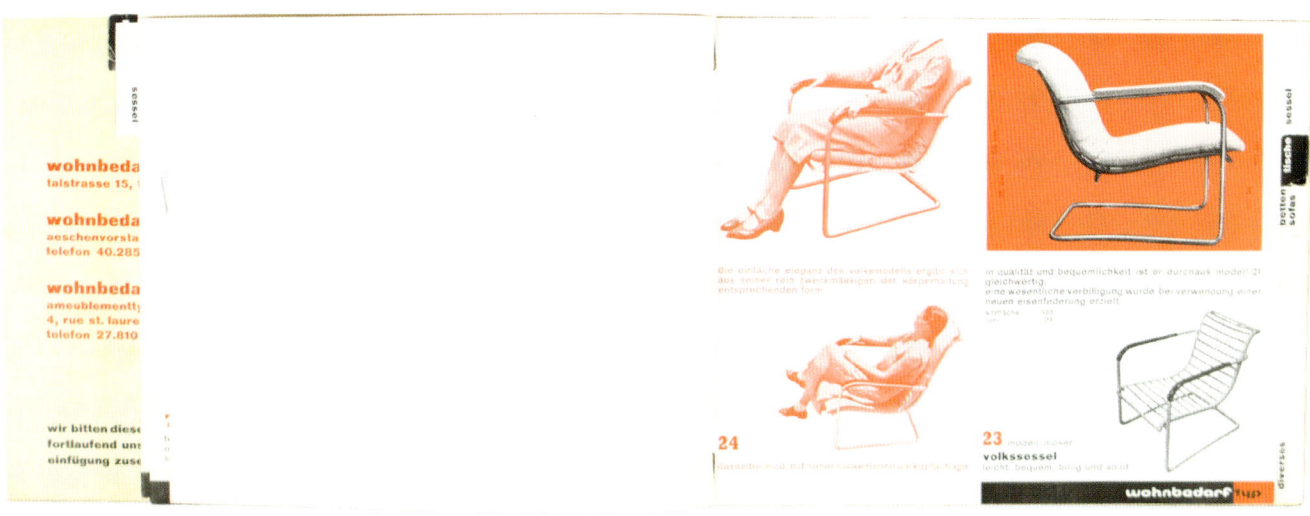

Herbert Bayer, brochure cover and spread, *Wohnbedarf*, 1933–1934.
14.9 x 21 cm
Private collection

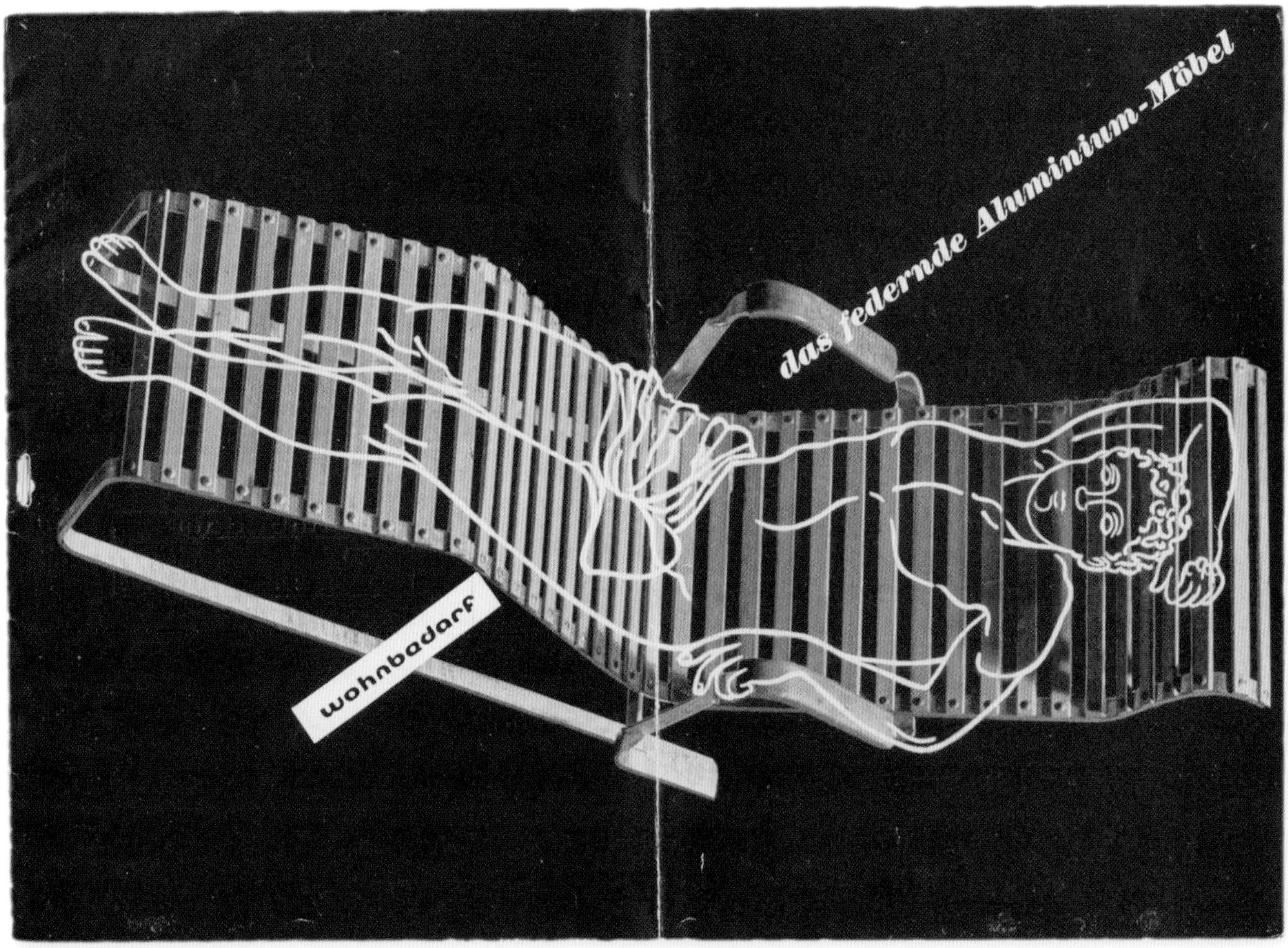

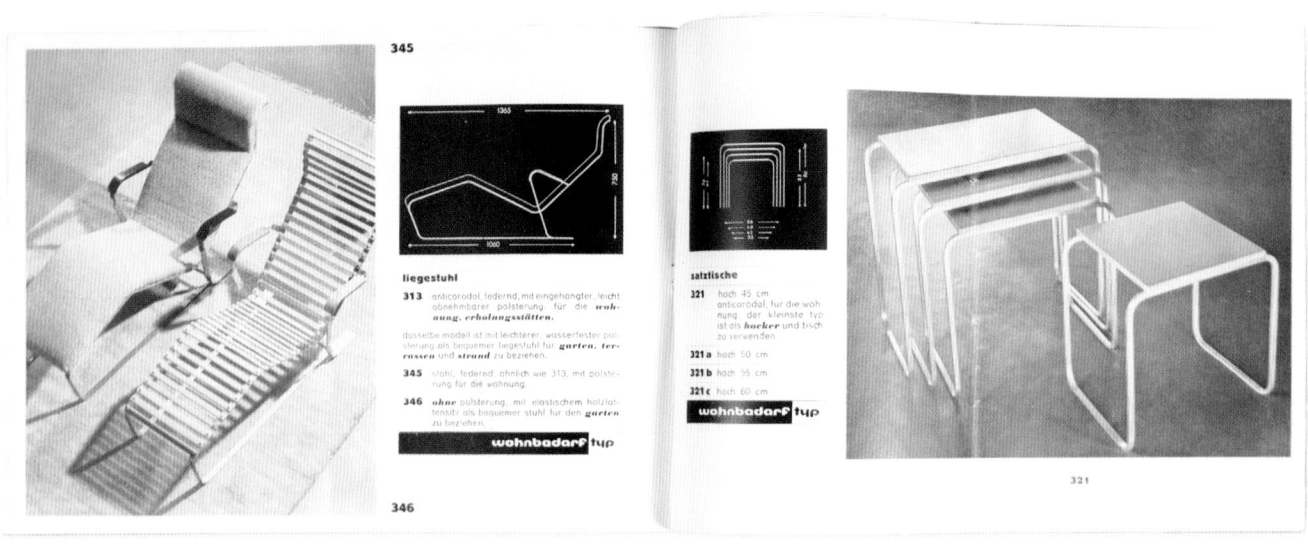

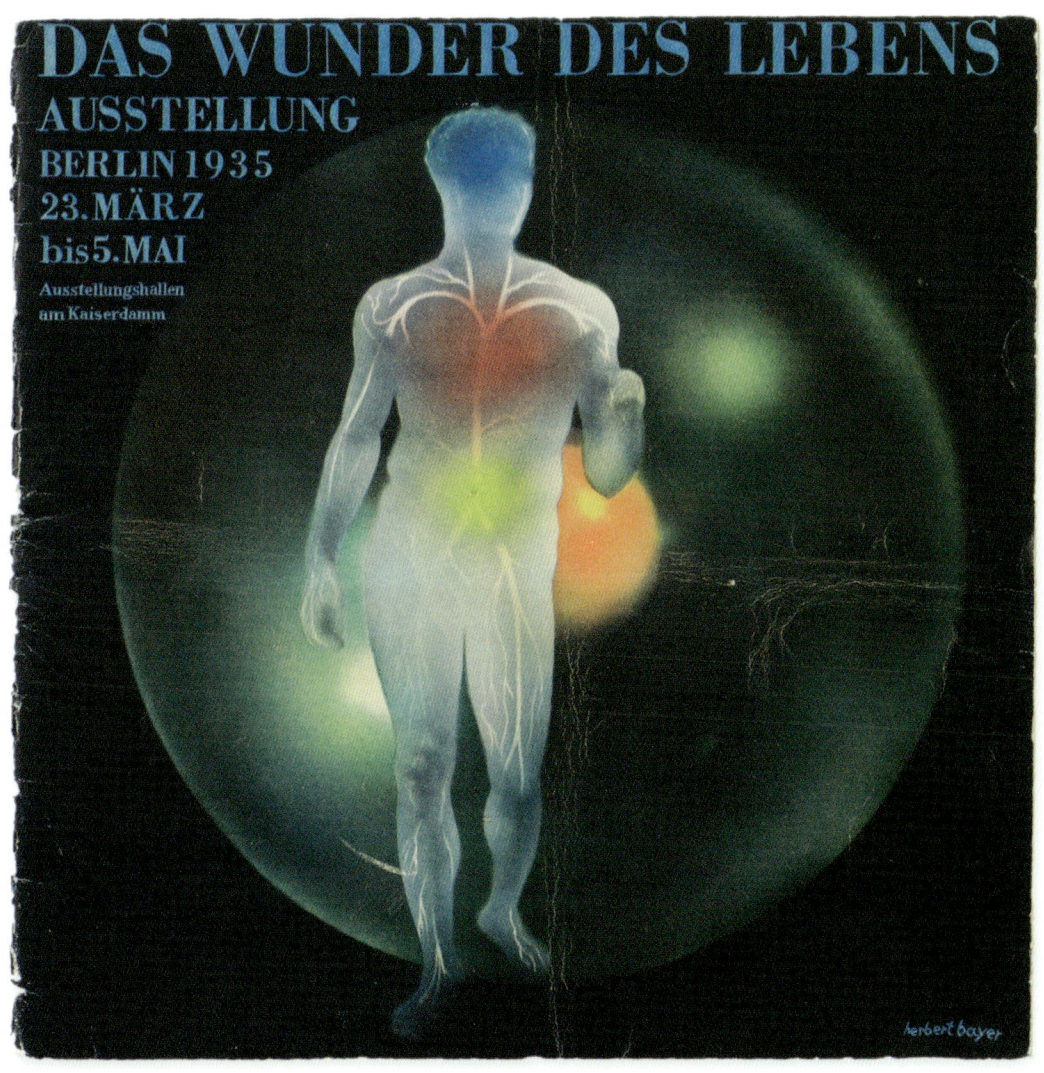

Herbert Bayer, cover and spread for *Das Wunder des Lebens*, 1935.
20.8 x 20.8 cm
Private collection

Herbert Bayer, spreads for *Das Wunder des Lebens*, 1935.
20.8 x 20.8 cm
Private collection

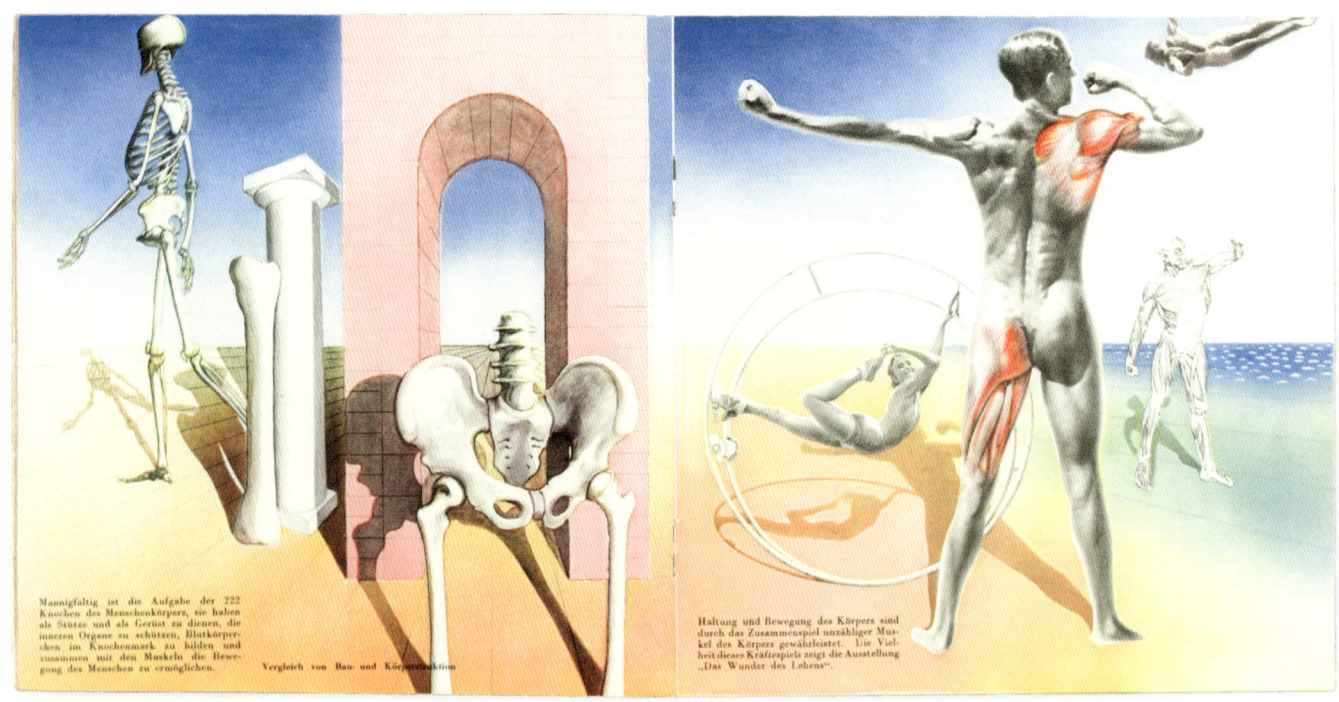

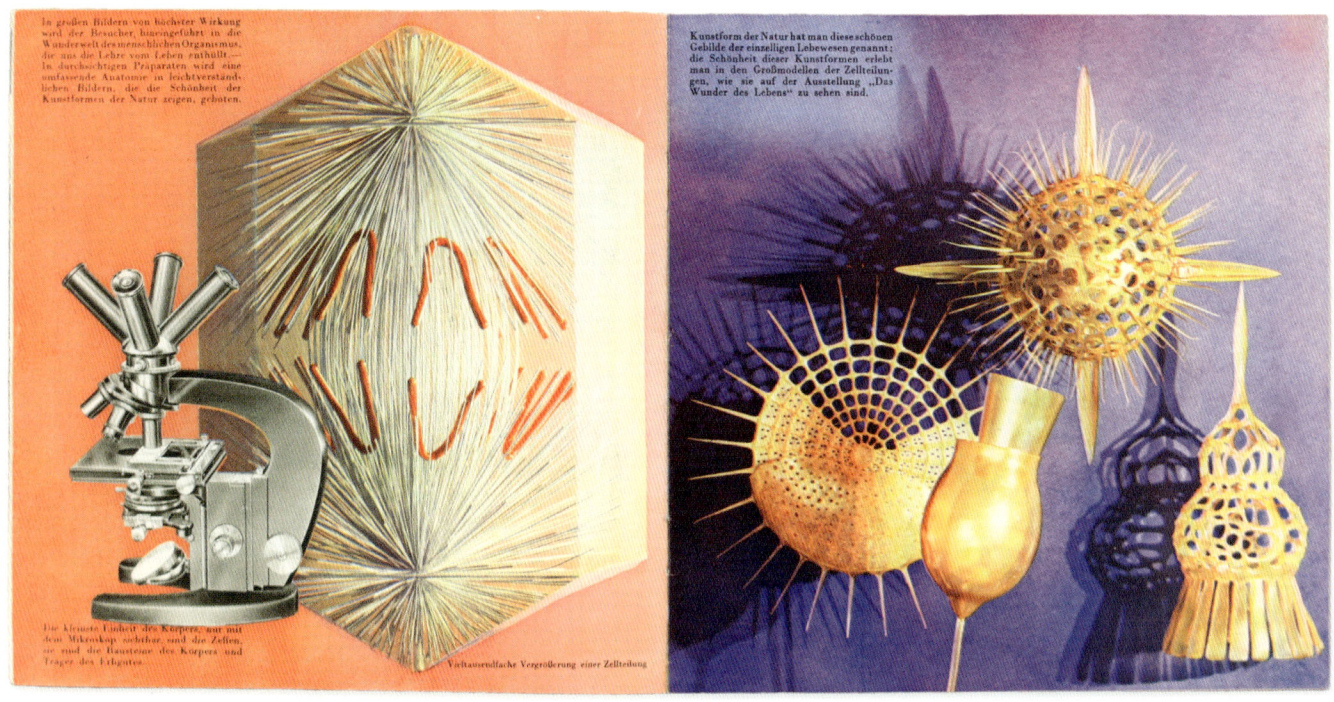

Herbert Bayer, cover and spreads for *Sport stählern gesehen*, 1936.
20.2 x 14.6 cm
Private collection

„Und auf dem Markte standen wir,
Zur Hand ein jeder sein Rapier.
Und Terz und Quart und Quartrevers —
Gib mir dein Glas nur wieder her —,
Die flogen links und rechts hinüber!"
Fritz Reuter, Hanne Nüte

DECHTSPORT

Das helle Klirren und das Blitzen der blanken Klingen, die gewandten Bewegungen der Fechter im schnellen Wechsel zwischen Angriff und Deckung geben dem Fechtsport schon einen hohen ästhetischen Reiz. Körperlich bringt er Elastizität und Auflockerung der ganzen Haltung mit sich. Das Augenmaß und die Fähigkeit zu rascher Beobachtung wird geübt, die Freude an fairem Kampf erweckt. Da das Florettfechten weniger körperliche Kraft als Geschicklichkeit und Schnelligkeit erfordert, eignet es sich auch für Frauen.

Bei allen wehrhaften Völkern gehört das Fechten zu den ältesten Leibesübungen, und die Schmiede erzielten dort schon früh bedeutende Leistungen in der Herstellung hochwertiger Schwerter. Die Meisterklingen, die in der Kriegerkaste der Samurais durch Generationen vererbt wurden, waren durch Aufeinanderschweißen von Stahlschichten erzeugt. Ein fertiges Schwert enthielt bis zu vier Millionen solcher Schichten, was ebensovielen Arbeitsvorgängen entsprach. Aber auch die alten deutschen Schmiede verstanden es, in mühevoller Arbeit erlesene Klingen zu schmieden, die weit über die Grenzen des Landes hinaus berühmt waren. Schon der Gotenkönig Dietrich scheute den weiten Weg ins Siegerland nicht, um ein kostbares Schwert zu gewinnen. Die deutschen Klingenschmiede sind der alten Tradition treu geblieben. Ihre Erzeugnisse gehen in alle Länder und haben vor allem in Zusammenhang mit dem Namen der Stadt Solingen Weltruf erlangt.

Baden ist ein sauber spil
Das ich auch immer preisen will.
Liederbuch der Augsburger
Nonne Klara Hätzerlin 1471

WASSERSPORT

Während sich in der Verborgenheit der mittelalterlichen Badestuben Gepflogenheiten entwickelten, die uns heute zum mindesten hygienisch höchst bedenklich erscheinen, schränkte Prüderie und Engherzigkeit das freie Baden und Schwimmen ein. Im Frankfurter Bürgermeisterbuch vom Jahre 1550 wird den „handtwercksgesellen und anderen, so im Main zu baden pflegen", streng befohlen, „gedeckt und zuchtig" zu baden. Noch vor 30 Jahren waren die Badeanzüge der Frauen so „züchtig", daß von einer Wirkung von Sonne und Luft auf den Körper kaum die Rede sein konnte. Und noch vor 20 Jahren meldete sich nur ein verhältnismäßig geringer Teil der Schüler, wenn in einer mittleren Schulklasse gefragt wurde, wer Freischwimmer sei.

Das ist heute anders. Der Schwimmunterricht in den Schulen ist Pflicht, und allenthalben finden sich schöne natürliche und künstlich angelegte Strandbäder. Das Verlangen nach freiem Zutritt von Sonne und Wind beim Baden hat auch bewirkt, daß heute gelegentlich nach oben völlig offene schwimmende Badeanstalten gebaut werden. Wenn man an die zeitweilig außerordentlich starke Benutzung der Umkleidezellen denkt, wird man zugeben, daß sich hier die hygienischen Vorteile der Stahlbauweise besonders geltend machen.

Das fortschrittlich eingerichtete Strandbad erkennt man heute schon aus der Ferne an den schmalen Linien des Sprungturms aus Stahl. Auch in Hallenschwimmbädern besitzen diese Türme den Vorzug, daß sie das Blickfeld möglichst frei lassen. Bei ihnen wie auch bei den Sprungbrettern aus Stahl wird die unbedingte Splitterfreiheit angenehm empfunden.

Alexander Rodchenko
1891–1956

Alexander Rodchenko, cover for *Novy LEF*, no. 1, 1923.
23.2 x 15.6 cm
Private collection

Alexander Rodchenko, cover for *Novy LEF*, no. 2, 1923.
23.2 x 15.6 cm
Private collection

Alexander Rodchenko, cover for *Novy LEF*, no. 3, 1923.
23.2 x 15.6 cm
Private collection

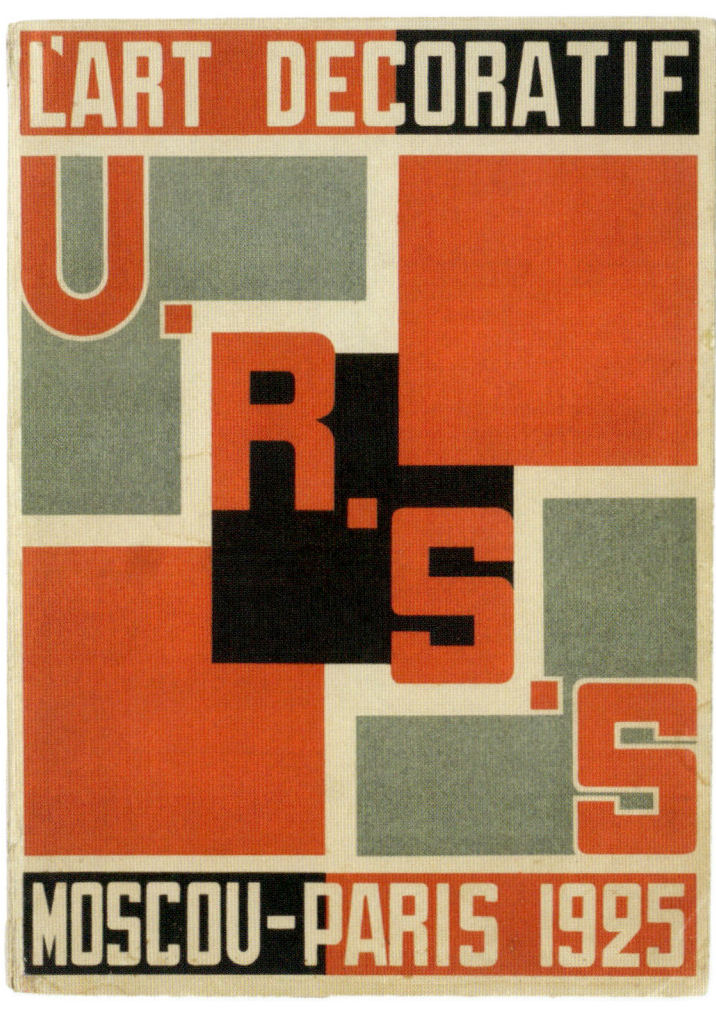

Alexander Rodchenko, cover for *U.R.S.S. L'Art Decoratif Moscou-Paris 1925*, 1925.
27 x 19.8 cm
Private collection

Alexander Rodchenko, cover for *De stem van Moskou*, 1930.
31 x 22.5 cm
Private collection

Alexander Rodchenko,
cover and spreads for
USSR im Bau, 1935.
42 x 29.6 cm
Private collection

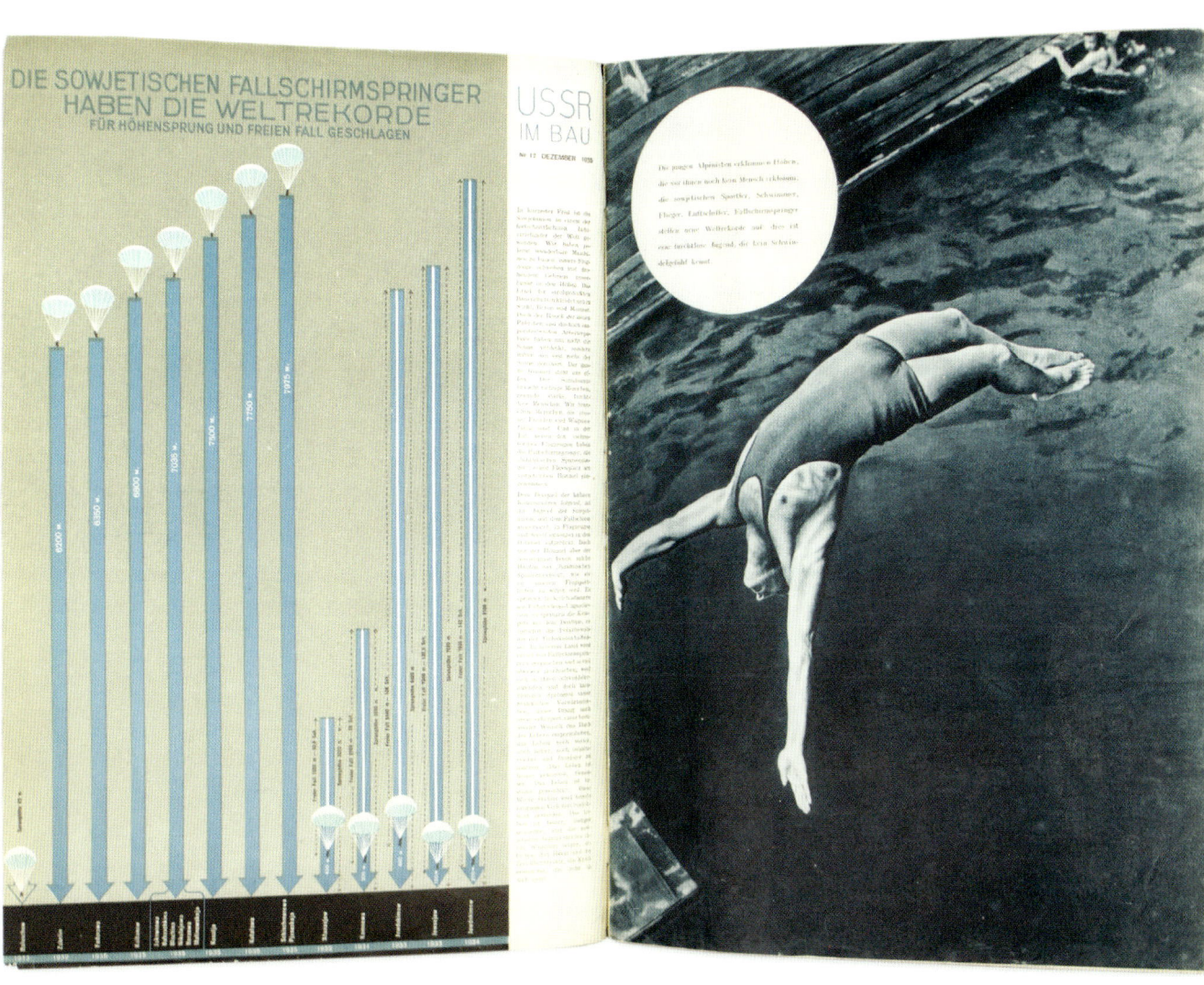

Alexander Rodchenko, spreads for *USSR im Bau,* 1935.
42 x 29.6 cm
Private collection

Karel Teige
1900–1951

Karel Teige, cover for
Město v slzách, 1923.
19.5 x 14 cm
Private collection

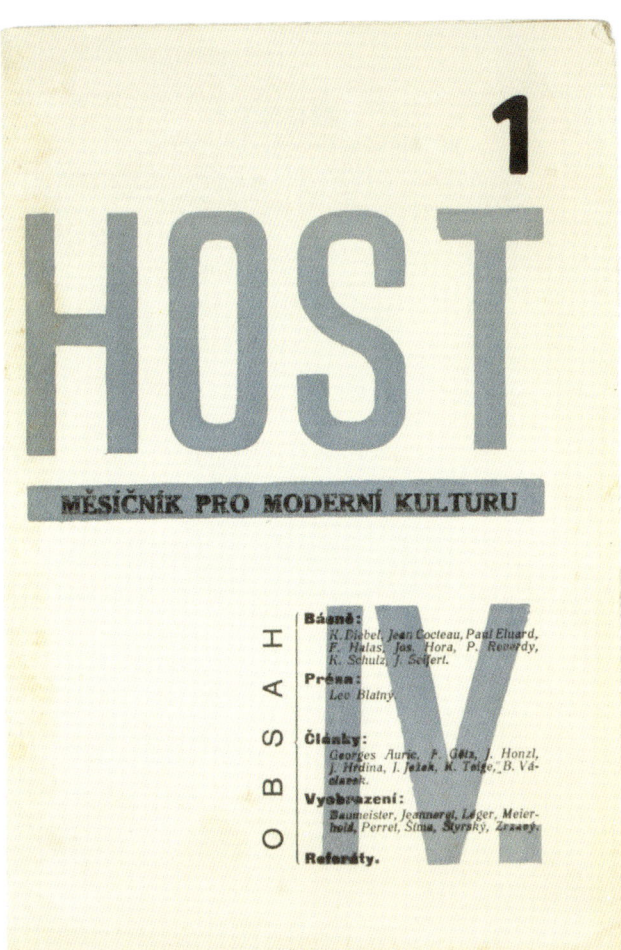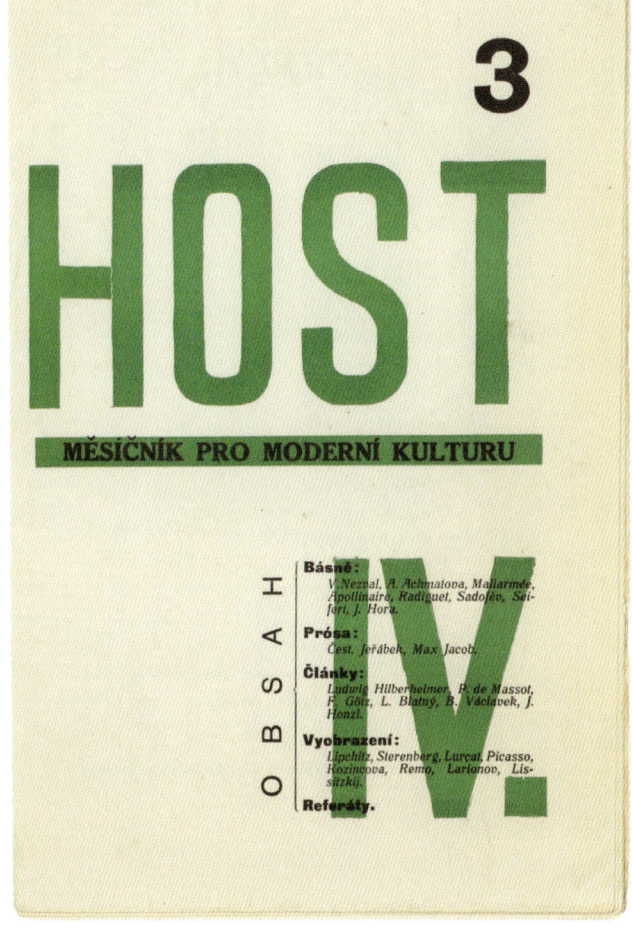

Karel Teige, covers for *Host*, nos. 1, 2 and 3, 1924.
28.2 x 19.1 cm
Private collection

Karel Teige, cover for
Chagrinová kůže, Praha, 1925.
16.9 x11.2 cm
Private collection

Karel Teige, cover for
Křižník Potěmkin, 1926.
19.2 x 14 cm
Private collection

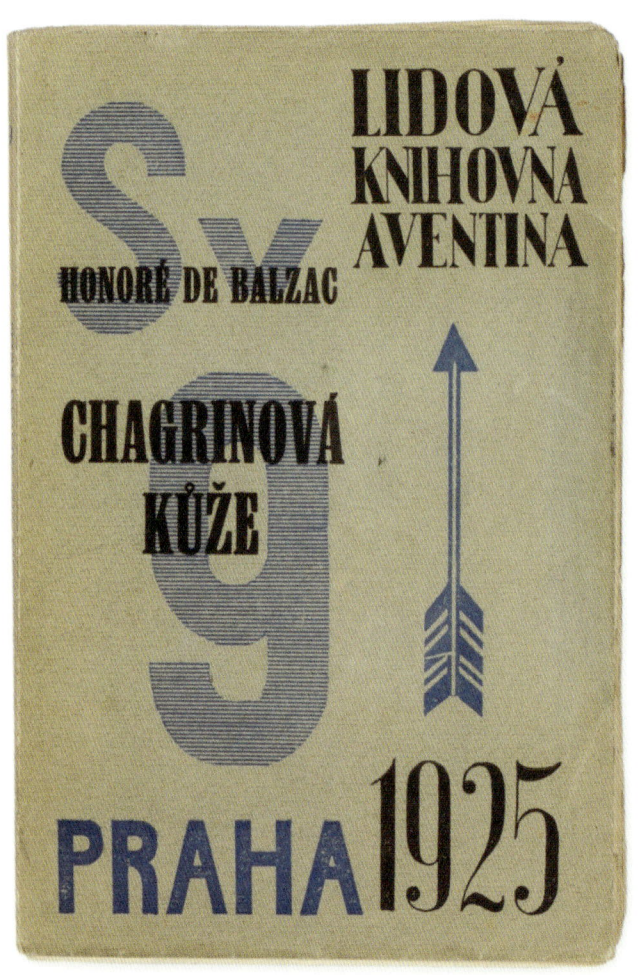

Karel Teige, cover for
Bas-Basina-Bulu, 1926.
19.7 x 13.5 cm
Private collection

Karel Teige, cover for
Fanfarlo, 1927.
18.8 x 12.7 cm
Private collection

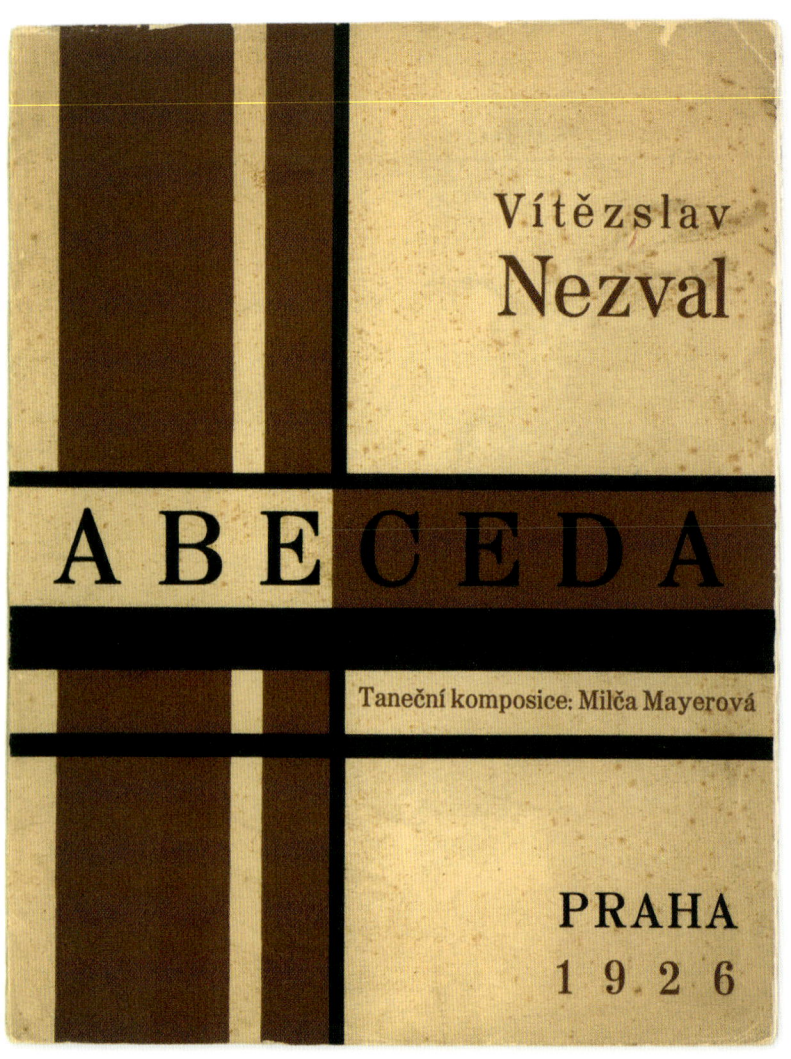

Karel Teige, cover and pages for *Abeceda* by Vítězslav Nezval, 1926.
Choreographer: Milča Mayerov.
Photographer: Karel Paspa.
30.6 x 23.8 cm
Universiteit van Amsterdam Bijzondere Collecties, Amsterdam

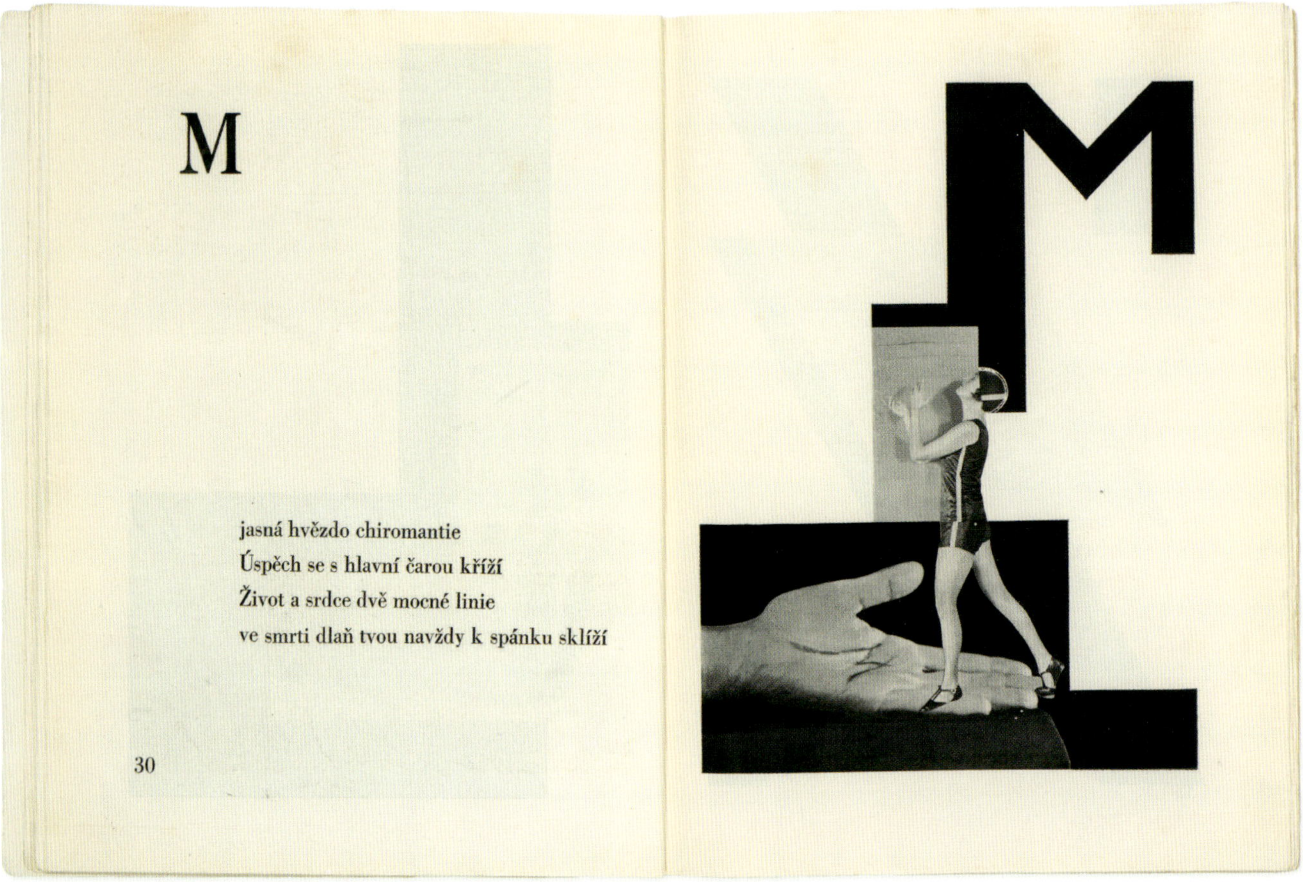

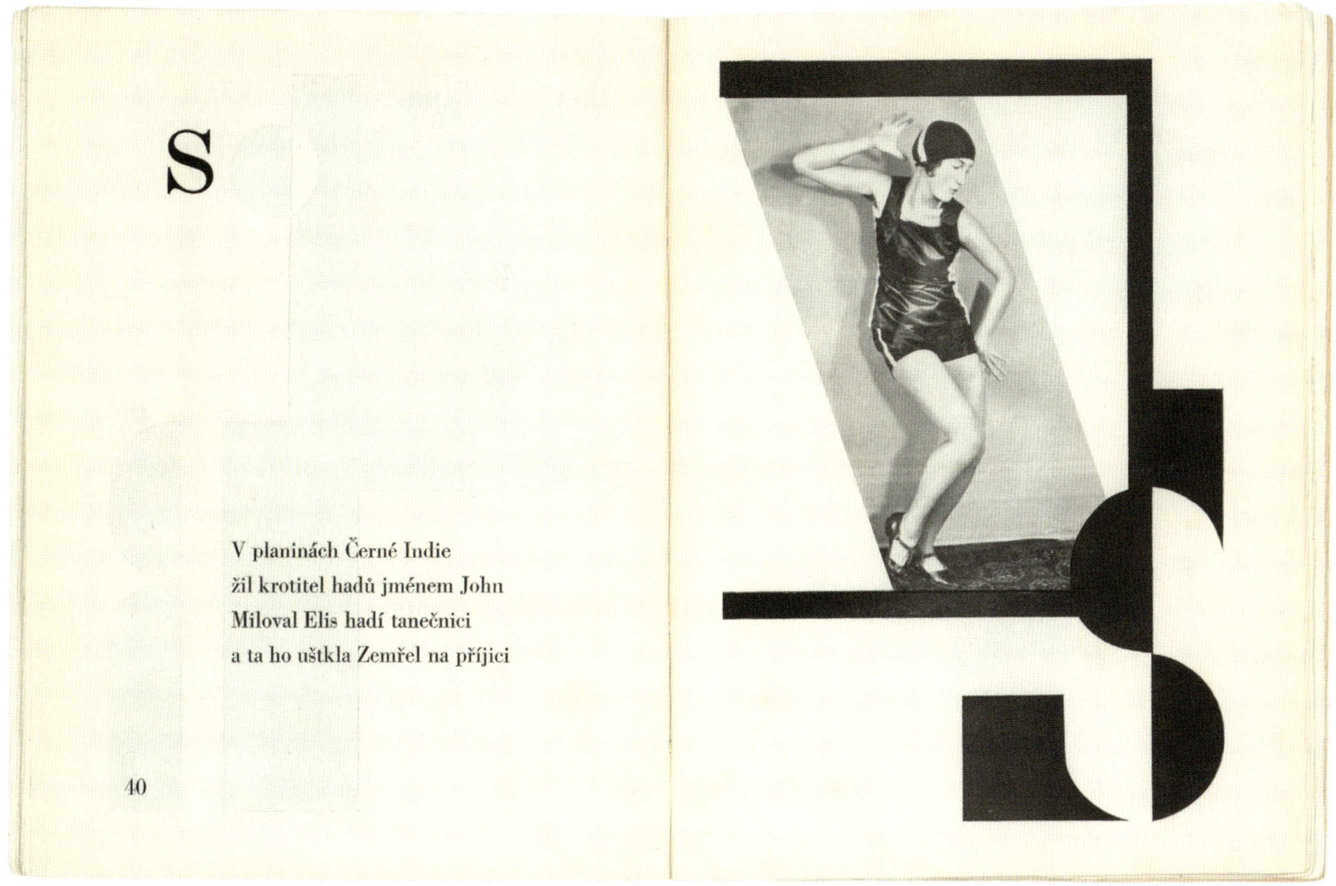

S

V planinách Černé Indie
žil krotitel hadů jménem John
Miloval Elis hadí tanečnici
a ta ho uštkla Zemřel na příjici

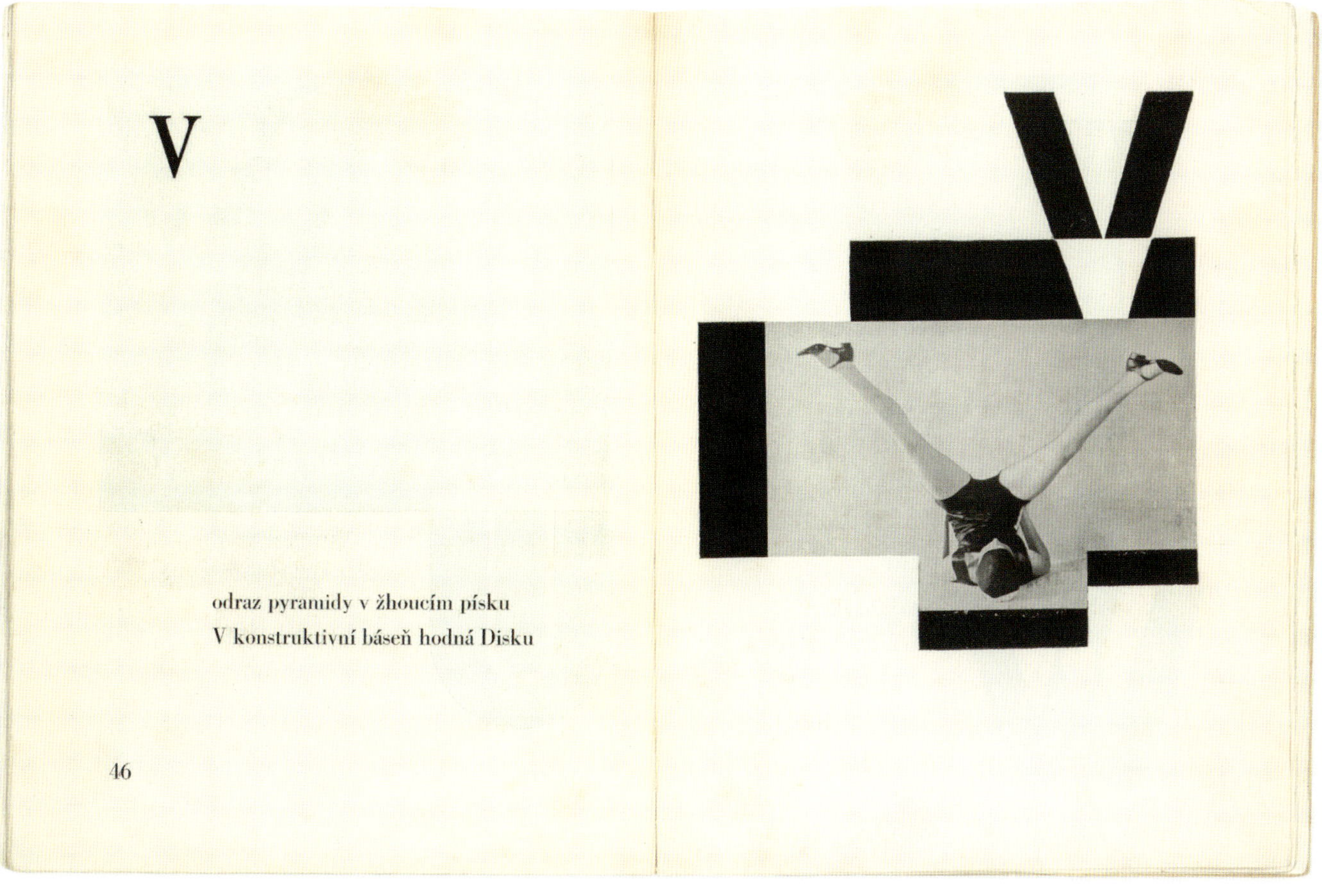

V

odraz pyramidy v žhoucím písku
V konstruktivní báseň hodná Disku

J Q

Přes Německo do Francie
dudák se svým měchem větry pluje
Chodské písně pomalu
hvízdá na svou píšťalu

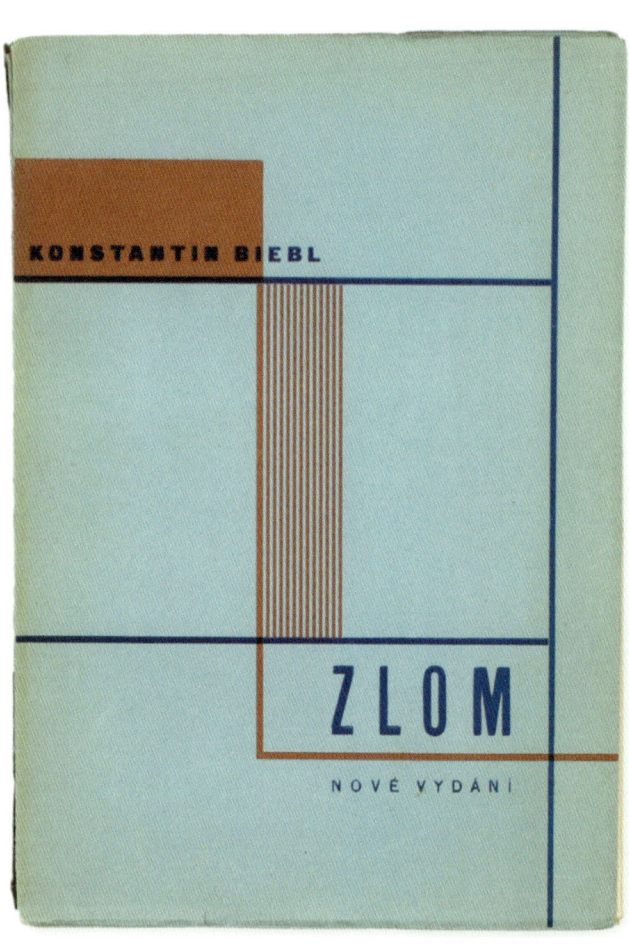
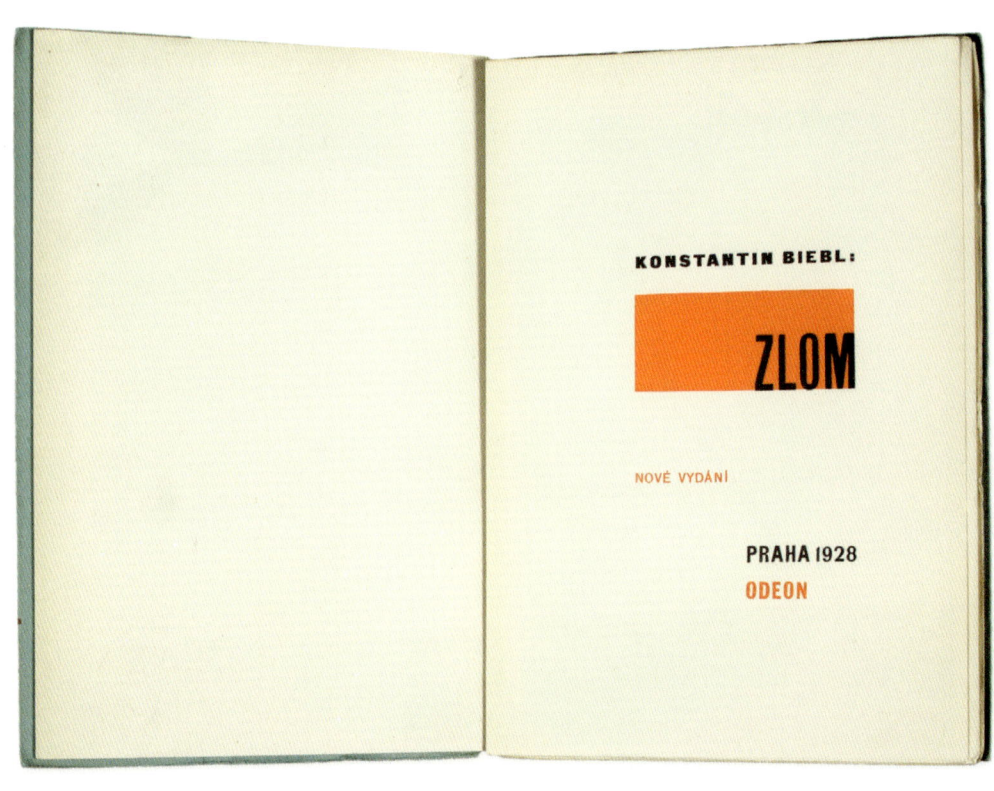

Karel Teige, cover and spreads for *Zlom*, 1928.
19.9 x 13.9 cm
Private collection

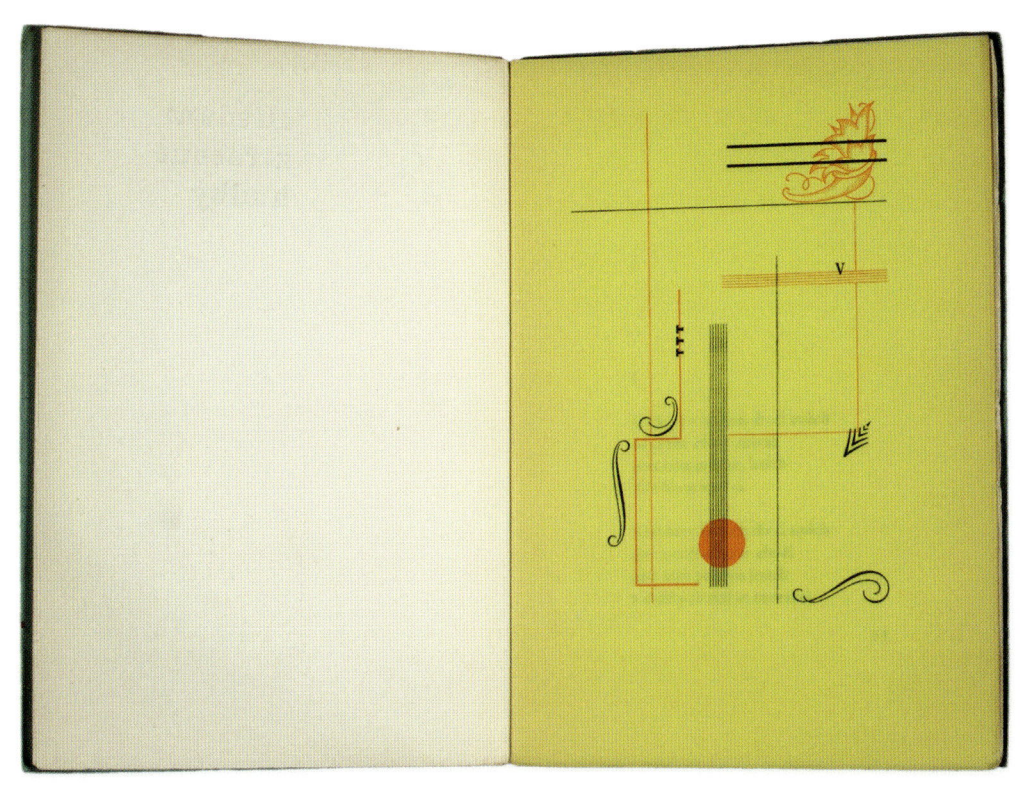

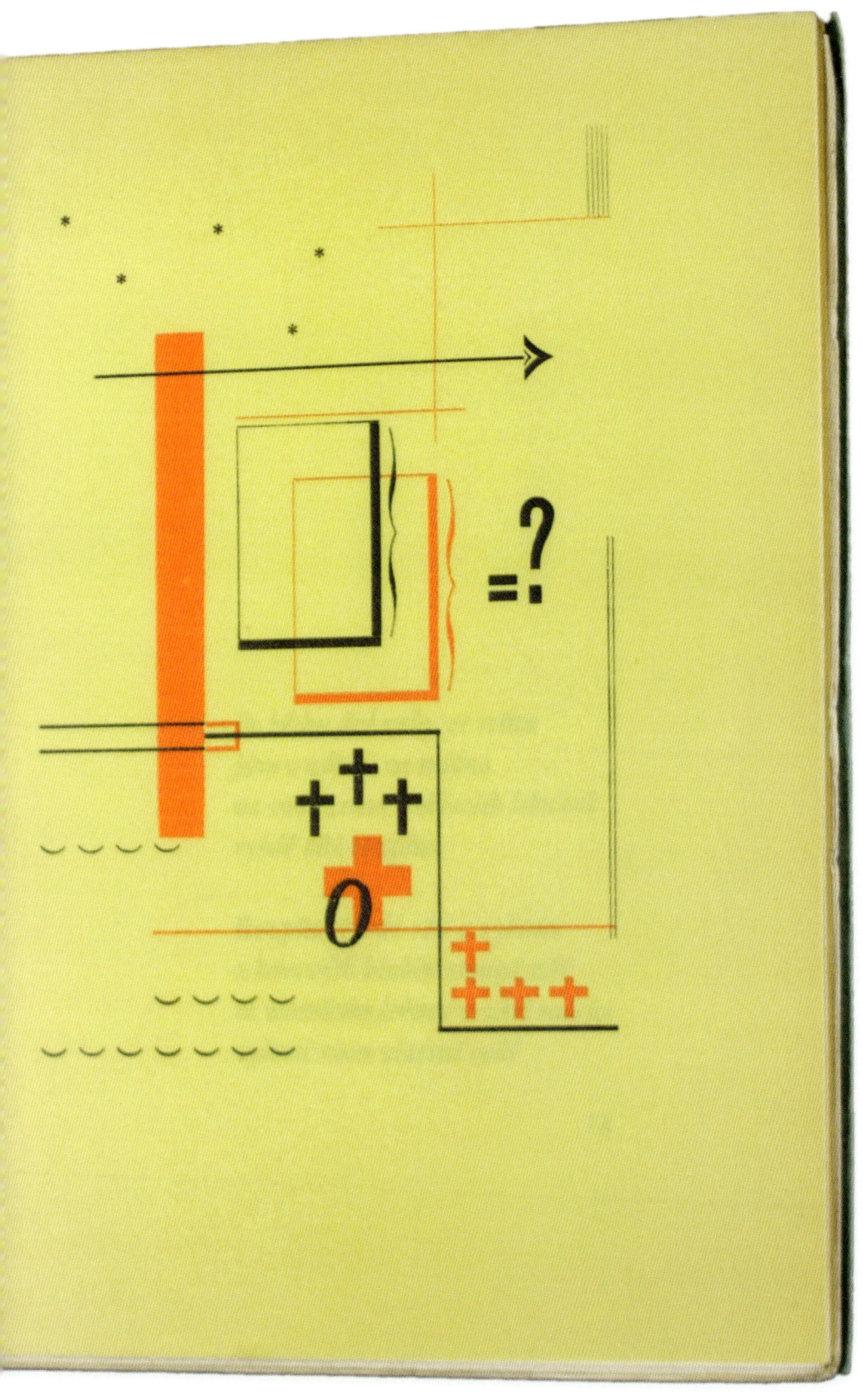

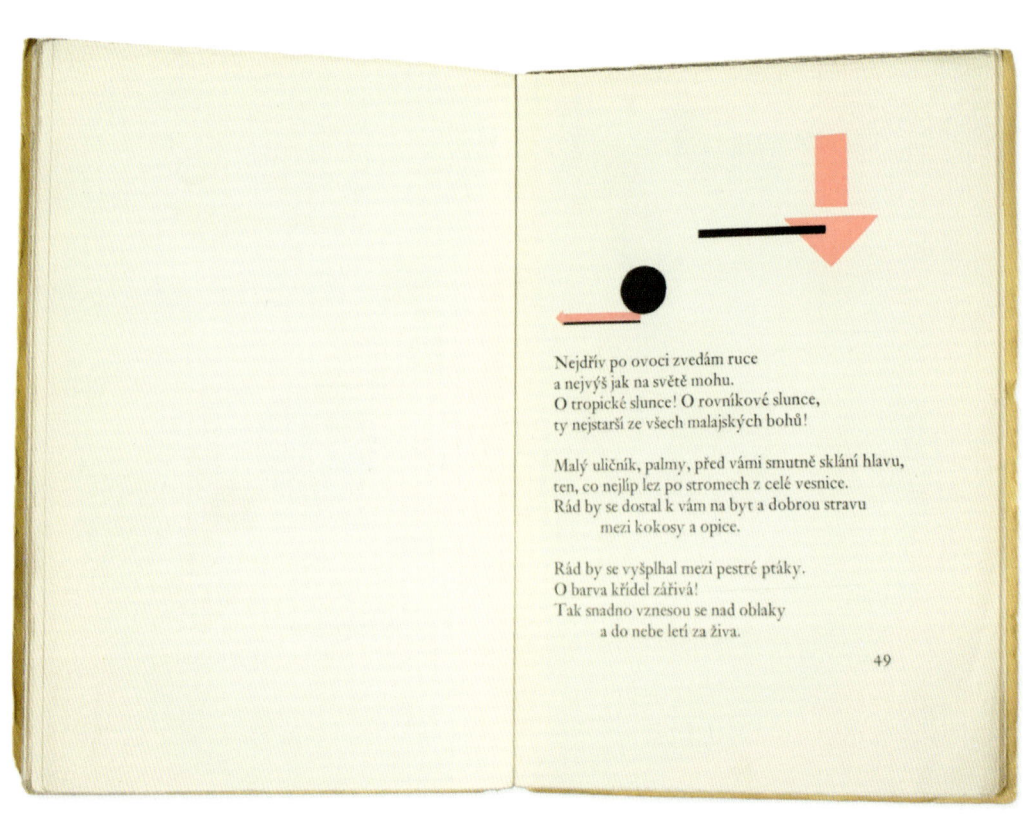

Karel Teige, cover and spreads for *S lodí jež dováží čaj a kávu*, 1928.
19.9 x 13.9 cm
Private collection

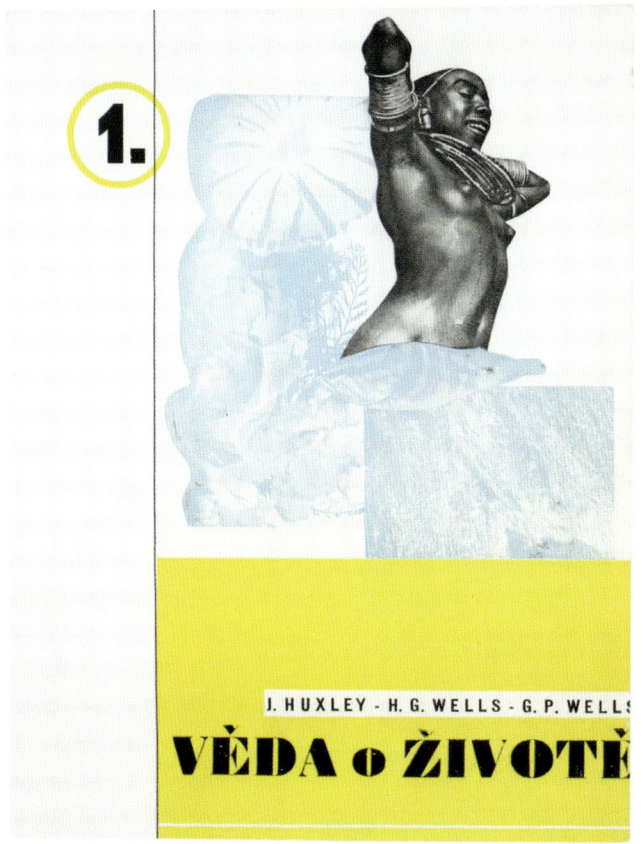

Karel Teige, magazine covers for *Věda o životě*, nos. 1, 2 and 3, 1932.
23.6 x 18.1 cm
Private collection

Joost Schmidt, exhibition poster for *Staatliches Bauhaus, Weimar*, 1923.
68 x 48 cm
Private collection
Courtesy www.iaddb.org

Joost Schmidt
1893-1948

Joost Schmidt, magazine cover and spreads for *Die Form: Zeitschrift für gestaltende Arbeit*, 1928.
30 x 21 cm
Private collection

Joost Schmidt, brochure cover for *Doppelkolben-Dieselmotoren*, Junkers, 1928.
29.6 x 20.7 cm
Private collection

Stenberg Brothers,
Georgii & Vladimir Stenberg,
poster for *Theater Kamerny
de Moscou, France*, 1923.
72 x 47 cm
Private collection
Courtesy www.iaddb.org

Stenberg Brothers

Georgii Stenberg
1900-1933

Vladimir Stenberg
1899-1982

Stenberg Brothers,
Georgii & Vladimir Stenberg,
movie poster for *The Miracle
of the Wolves*, c. 1927.
105.5 x 76 cm
Private collection
Courtesy www.iaddb.org

Stenberg Brothers,
Georgii & Vladimir Stenberg,
movie poster for *The Eleventh
Year of the Revolution*, 1928.
104.6 x 70.7 cm
Private collection
Courtesy www.iaddb.org

Friedrich Kiesler, poster on two sheets, *Internationale Ausstellung neuer Theatertechnik Konzerthaus*, 1924.
126.7 x 189 cm
Private collection
Courtesy www.iaddb.org

Friedrich Kiesler
1890-1965

1924

Oskar Fischer
1892–1955

Oskar Fischer, cover for
Die Gegenwart über Lenin,
1924.
22 x 15.2 cm
Private collection

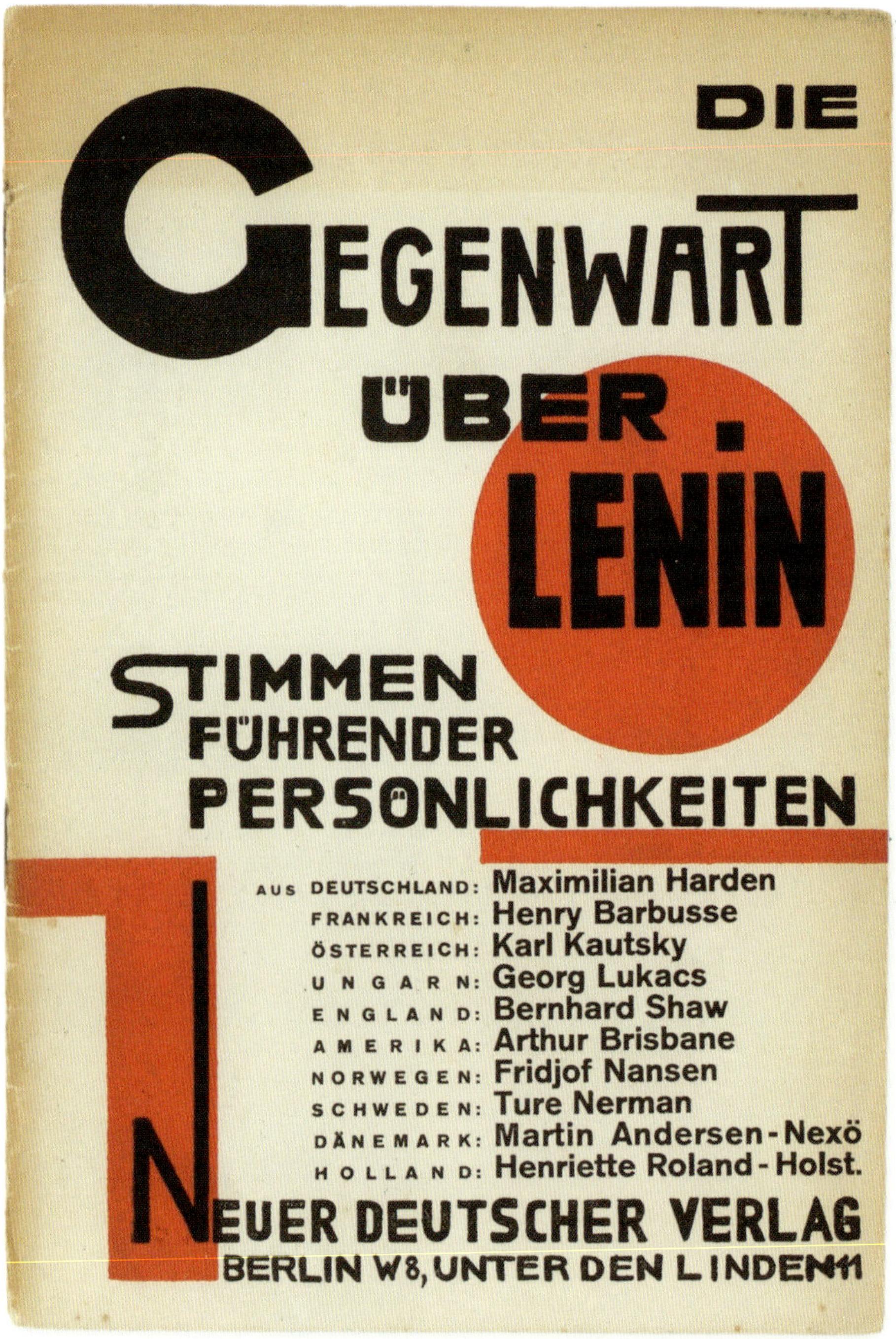

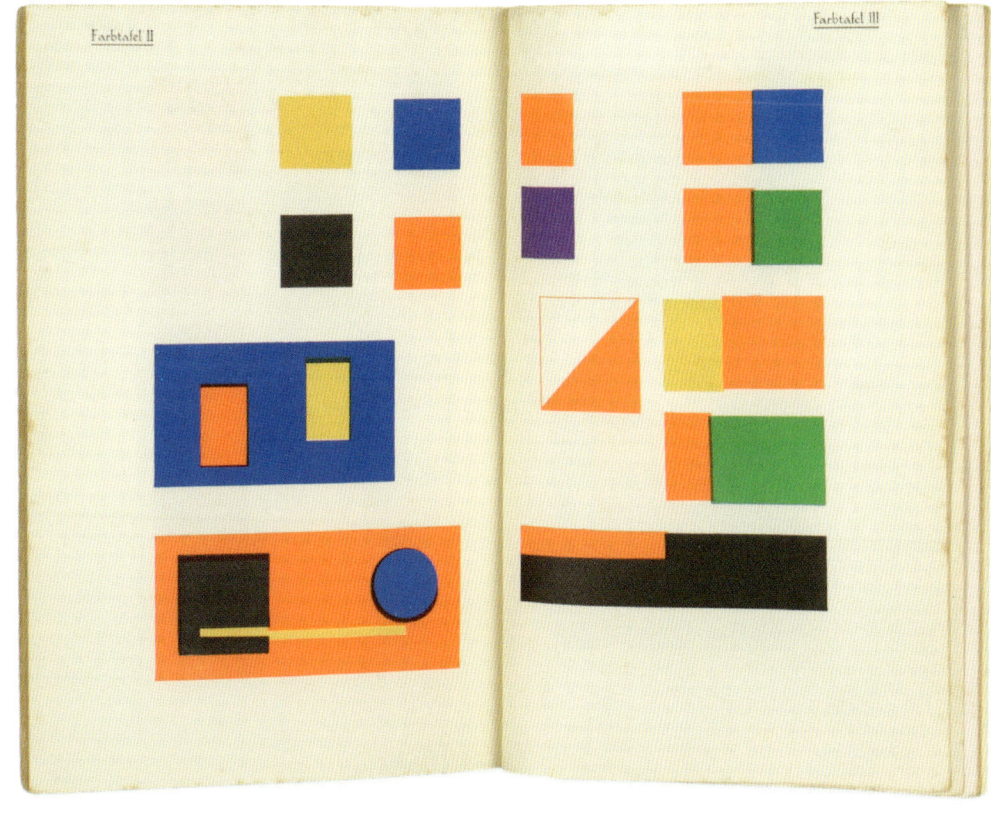

Oskar Fischer, cover and spread for *Von Kunst zur Gestaltung*, 1925.
21 x 14 cm
Private collection

H. Th. Wijdeveld, exhibition poster, *Tentoonstelling Buitenlandsch Bindwerk van dezen tijd*, Gemeentemuseum Den Haag, Stedelijk Museum Amsterdam, 1924.
66 x 42.2 cm
Private collection
Courtesy www.iaddb.org

H. Th. Wijdeveld
1885–1987

H. Th. Wijdeveld, exhibition poster, *Internationale Economisch-Historische Tentoonstelling*, Stedelijk Museum Amsterdam, 1929.
65 x 51 cm
Private collection

1925

Max Burchartz
1887–1961

Max Burchartz, cover and spreads for *Feierspiele Münster Pfingsten*, 1925.
21 x 19 cm
Private collection

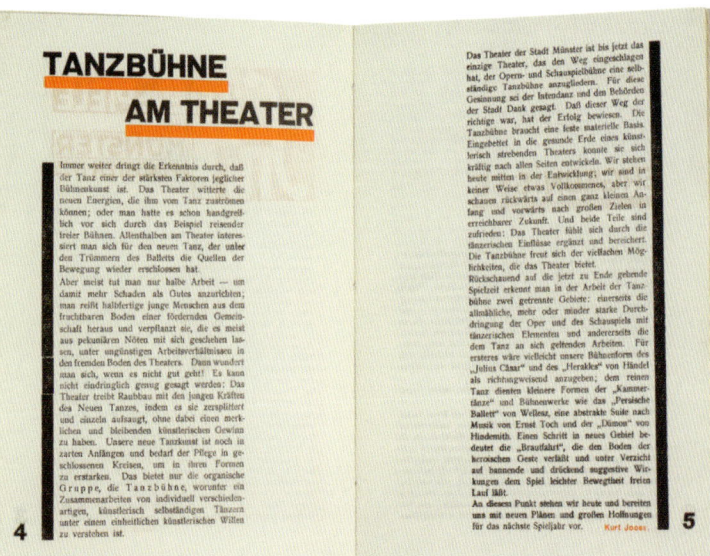

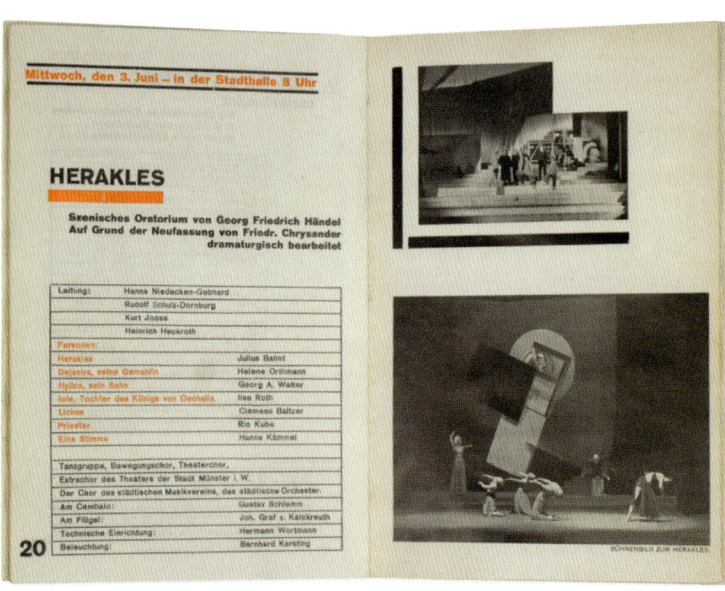

Max Burchartz, cover for
Agrandissement, 1938.
16.8 x 12 cm
Private collection

Max Burchartz, poster for
Tanz Festspiele Essen, 1928.
89.5 x 83.1 cm.
Private collection
Courtesy www.iaddb.org

1925

Bauhausbücher published from 1925 to 1930 by Walter Gropius and László Moholy-Nagy. Langen Verlag, Munich. 14 books, 23 x 17 cm.

Walter Gropius, *Internationale Architektur*, no. 1, Munich, 1925. Jacket design Farkas Molnár.
Private collection
Courtesy www.iaddb.org

Paul Klee, *Pädagogisches Skizzenbuch*, no. 2, Munich, 1925. Jacket design László Moholy-Nagy.
Private collection
Courtesy www.iaddb.org

Adolf Meyer, *Ein Versuchshaus des Bauhauses in Weimar*, no. 3, Munich, 1925.
Jacket design Adolf Meyer.
Private collection
Courtesy www.iaddb.org

Oskar Schlemmer, *Die Bühne im Bauhaus*, no. 4, Munich, 1925.
Jacket design Oskar Schlemmer.
Private collection
Courtesy www.iaddb.org

Piet Mondrian, *Neue Gestaltung* (translated by Max Burchartz and Rudolf Franz Hartogh), no. 5, Munich, 1925. Jacket design László Moholy-Nagy.
Private collection
Courtesy www.iaddb.org

Theo van Doesburg, *Grundbegriffe der neuen gestaltenden Kunst* (translated by Theo van Doesburg and Max Burchartz), no. 6, Munich, 1925. Jacket design Theo van Doesburg.
Private collection
Courtesy www.iaddb.org

Walter Gropius, *Neue Arbeiten der Bauhauswerkstätten*, no. 7, Munich, 1925. Jacket design László Moholy-Nagy.
Private collection
Courtesy www.iaddb.org

László Moholy-Nagy, *Malerei, Fotografie, Film*, no. 8, Munich, 1925. Jacket design László Moholy-Nagy.
Private collection
Courtesy www.iaddb.org

Wassily Kandinsky, *Punkt und Linie zur Fläche*, no. 9, Munich, 1926. Jacket design Herbert Bayer.
Private collection
Courtesy www.iaddb.org

Jacobus Johannes Pieter Oud, *Holländische Architektur*, no. 10, Munich, 1926. Jacket design László Moholy-Nagy.
Private collection
Courtesy www.iaddb.org

Kasimir Malewitsch, *Die gegenstandslose Welt* (translated by Alexander van Riesen), no. 11, Munich, 1927. Jacket design László Moholy-Nagy.
Private collection
Courtesy www.iaddb.org

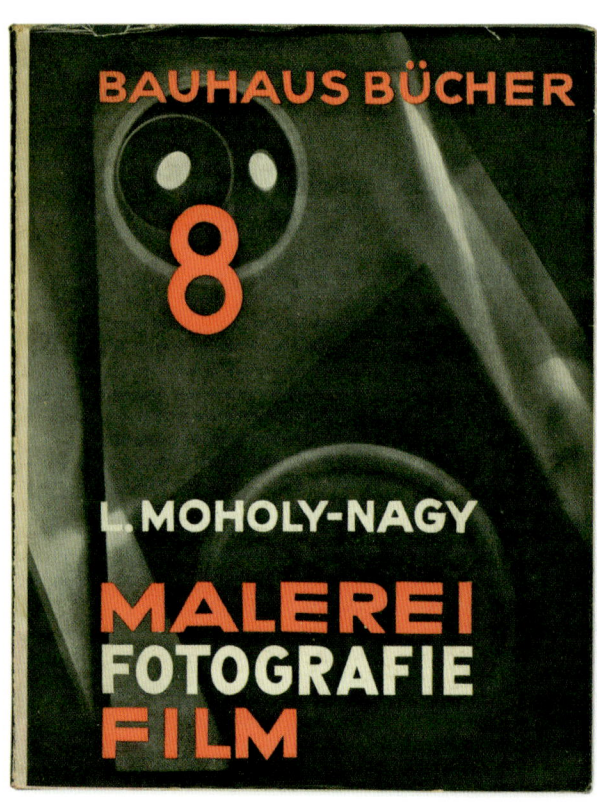

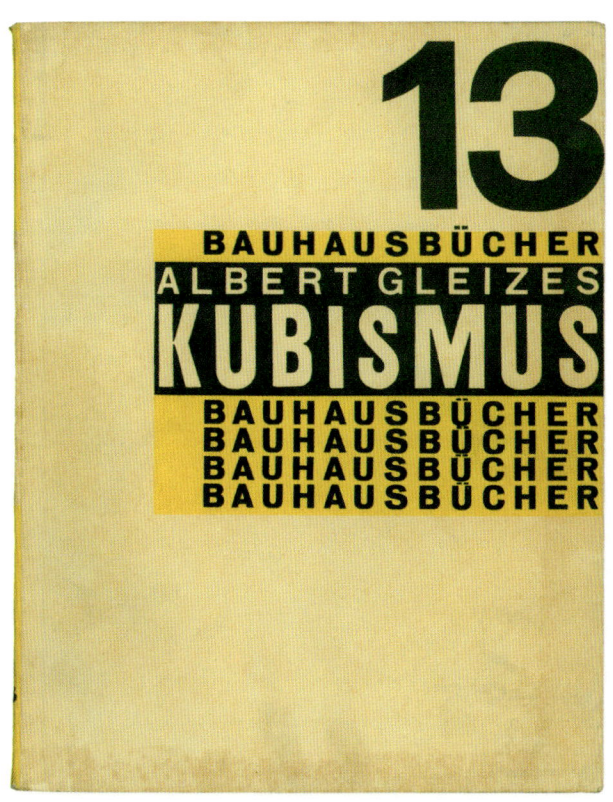

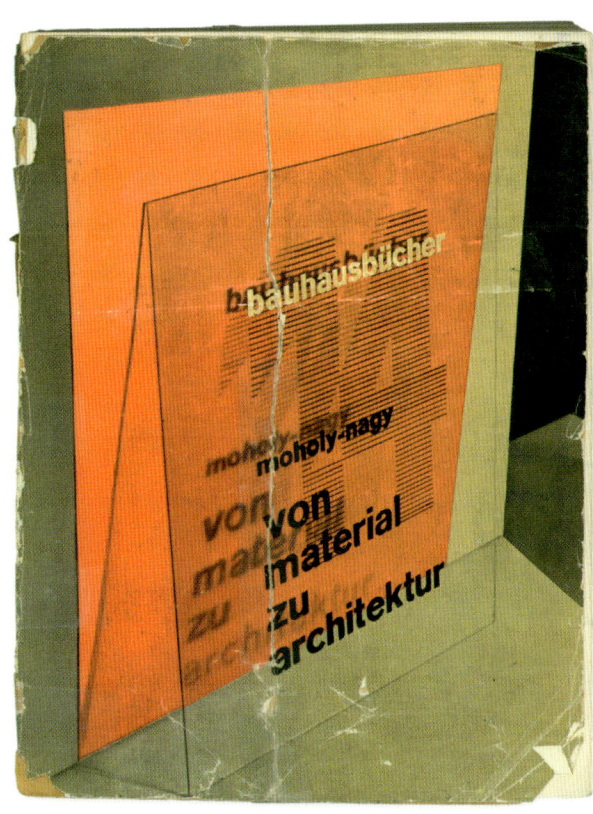

Walter Gropius, *Bauhausbauten Dessau*, no. 12, Munich, 1930. Jacket design László Moholy-Nagy.
Private collection
Courtesy www.iaddb.org

Albert Gleizes, *Kubismus* (translated by Eulein Grohmann), no. 13, Munich, 1928. Jacket design László Moholy-Nagy.
Private collection
Courtesy www.iaddb.org

László Moholy-Nagy, *Von Material zu Architektur*, no. 14, Munich, 1929. Jacket design László Moholy-Nagy.
Private collection
Courtesy www.iaddb.org

Hendrik N. Werkman, poster
for *Exposition du Congrès,*
Le cercle d'art de Gronigue,
"De Ploeg", Groningen, 1926.
93 x 57.7 cm
Private collection
Courtesy www.iaddb.org

Hendrik N. Werkman
1882–1945

1925

László Moholy-Nagy
1895–1946

László Moholy-Nagy, magazine cover for *i10*, nos. 5, 17, 18 and 19, 1927–1928.
29.8 x 21 cm
Private collection

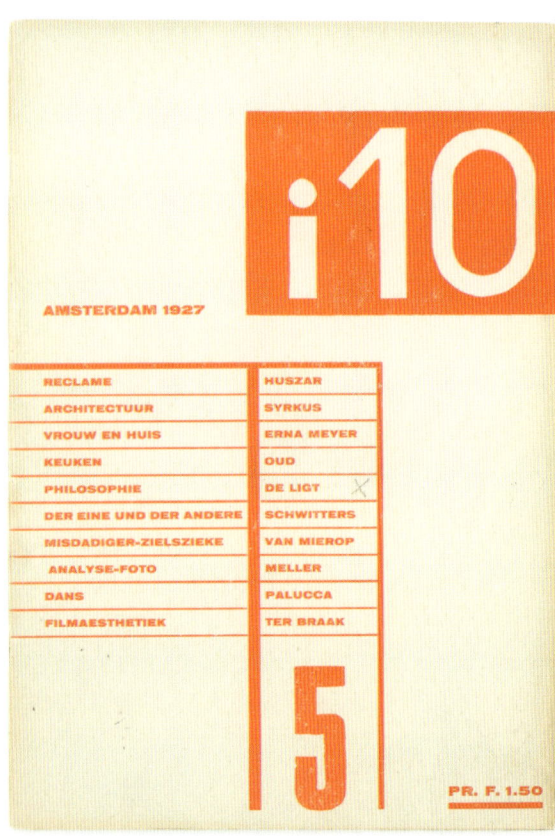

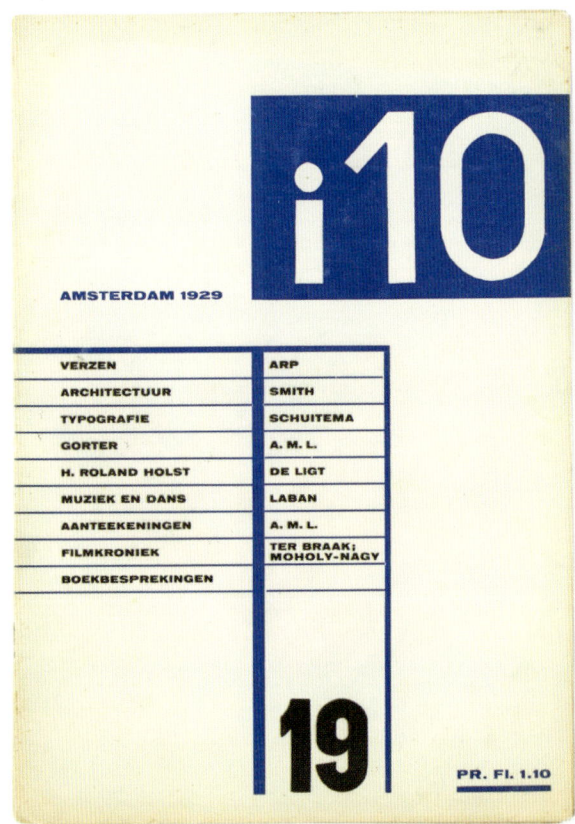

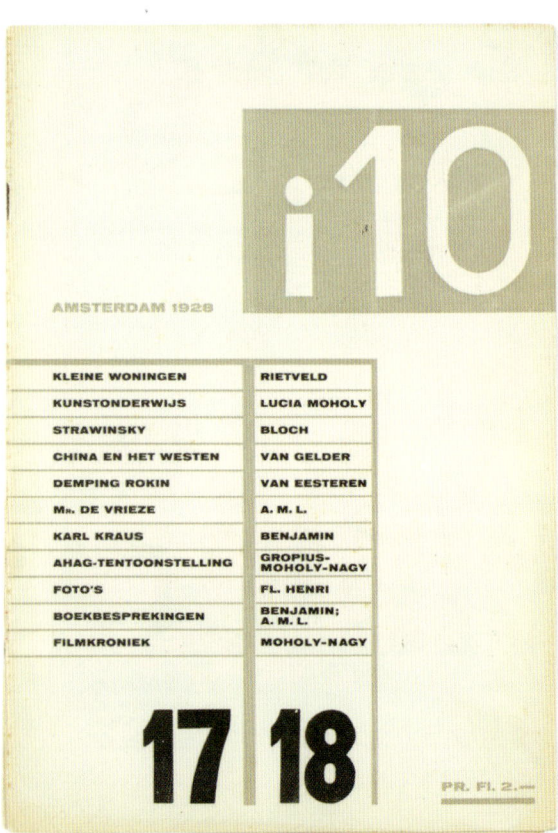

László Moholy-Nagy, magazine cover for *Die neue Linie*, 1931.
36.6 x 26.7 cm
Private collection

László Moholy-Nagy, magazine cover for *Die neue Linie*, 1932.
36.6 x 26.7 cm
Private collection

1925

Štýrský & Toyen

Jindřich Štýrský
1899–1942

Marie Čermínová
1902–1980

Štýrský & Toyen, cover for *Tono-Bungay*, 1925.
29.7 x 14 cm
Private collection

Štýrský & Toyen, cover for *Dáma u vodotrysky*, 1926.
17.6 x 11.1 cm
Private collection

Theo van Doesburg,
Käte Steinitz, and
Kurt Schwitters,
cover and pages for
Die Scheuche: Märchen
by Kurt Schwitters, 1925.
20.5 x 24.5 cm
Universiteit van Amsterdam,
Bijzondere Collecties,
Amsterdam

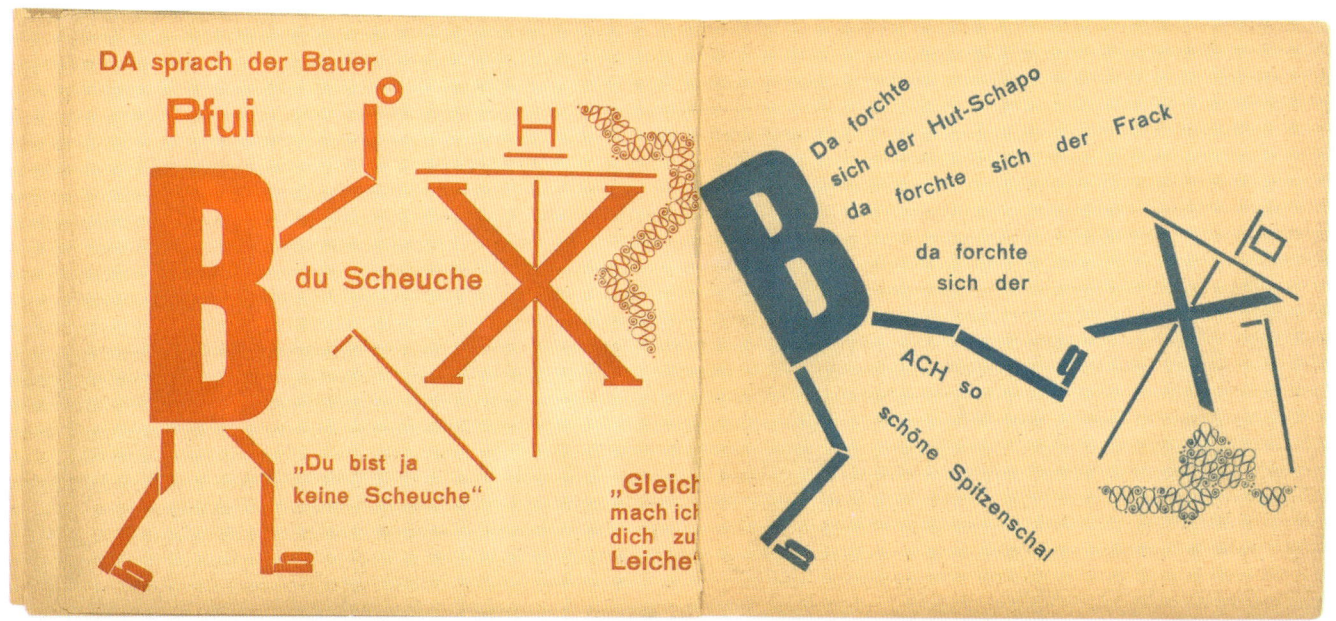

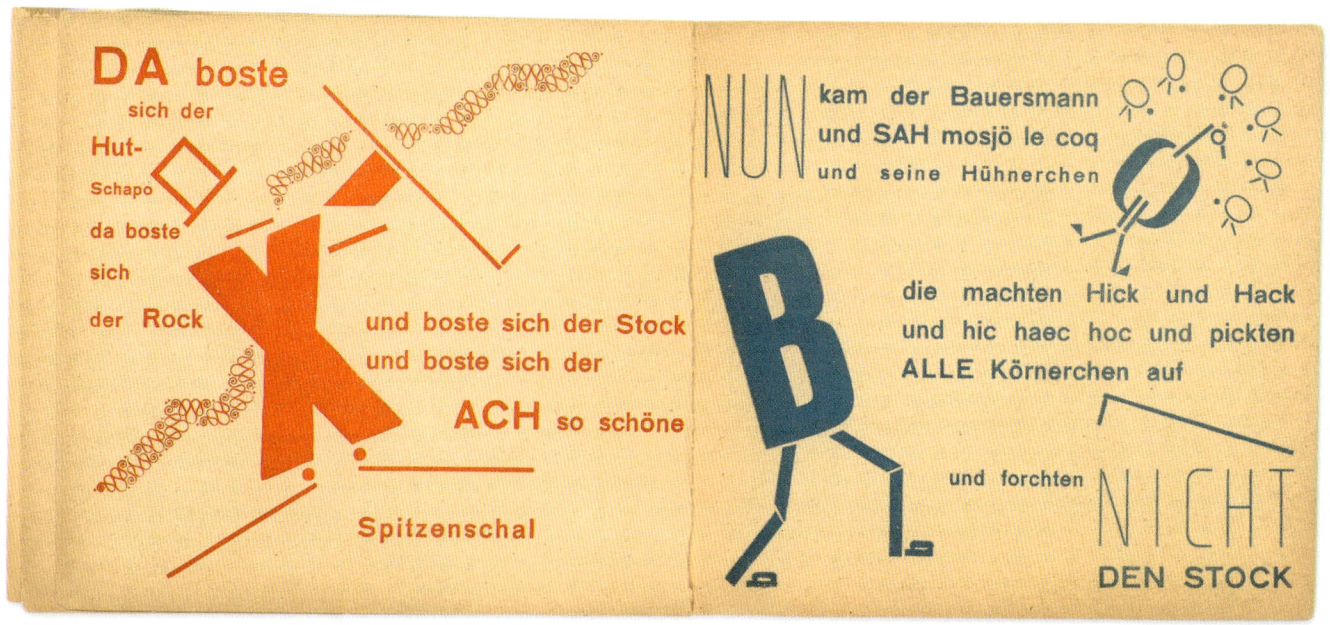

1926

John Heartfield
1891–1968

John Heartfield, cover for *Maxim Gorki: Der 9. Januar*, 1926.
18 x 12.2 cm
Private collection

John Heartfield, cover for *Das deutsche Wirtschaftswunder*,
Size unknown
Private collection
Courtesy www.iaddb.org

John Heartfield, cover for
Richter und Gerichtete, 1928.
22.1 x 32.2 cm
Private collection

John Heartfield, cover and spreads for *Deutschland, Deutschland über alles*, 1929.
23.1 x 18.6 cm
Private collection

John Heartfield, cover
for *Drei Soldaten*, 1929.
18.8 x 12.9 cm
Private collection

John Heartfield, cover for
*Illustrierte Geschichte der
Deutschen Revolution*, 1929.
28.5 x 21.4 cm
Private collection

John Heartfield, cover for
*Illustrierte Geschichte des
Bürgerkrieges in Russland*,
1917-1921, 1929.
28.5 x 21 cm
Private collection

John Heartfield, cover for
Das Geld schreibt, 1930.
19.2 x 12.7 cm
Private collection

John Heartfield, cover for
So macht man Dollars, 1932.
18.9 x 12.7 cm
Private collection

John Heartfield, cover
for *Alkohol*, 1932.
18.9 x 12.7 cm
Private collection

John Heartfield, poster,
*Das letzte Stück Brot raubt
ihnen der Kapitalismus.
Wählt Kommunisten!
Wählt Thälmann!*, 1932.
96.7 x 71.7 cm
Private collection
Courtesy www.iaddb.org

John Heartfield, election poster for *Kämpfe mit der Kommunistischen Partei!*, 1932.
100.5 x 70.5 cm
Private collection
Courtesy www.iaddb.org

Nikolai Prusakov & Grigori Ilyich, poster, 1927.
72 x 105 cm
Private collection
Courtesy www.iaddb.org

1927

Cyril Bouda
1901–1984

Cyril Bouda, cover for *Jen země*, 1927.
20 x 13.8 cm
Private collection

Wyndham Lewis
1882–1957

Wyndham Lewis, cover for
The Enemy, 1927.
28.1 x 18.2 cm
Private collection

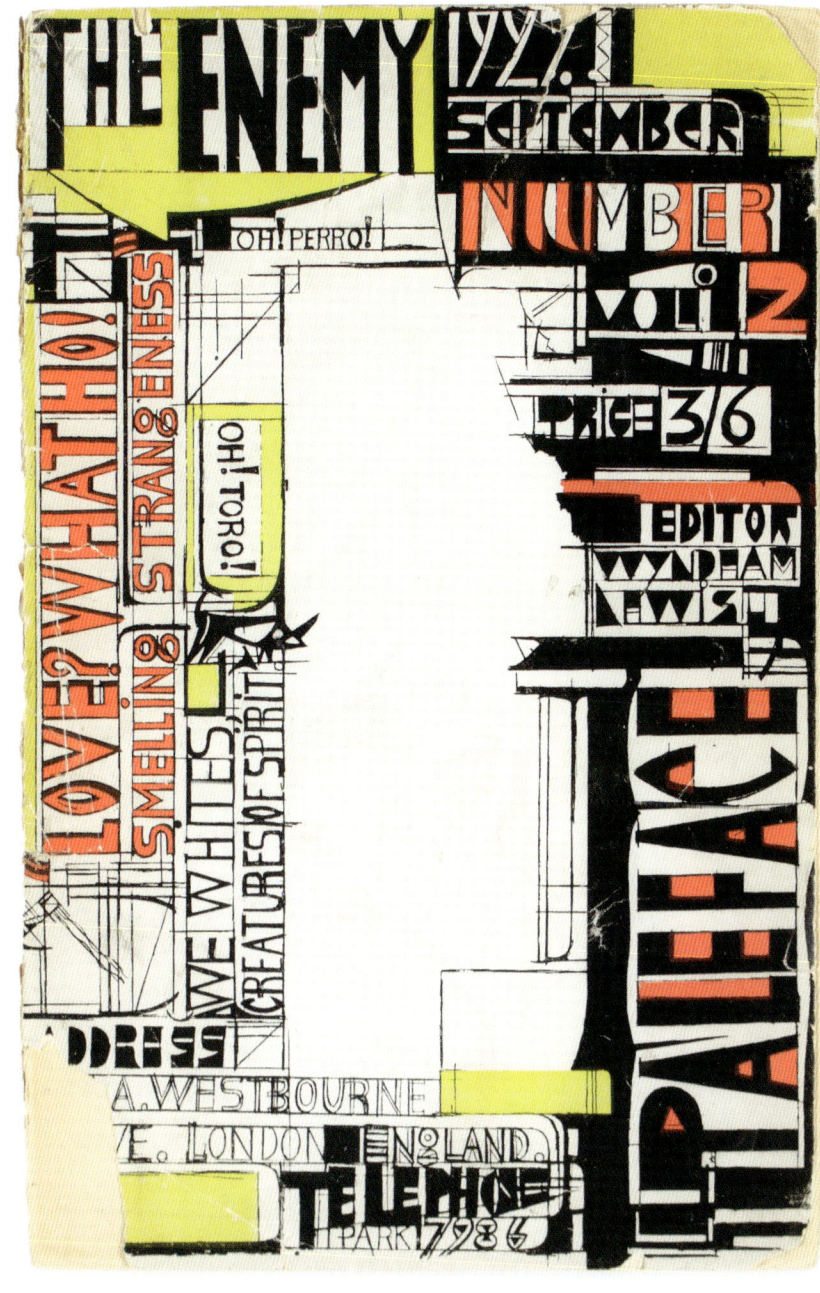

Walter Käch, poster for *Ausstellung Form ohne Ornament*, c. 1927.
128 x 89.8 cm
Private collection
Courtesy www.iaddb.org

Walter Käch
1901-1970

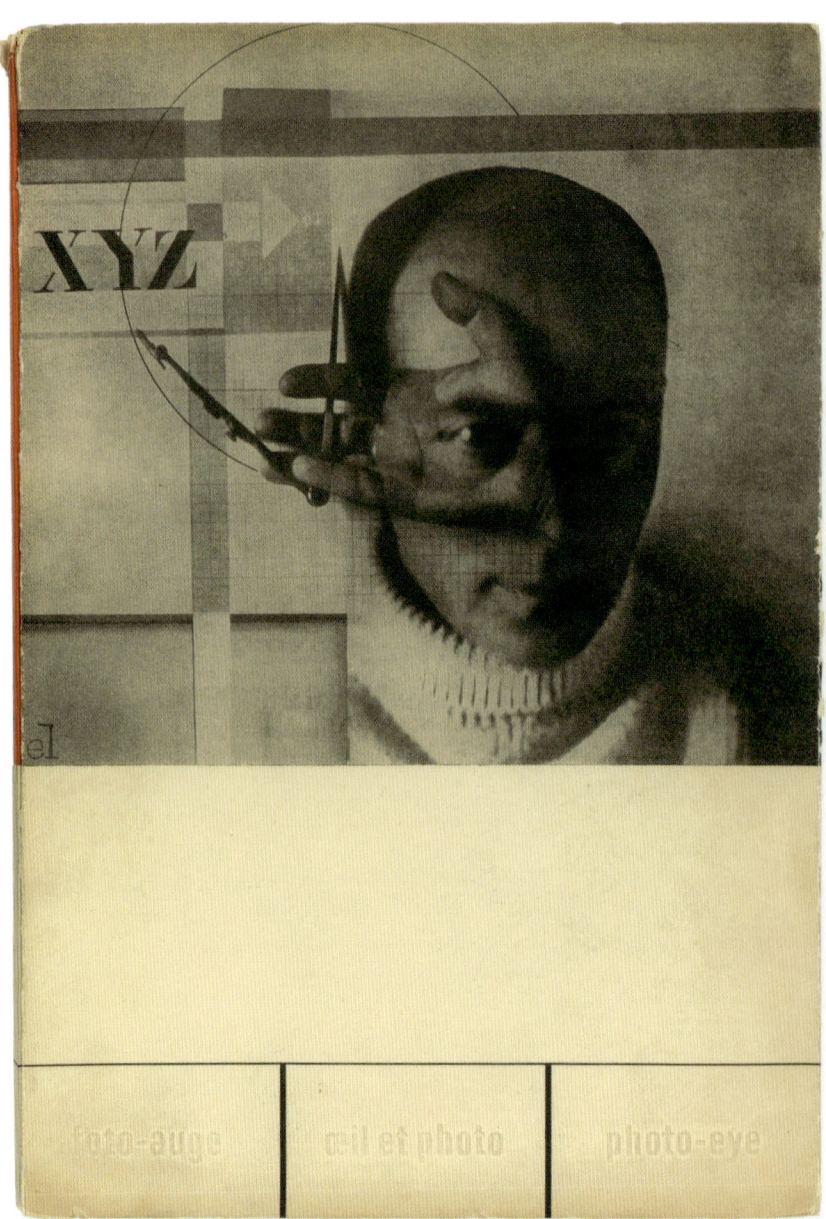

Jan Tschichold, cover and pages for *Foto-Auge: 76 Fotos der Zeit*, 1929. Photographer (cover), El Lissitzky.
29.6 x 20.6 cm
Universiteit van Amsterdam, Bijzondere Collecties, Amsterdam

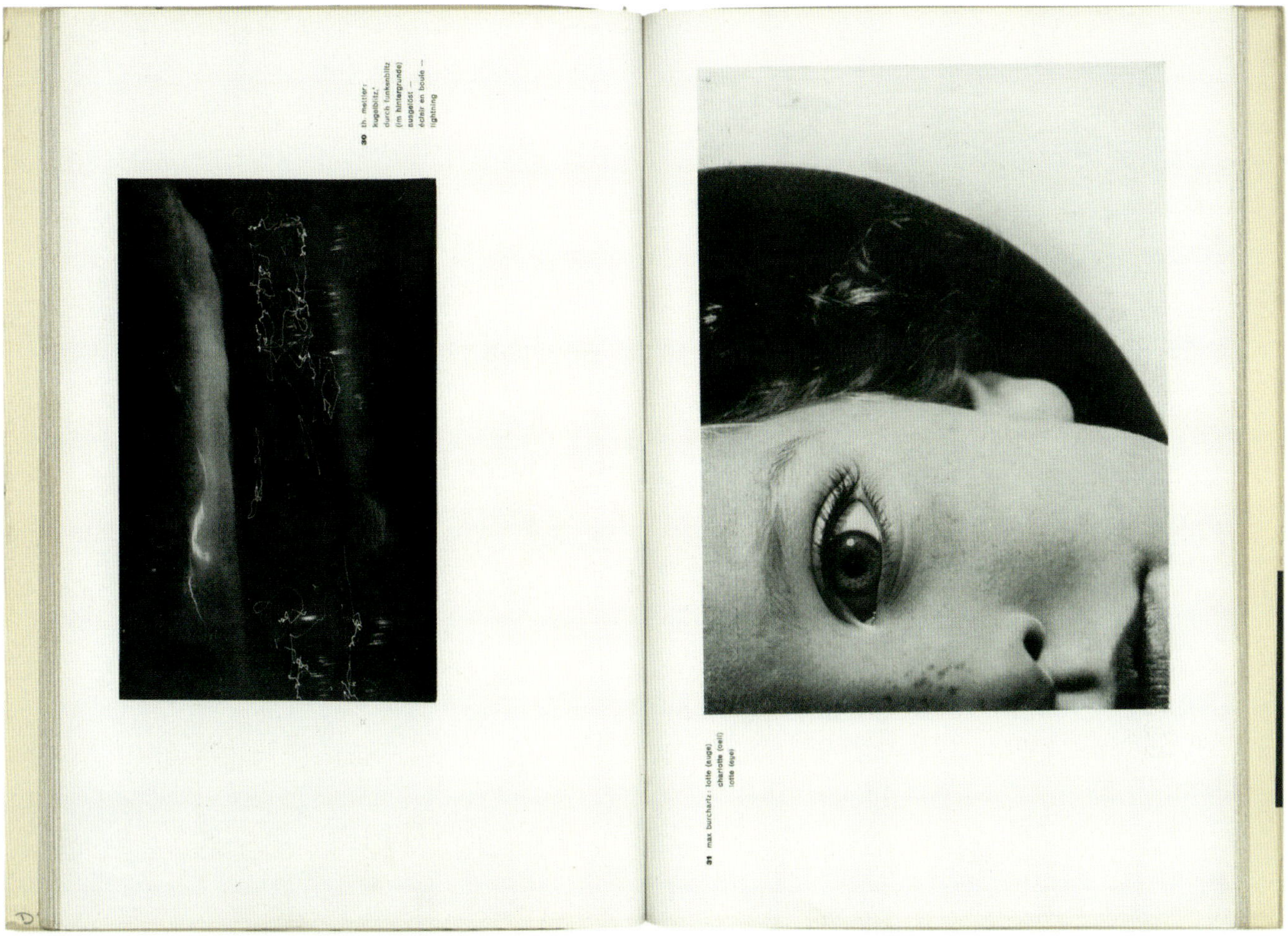

30 th. meister: kugelblitz, durch funkenschluss (im hintergrunde) ausgelöst — éclair en boule — lighting

31 max burchartz: lotte (auge) charlotte (oeil) lotte (eye)

34 brett weston: wellblechdächer — toits de tôle ondulée — roofs of corrugated iron

35 herbert bayer: beine — jambes — legs

243

Jan Tschichold,
cover and spread for
Aenne Biermann, 1930.
25 x 17.6 cm
Private collection

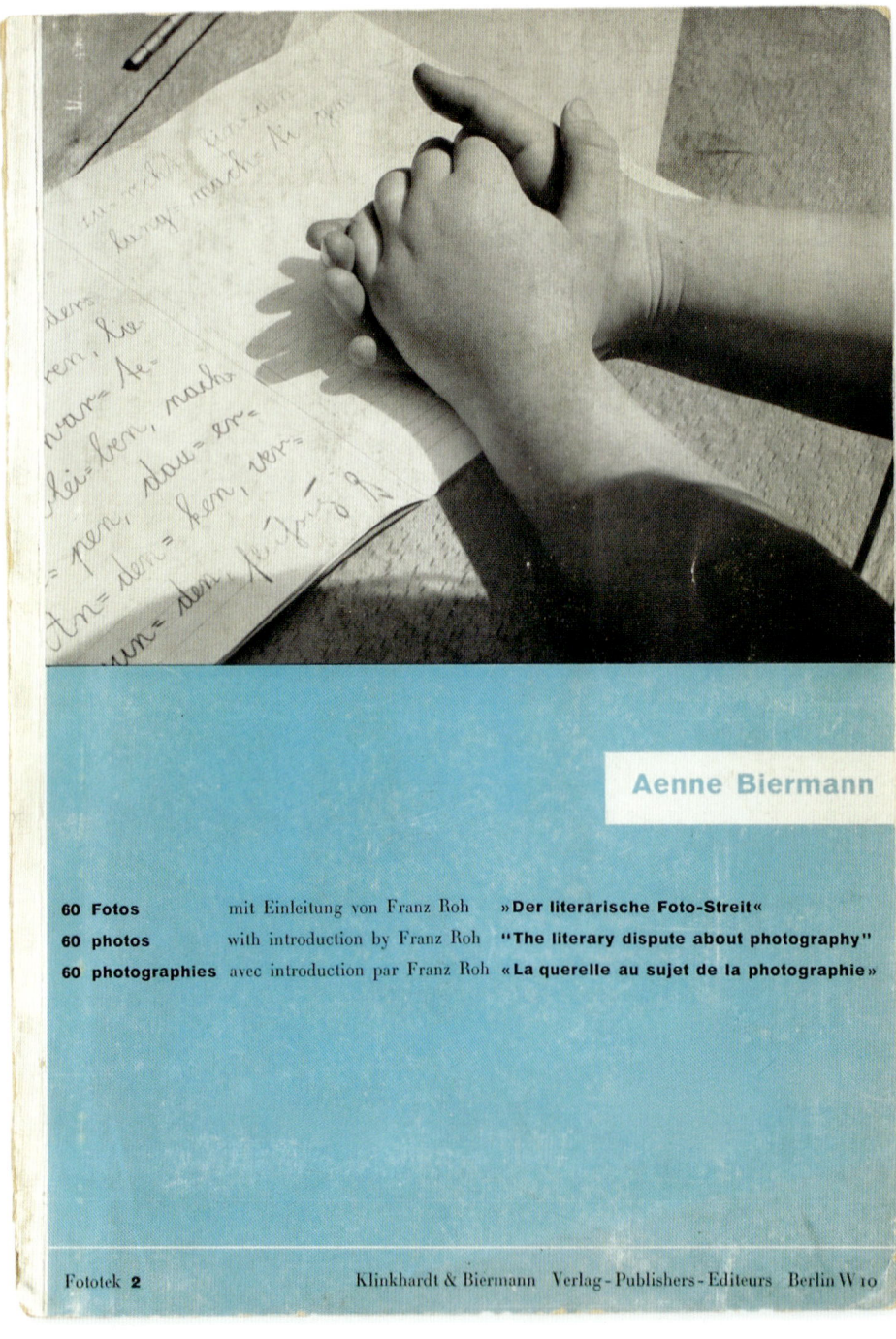

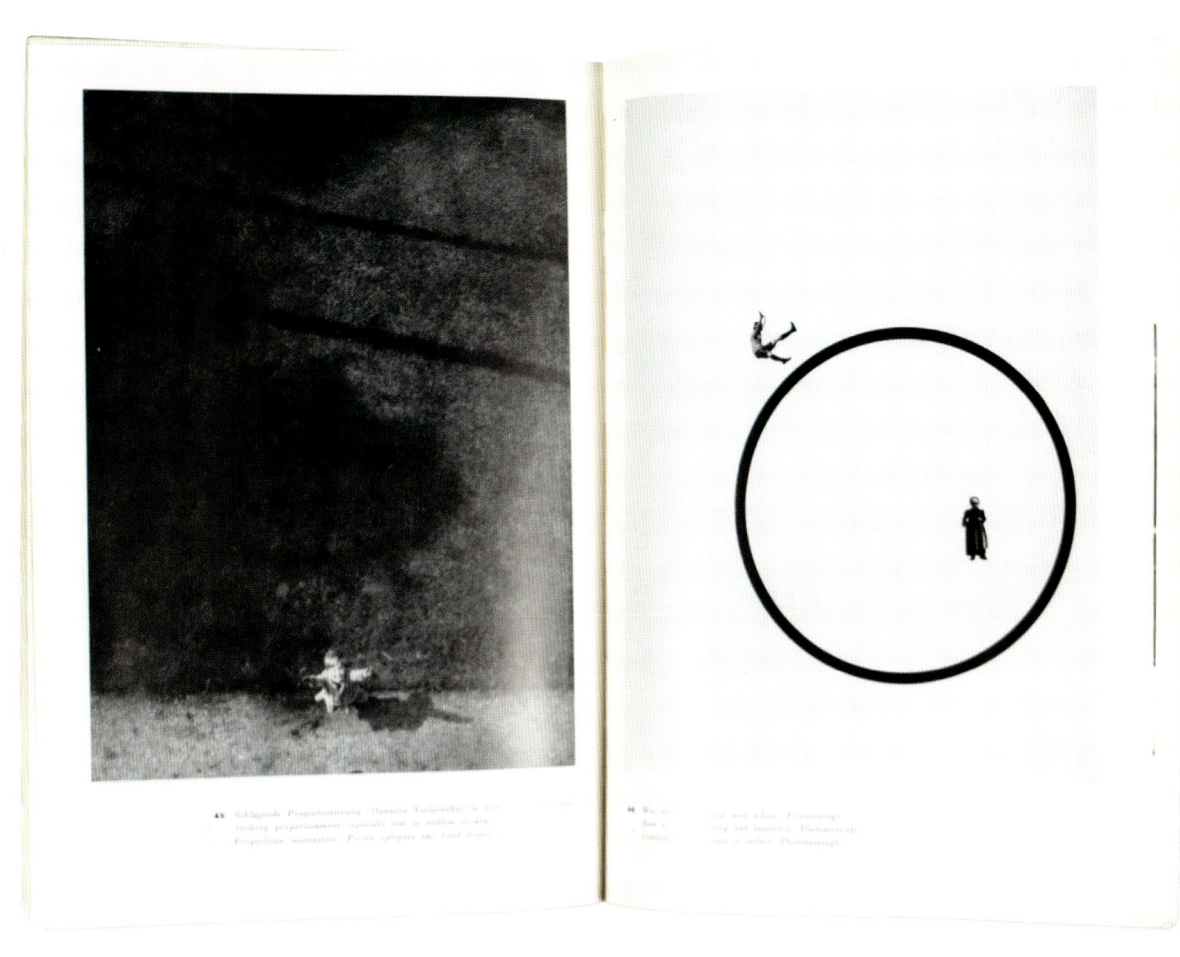

Jan Tschichold, cover and spread for *Moholy-Nagy*, 1930.
25 x 17.6 cm
Private collection

Jan Tschichold, cover and spreads for *Eine Stunde Druckgestaltung*, 1930.
29.6 x 21 cm
Private collection

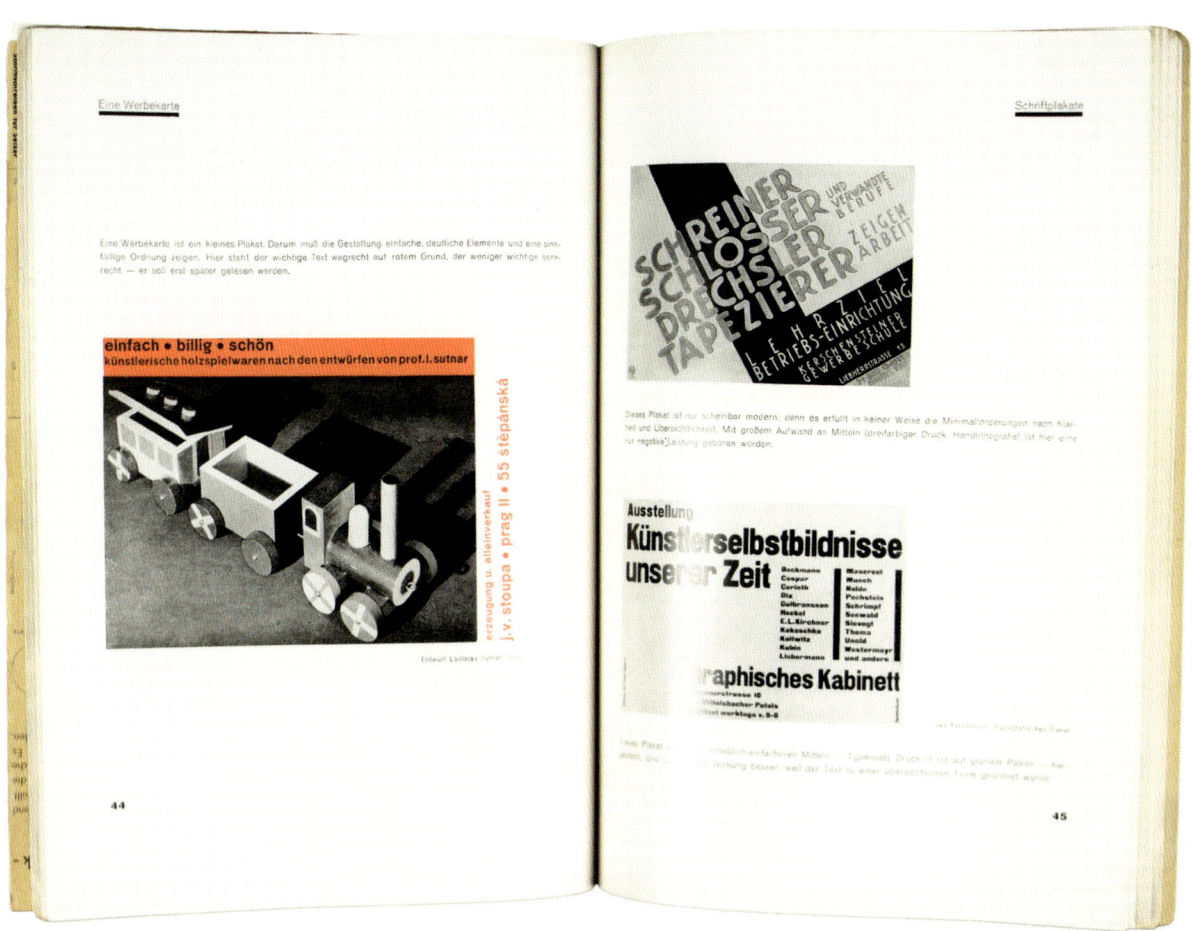

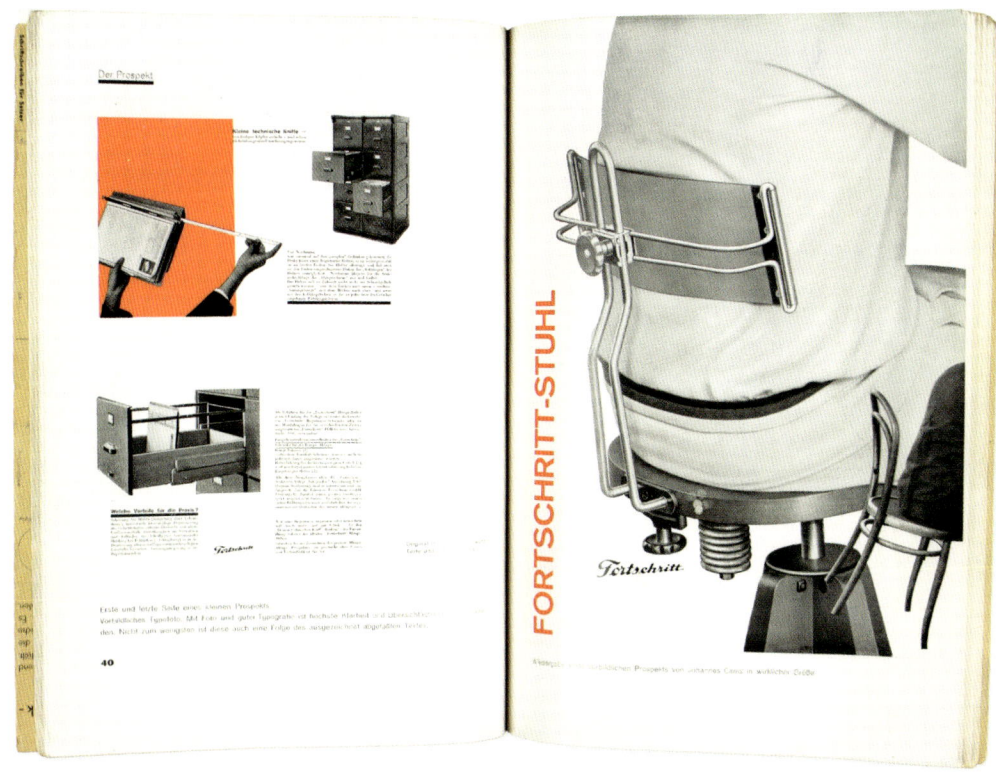

Jan Tschichold, spread for
Eine Stunde Druckgestaltung,
1930.
29.6 x 21 cm
Private collection

Das Fotoplakat

47

Jan Tschichold, cover for
Arbeiter in U.S.A., 1930.
18.2 x 12.3 cm
Private collection

Jan Tschichold, cover for
Drittel der Menschheit, 1932.
22.4 x 14.7 cm
Private collection

Jan Tschichold, cover and
spread for *Der Sieg*, 1932.
24 x 17.5 cm
Private collection

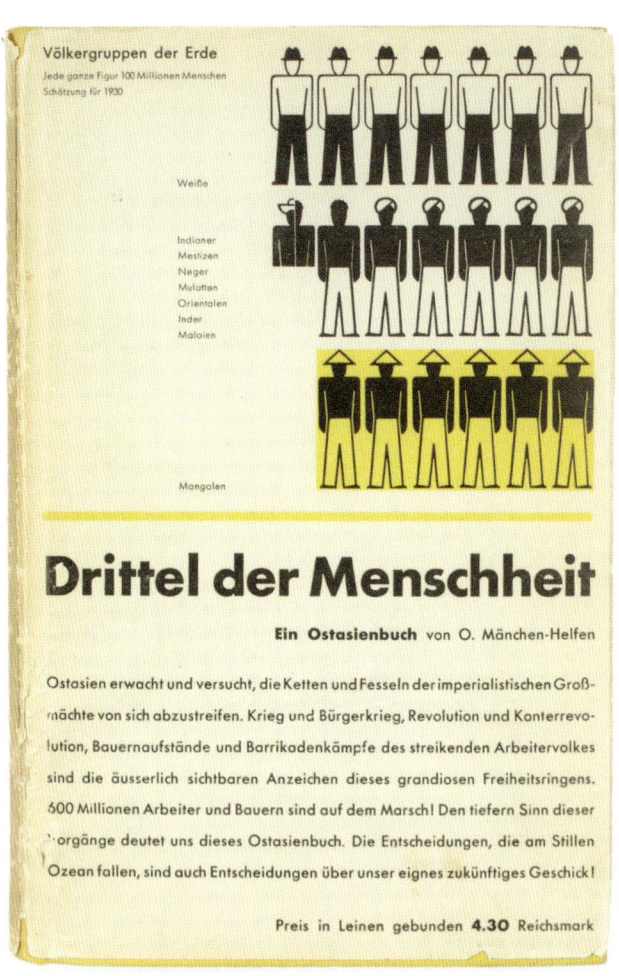

Jan Tschichold, exhibition poster
Der Berufsphotograph, 1938.
63 x 89 cm
Private collection
Courtesy www.iaddb.org

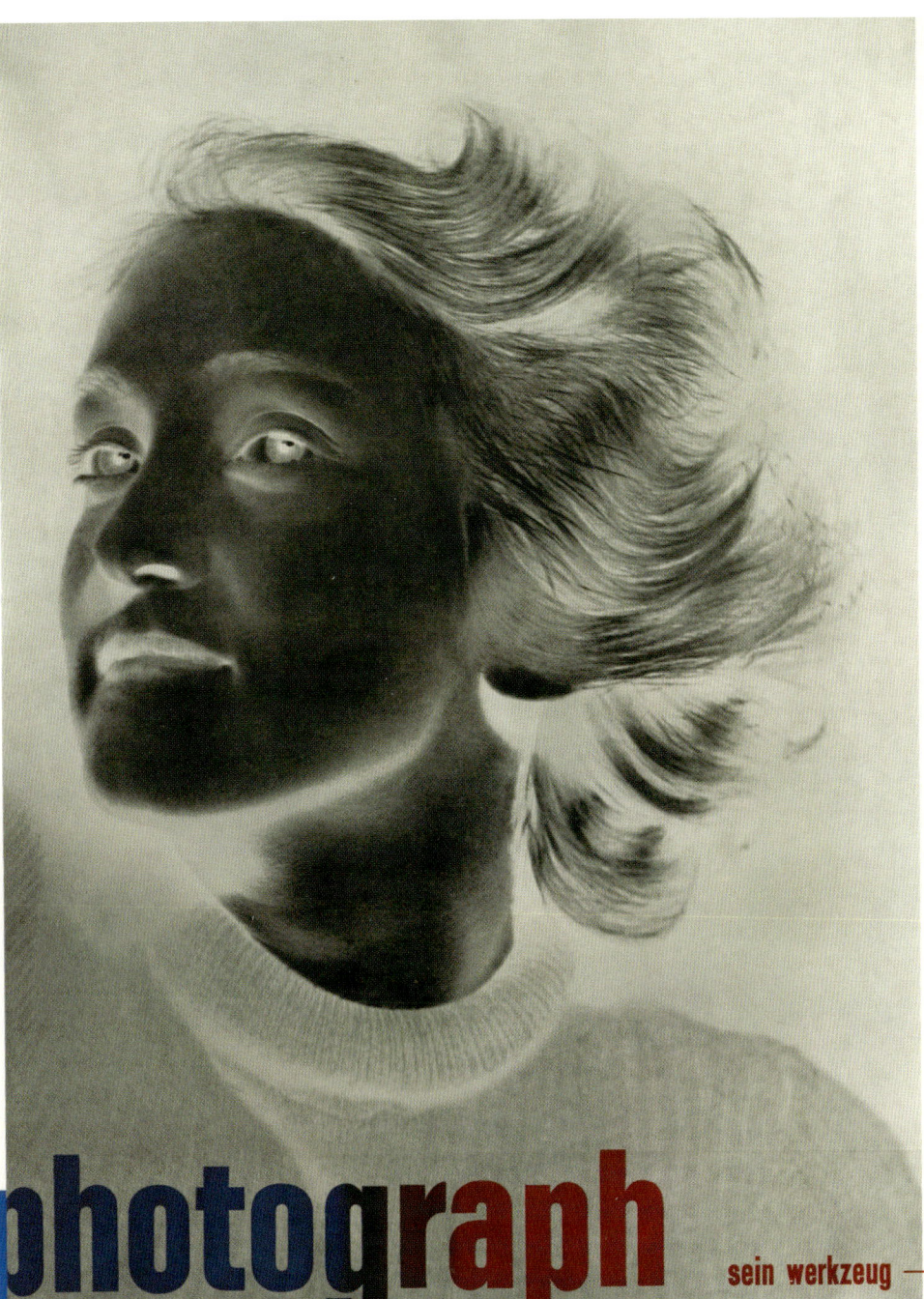

Carl Otto Müller, movie poster for Elisabeth Bergner in *Donna Juana*, Phoebus Palast, c. 1927.
119 x 85 cm
Private collection
Courtesy www.iaddb.org

Carl Otto Müller
1901–1970

Carl Otto Müller, poster
for *Fürst oder Clown*,
Phoebus Palast, 1928.
119 x 84.5 cm
Private collection
Courtesy www.iaddb.org

Carl Otto Müller, poster for
Der Fluch der Vererbung,
Phoebus Palast, 1928.
85 x 119 cm
Private collection
Courtesy www.iaddb.org

Fortunato Depero
1892–1960

Fortunato Depero, cover and spread for *Secolo XX*, 1928.
28.1 x 20 cm
Private collection

Fortunato Depero,
Christmas Wish, 1932.
11 x 8 cm
Private collection

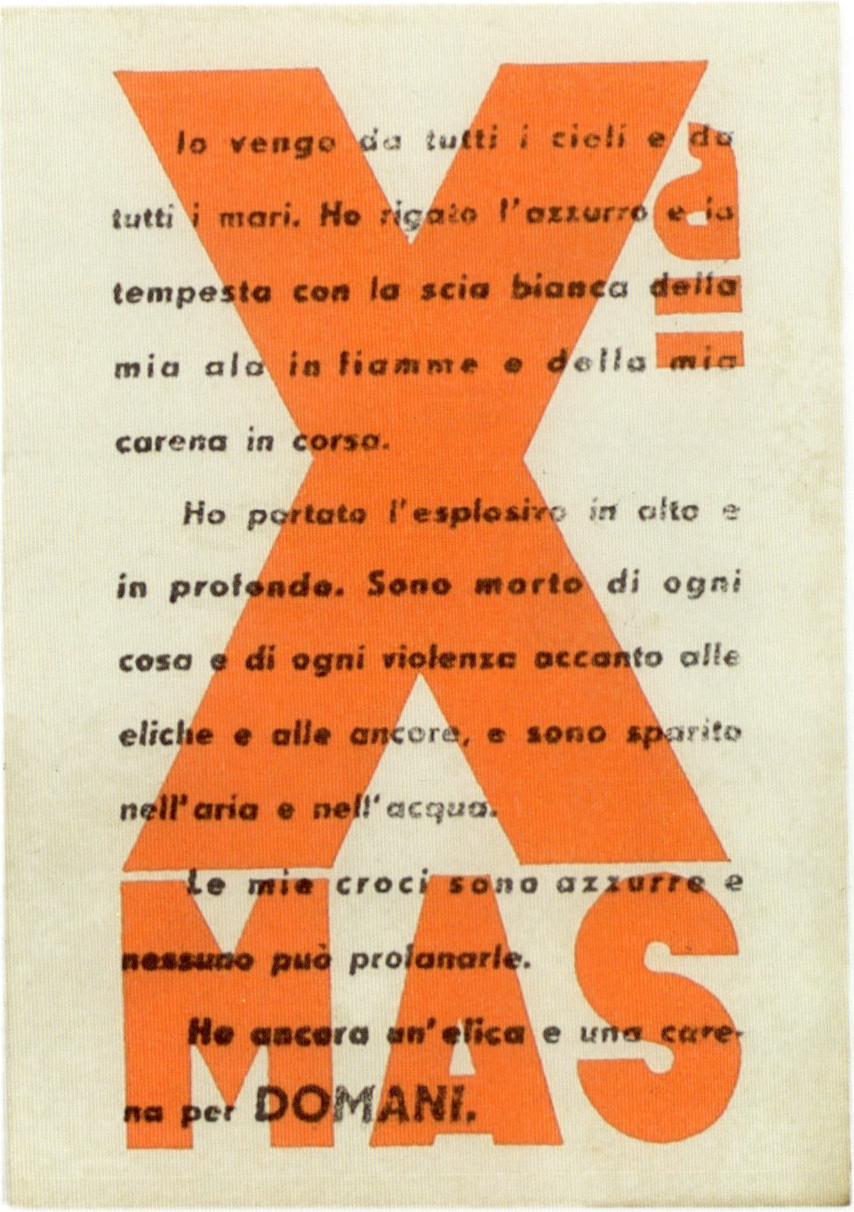

Fortunato Depero, cover
and pages for the publication
Parole in libertà, 1932.
24 x 24 cm
Private collection

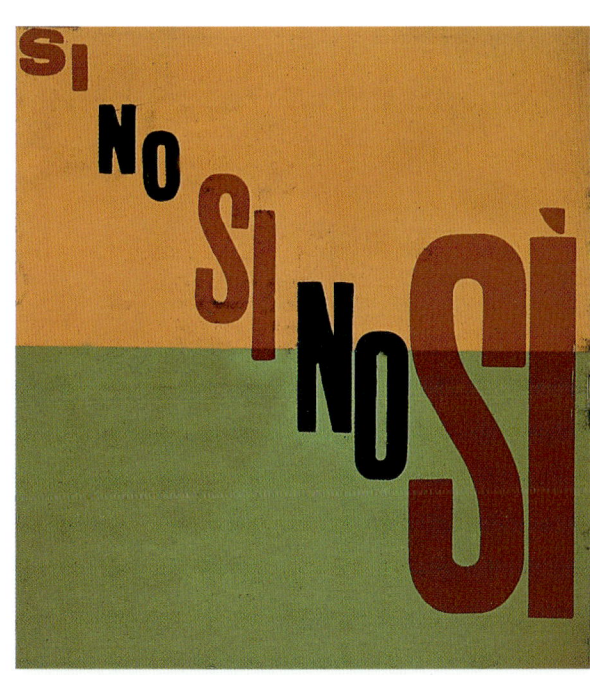

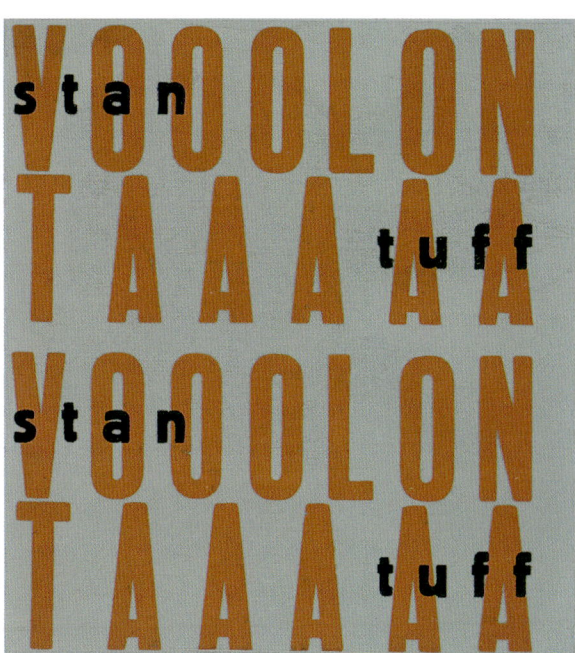

Otto Baumberger,
poster for a carpet sale,
Forster Teil Ausverkauf, 1928.
128 x 90 cm
Private collection
Courtesy www.iaddb.org

Otto Baumberger
1889-1961

1928

César Domela
1900–1992

César Domela, cover for
25 Jahre Dampfturbinen,
AEG, 1928.
29.5 x 21 cm
Private collection

1928

Gustav Klutsis
1895–1938

Gustav Klutsis (1895–1938)
and Sergei Senkin (1894–1963),
magazine cover for
*Film und Filmkunst in der UdSSR
1917-1928*.
21.1 x 11.9 cm
Private collection

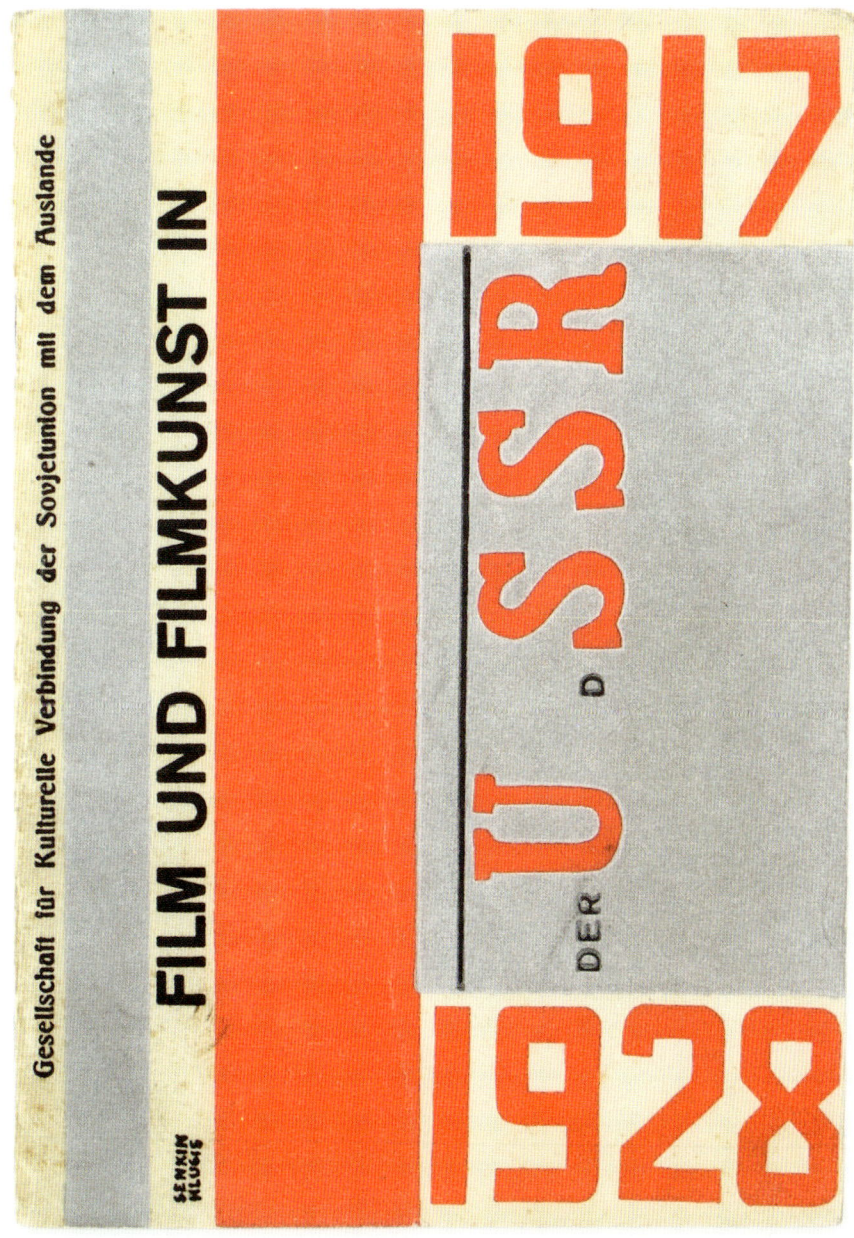

Gustav G. Klutsis, poster for
*The USSR is the Avant-Garde
of the World Proletariat*, 1931.
144 x 104 cm
Private collection
Courtesy www.iaddb.org

Gustav G. Klutsis, poster
*In Our Country the Victory
of Socialism is Guaranteed,
Communist Party*, 1932.
145 x 102 cm
Private collection
Courtesy www.iaddb.org

Gustav Klutsis, magazine covers for *Sovetsky teatr*, nos. 3, 5, 9, 12, 1932–1933.
29.6 x 21.5 cm
Private collection

Gustav G. Klutsis, poster
Hail to the Worldwide October Celebration, Communist Party, 1933.
159.5 x 103 cm
Private collection
Courtesy www.iaddb.org

Gustav G. Klutsis, poster
Be Proud, Be Happy to Become a Soldier in the Red Army, 1936.
95 x 63 cm
Private collection
Courtesy www.iaddb.org

1928

Hans Leistikow
1892–1962

Hans Leistikow, covers for *Das neue Frankfurt*, nos. 6, 7/8, 9, 9 and 11/12, 1928–1929.
26.1 x 24.2 cm
Private collection

Hans Leistikow, brochure cover for *Was wissen Sie von der Städtischen Sparkasse zu Frankfurt am Main*, c. 1929.
21 x 15 cm
Private collection

Hans Leistikow, brochure cover for *Uraltes Frankfurt a. M.*, c. 1929.
21.8 x 11.6 cm
Private collection

Hans Leistikow, magazine cover and spread for *Ruhr-Anthrazit-Eiformbriketts*, c. 1930.
21 x 14.9 cm
Private collection

Ruhr-Anthrazit-Eiformbriketts im irischen Ofen — billiger Dauerbrand

Der irische Ofen hat einen hohen, mit Schamottesteinen ausgemauerten Schacht, der einen Brennstoffvorrat für etwa 12stündigen Betrieb faßt. Alle Türen sind dicht schließend, so daß die Verbrennungsluft nur durch die einstellbare Regulieröffnung in der Aschfalltür eintreten kann, wodurch eine sehr gute Regulierfähigkeit des Ofens erreicht wird. Der Rost hat ein bewegliches Mittelteil; durch Betätigung dieses Rüttelrostes von außen fällt die sich ansammelnde Asche in den Aschkasten. Ruhr-Anthrazit-Eiformbriketts sind der einzige Brennstoff, mit dem sich diese einfachen Öfen als Dauerbrenner betreiben lassen.

Immer ein warmes Zimmer

Der mit Ruhr-Anthrazit-Eiformbriketts betriebene irische Ofen geht nie aus. Über Nacht und für die übrigen Zeiten, in denen der Raum nicht benutzt wird, kann die Ofenleistung so klein eingestellt werden, daß ein nennenswerter Kohlenverbrauch nicht eintritt, die unwirtschaftliche Auskühlung der Zimmerwände aber verhindert wird. Im Bedarfsfalle wird lediglich die Luftzufuhr verstärkt, d. h. der Ofen auf „Stark" gestellt, in wenigen Augenblicken ist er dann in heller Glut und die Stube angenehm durchwärmt.

Das lästige, tägliche Feueranmachen fällt fort

Zu Beginn der Heizzeit wird der Ofen angezündet, und wenn weiterhin morgens und abends nachgelegt wird, brennt er den ganzen Winter über in einwandfreiem Dauerbrand durch. Der Nachteil der Einzelofenheizung ist also beseitigt, die noch verbleibende Wartung — Nachfüllen, Freirütteln des Rostes, Entleeren des Aschkastens — kann demgegenüber kaum noch als besondere Arbeit angesehen werden. Es ist zweckmäßig, mit dem Nachfüllen nicht so lange zu warten, bis die Glut schon zu weit heruntergebrannt ist. Ein- bis zweimal am Tage wird das Feuer durch Betätigung des Rüttelrostes gereinigt.

Das Zimmer und die Hände bleiben sauber

Der Dauerbrand mit Ruhr-Anthrazit-Eiformbriketts im irischen Ofen beseitigt die schlimmste Quelle von Unsauberkeit, das wiederholte Feueranzünden. Der Ofen braucht nicht ausgenommen zu werden, und mit dem Brennstoff und Anmacheholz kommt man überhaupt nicht in Berührung. Auch das sonst unvermeidliche Verstauben des Zimmers ist beseitigt. Das Reinigen des Rostes ist durch die Rüttelvorrichtung einfach und ohne Verschmutzung möglich, das Nachfüllen geschieht unmittelbar aus der Kohlenschütte.

Hans Leistikow, brochure cover and spread for *Ruhr-Brechkoks,* c. 1930.
20.9 x 14.7 cm
Private collection

Otakar Mrkvička
1898–1957

Otakar Mrkvička, cover and spread, *Jak se vlastně dělá film*, 1928.
17.3 x 11.9 cm
Private collection

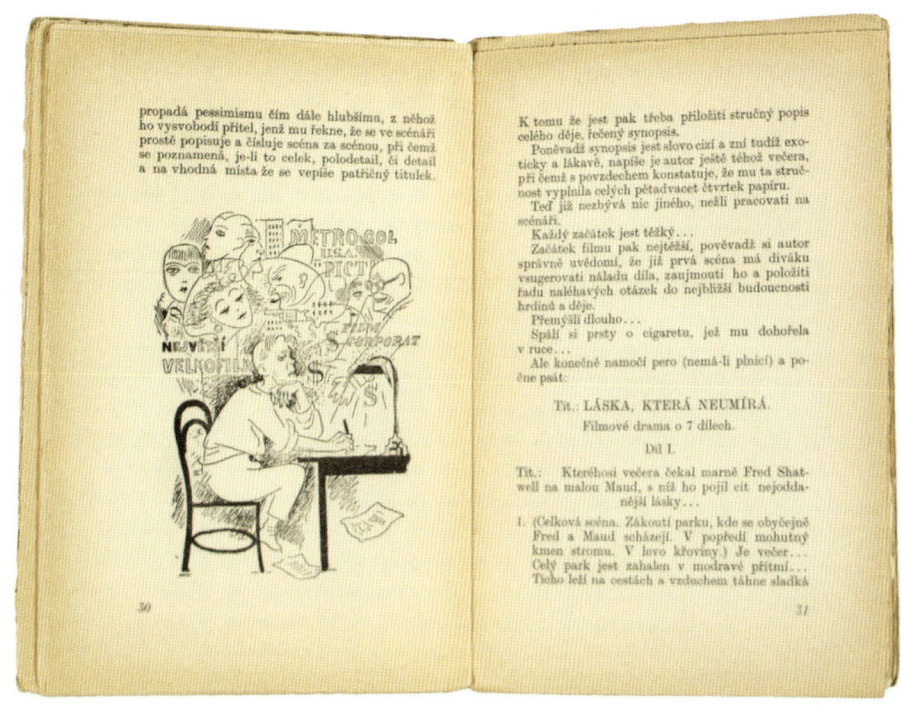

Louis Heijmans, *Zon Zee Zand voor 't jonge volkje*, poster for Middelburgsche Vacantieschool, c. 1928.
65 x 45 cm
Private collection
Courtesy www.iaddb.org

Louis Heijmans
1890–1977

1928

Paul Schuitema
1897–1973

Paul Schuitema, brochure cover for *Toledo-Berkel Snelwegers*, Rotterdam, 1928.
20.2 x 14.1 cm
Private collection

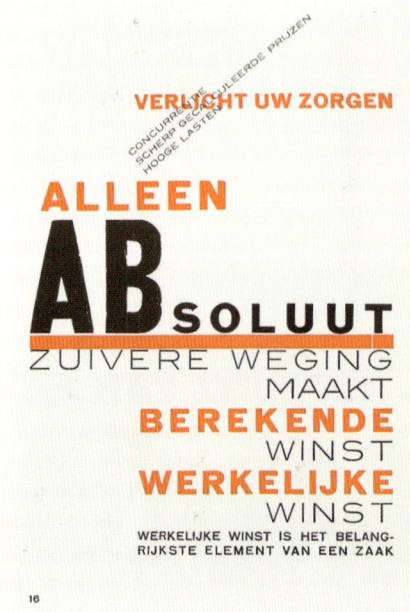

Paul Schuitema, leaflet for Berkel, *Hij sloeg het hoogst*, 1928.
28.5 x 21.1 cm
Private collection

Paul Schuitema, brochure cover for Berkel: *Aanwijzingen voor het onderhoud van de VBP vlees- en kaassnijmachine*, 1930.
21 x 11 cm
Private collection

Paul Schuitema, *Hoe groter*, leaflet for Berkel, c. 1929.
28.5 x 21.1 cm
Private collection

Paul Schuitema, union poster
for Centrale Bond: *30 000
Transportarbeiders,* 1930.
115.5 x 75.5 cm
Private collection
Courtesy www.iaddb.org

Paul Schuitema, magazine
cover for *De gemeenschap*,
vol. 6e, 1930.
25.2 x 18.6 cm
Private collection

Paul Schuitema, magazine
cover for *Film Liga Nr. 10:
Onafhankelijk maandblad
voor filmkunst, 1930–1932.*
29.2 x 20.5 cm
Private collection

Paul Schuitema, brochure cover for *Stalen meubelen d3*, Rotterdam, 1932.
27.9 x 21.2 cm
Private collection

Donald Brun, poster,
Die kluge Hausfrau kauft bei den Mitgliedern der Einkaufs-Rabattvereinigung LIGA – 6% Rabattmarken, 1928.
128 x 90.5 cm
Private collection
Courtesy www.iaddb.org

Donald Brun
1909-1999

Willem Hendrik Gispen,
poster for *Giso lampen*, 1928.
100 x 71 cm
Private collection
Courtesy www.iaddb.org

Willem Hendrik Gispen
1890-1981

Willem Hendrik Gispen, cover for *1e supplement metalen meubels,* Gispen, 1933.
21.1 x 18.2 cm
Private collection

Karl Gossow
1904–1962

Karl Gossow, cover for
Schkid: Die Republik der Strolche, 1929.
18.7 x 12.7 cm
Private collection

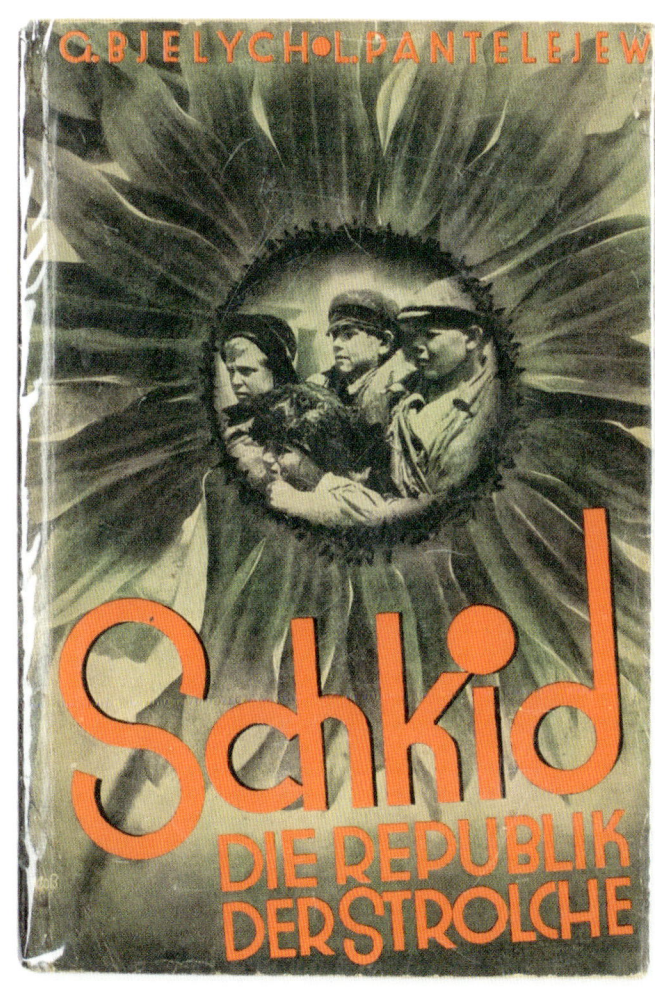

Franz Ehrlich, poster for
*Bauhaus, Dessau, im
Gewerbemuseum Basel*, 1929.
84 x 59 cm
Private collection
Courtesy www.iaddb.org

Franz Ehrlich
1907-1984

Jean Carlu, poster for
*Eclairages, Machinerie,
Théâtre Pigalle, Paris*, 1929.
155 x 102 cm
Private collection
Courtesy www.iaddb.org

Jean Carlu
1900-1997

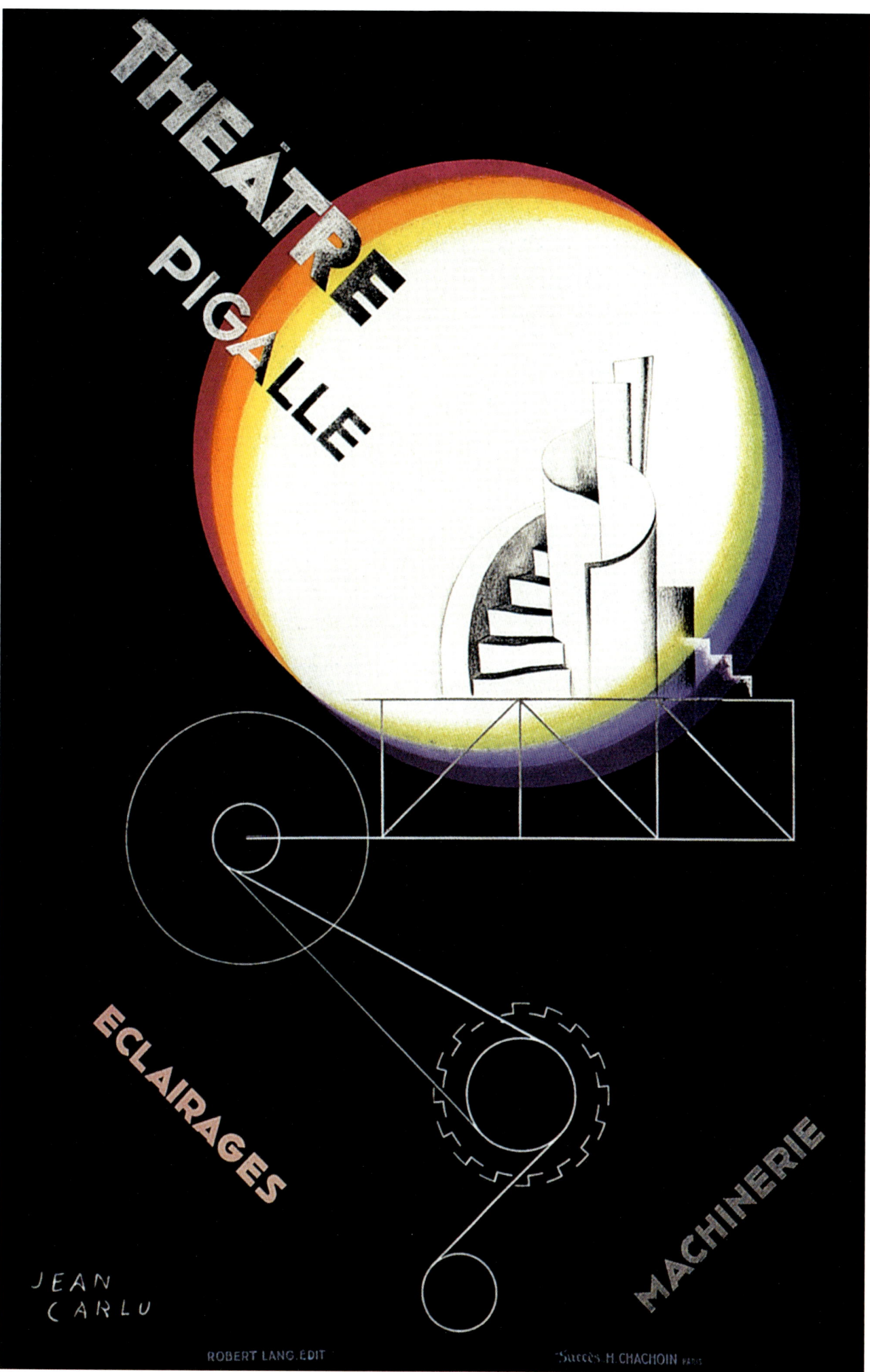

Jean Carlu, poster for a lottery
to benefit war veterans in
France, *La dette*, 1931.
106 x 75 cm
Private collection
Courtesy www.iaddb.org

Jean Carlu, *Je sais tout*, 1936.
26.7 x 20.9 cm
Private collection

1929

Vilmos Huszár
1884–1960

Vilmos Huszár, cover for *Jaarboek van de Nederlandsche ambachts- & nijverheidskunst: Ruimte*, 1929.
25.9 x 19.5 cm
Private collection

Vilmos Huszár, leaflet for *Dienst P.T.T.: Radiobrieftelegram*, 1931.
11.1 x 15.5 cm
Private collection

Vilmos Huszár, cover for magazine *Wendingen*, Diego Rivera, 1929.
33.5 x 33.7 cm
Private collection

Jean (Hans) Arp, Walter Cyliax, exhibition poster for *Kunsthaus Zürich, Abstrakte und Surrealistische Malerei und Plastik*, 1929.
128.3 x 90 cm
Private collection
Courtesy www.iaddb.org

Jean (Hans) Arp
1886-1966

Walter Cyliax
1899-1945

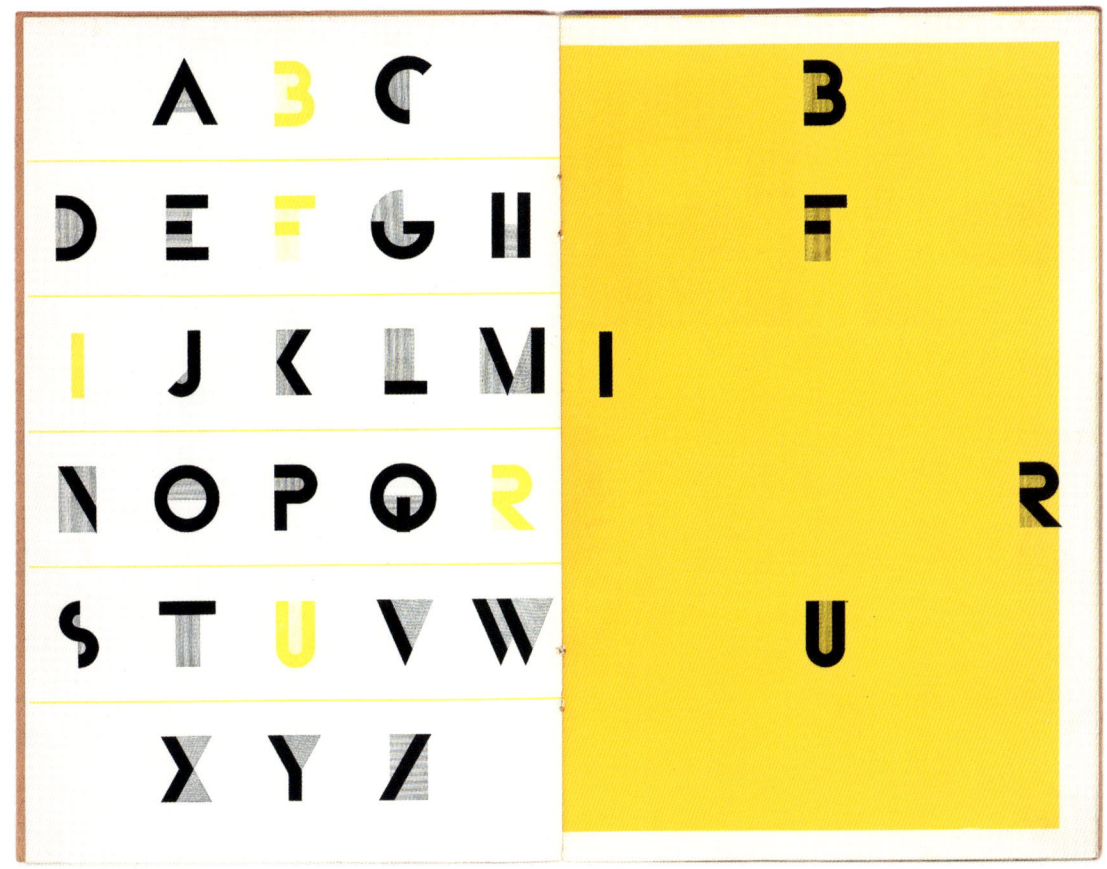

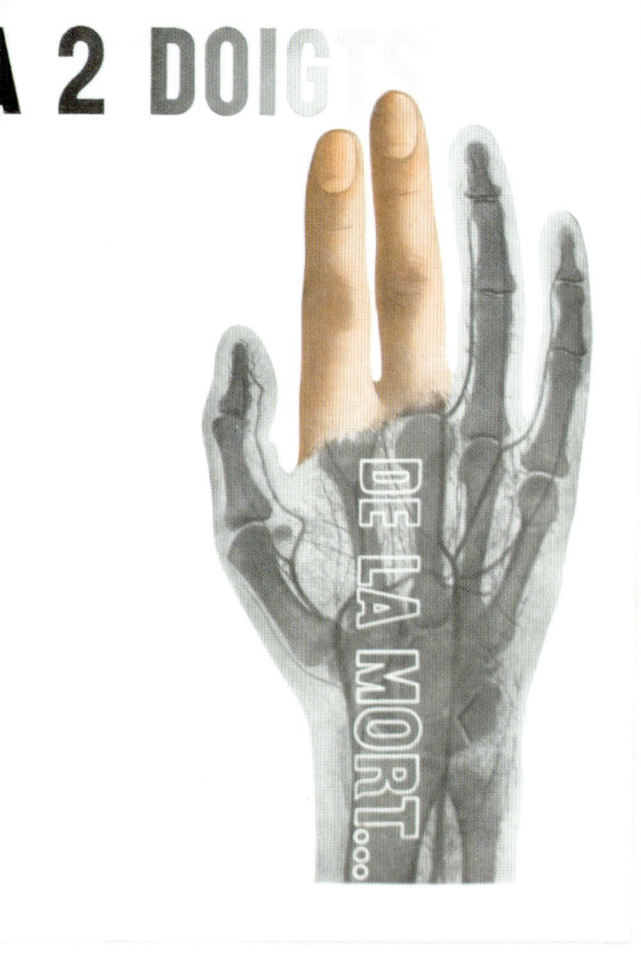

A. M. Cassandre, cover and brochure spread for *A 2 doigts de la mort...*, 1931.
26.1 x 20.2 cm
Private collection

1929

Man Ray
1890–1976

Man Ray, cover and spread for *Transition*, no. 15, 1929.
22.7 x 16.5 cm
Private collection

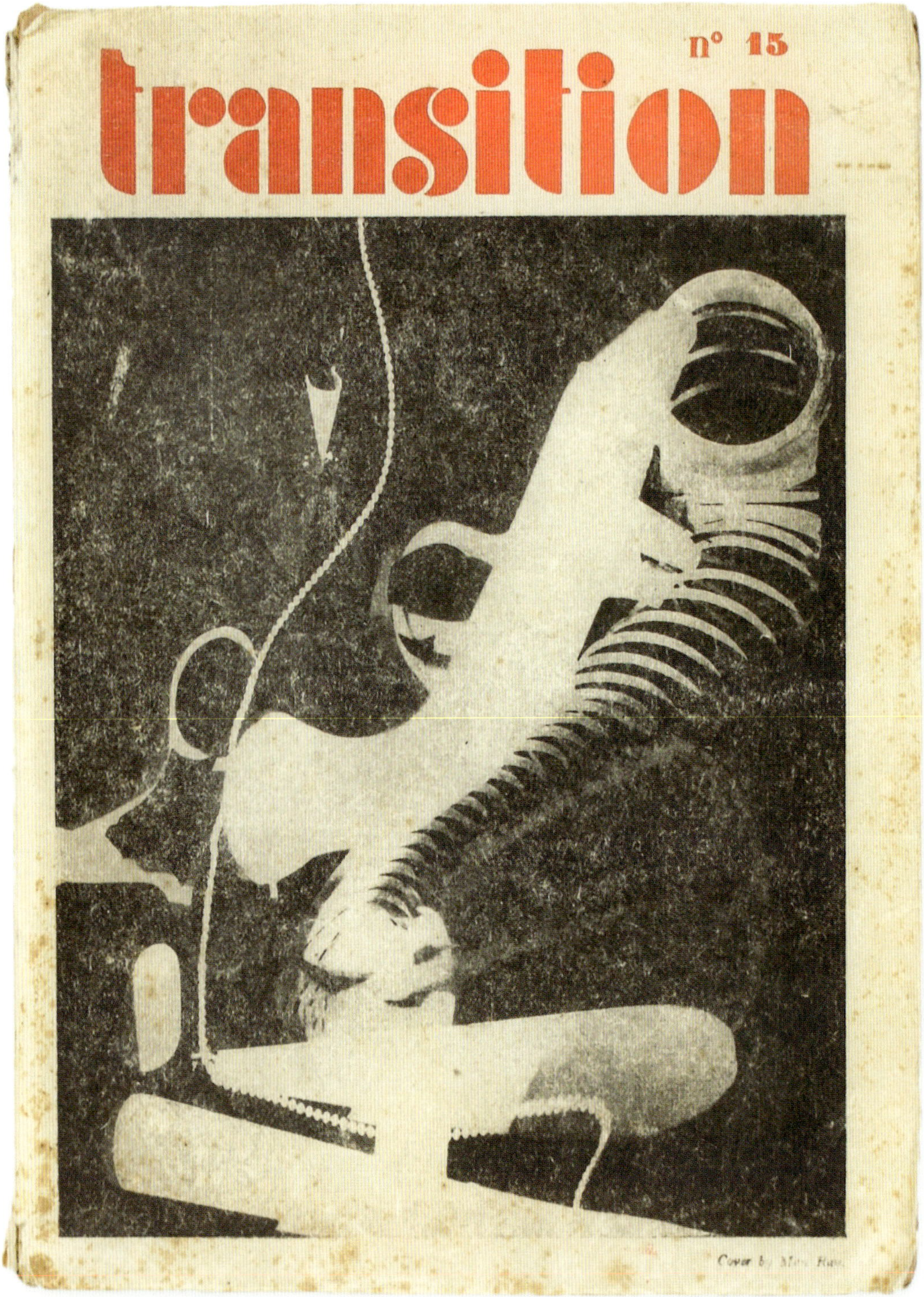

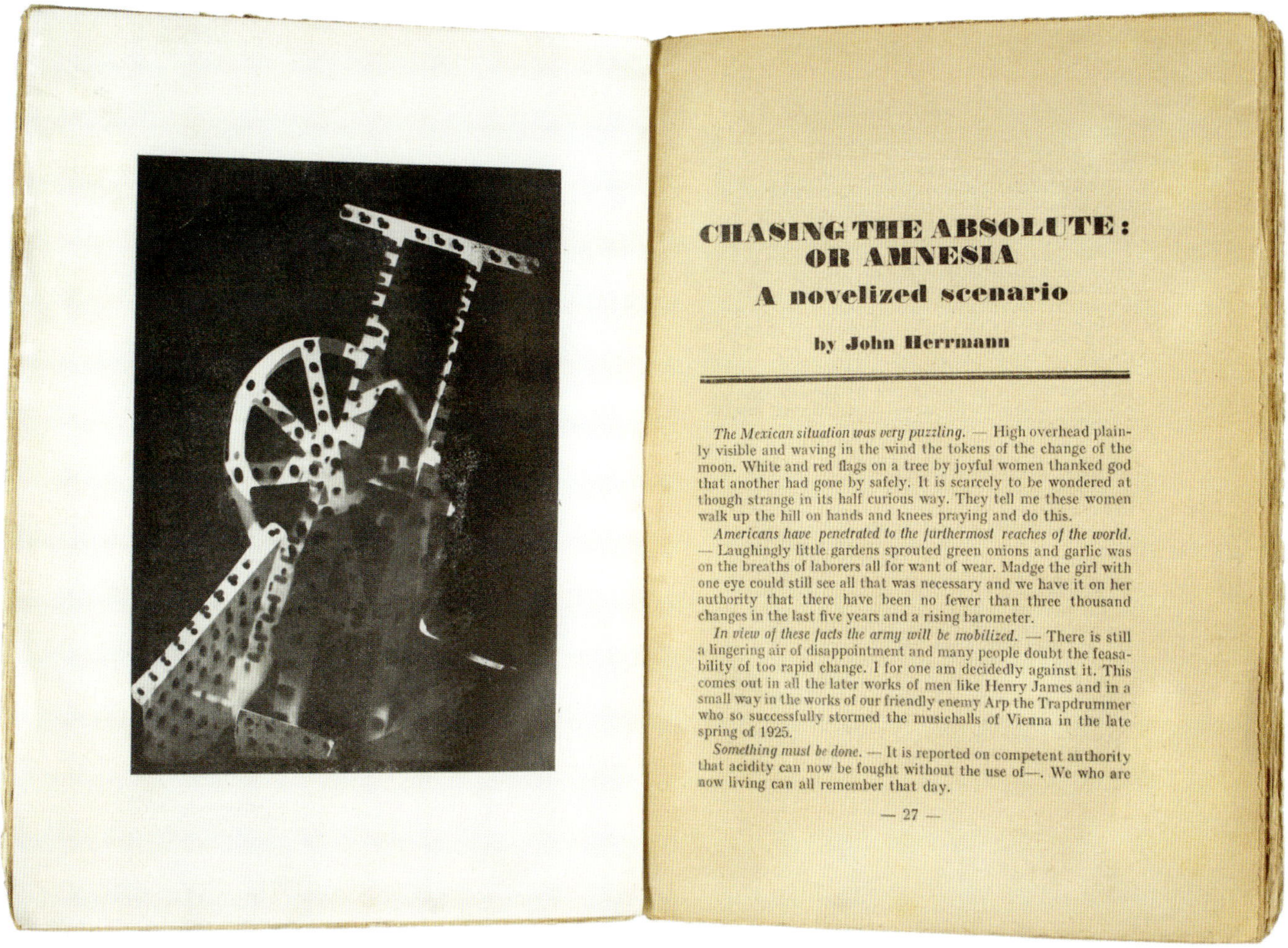

CHASING THE ABSOLUTE: OR AMNESIA
A novelized scenario

by John Herrmann

The Mexican situation was very puzzling. — High overhead plainly visible and waving in the wind the tokens of the change of the moon. White and red flags on a tree by joyful women thanked god that another had gone by safely. It is scarcely to be wondered at though strange in its half curious way. They tell me these women walk up the hill on hands and knees praying and do this.

Americans have penetrated to the furthermost reaches of the world. — Laughingly little gardens sprouted green onions and garlic was on the breaths of laborers all for want of wear. Madge the girl with one eye could still see all that was necessary and we have it on her authority that there have been no fewer than three thousand changes in the last five years and a rising barometer.

In view of these facts the army will be mobilized. — There is still a lingering air of disappointment and many people doubt the feasability of too rapid change. I for one am decidedly against it. This comes out in all the later works of men like Henry James and in a small way in the works of our friendly enemy Arp the Trapdrummer who so successfully stormed the musichalls of Vienna in the late spring of 1925.

Something must be done. — It is reported on competent authority that acidity can now be fought without the use of—. We who are now living can all remember that day.

— 27 —

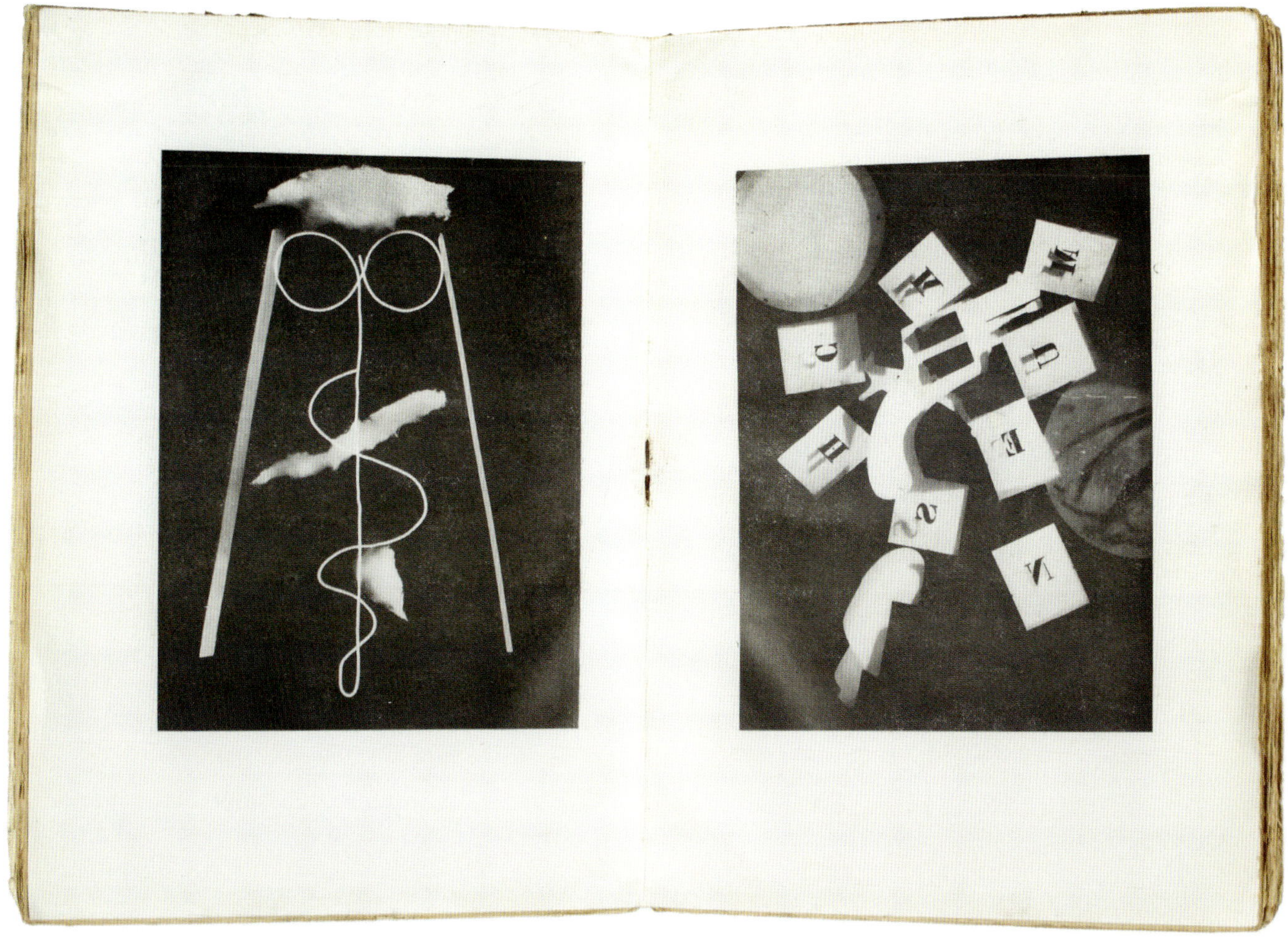

Myron Chepovskyi, poster for the movie *Man with the Movie Camera* by Dziga Vertov, 1929.
63.5 x 104 cm
Private collection
Courtesy www.iaddb.org

Myron Chepovskyi
1909-unknown

1930

Ladislav Sutnar
1897–1976

Ladislav Sutnar, cover for *Praha-Bukurešť*, 1930.
20.9 x 15 cm
Private collection

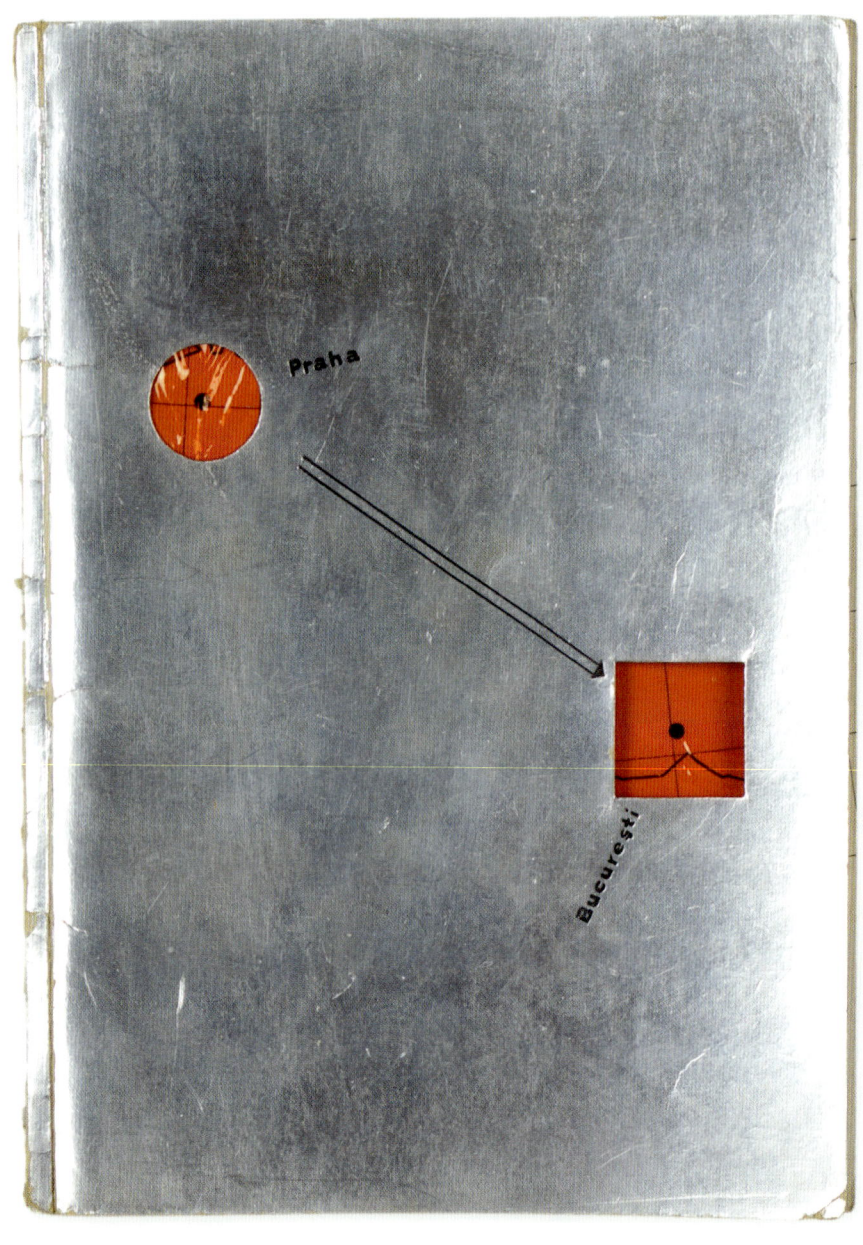

Ladislav Sutnar, cover for *Ženění a vdávání*, 1931.
19 x 14 cm
Private collection

Ladislav Sutnar, cover and spreads for *Nejmenší dům*, 1931.
29.7 x 21.2 cm
Private collection

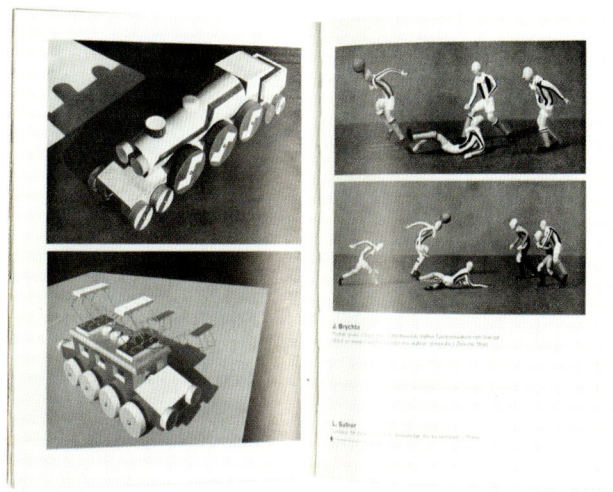

Ladislav Sutnar, cover and spreads for *Tjeckoslovakisk arkitektur och konstindustri*, 1931.
21 x 14.9 cm
Private collection

Ladislav Sutnar, cover and spread for advertising brochure, no. 3, 1932. Photography by Josef Sudek (1896–1976).
23.7 x 17.2 cm
Private collection

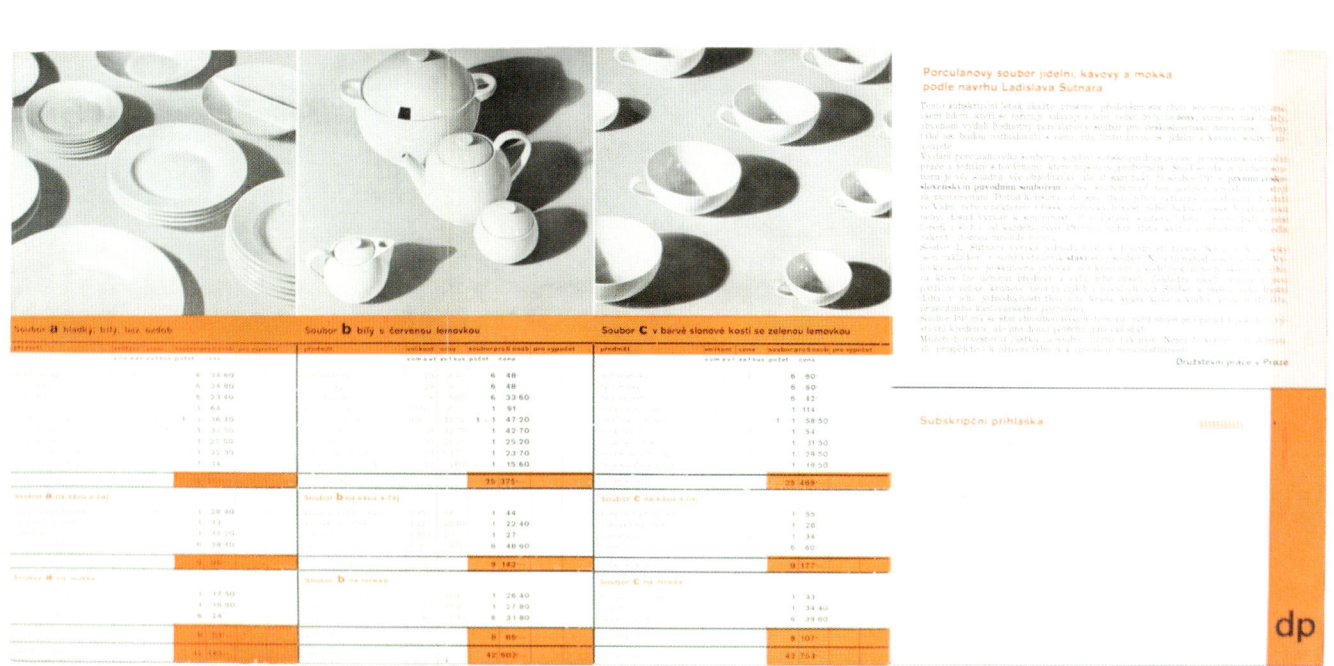

Ladislav Sutnar, cover for
10 let družstevní práce, 1932.
18.8 x 13.5 cm
Private collection

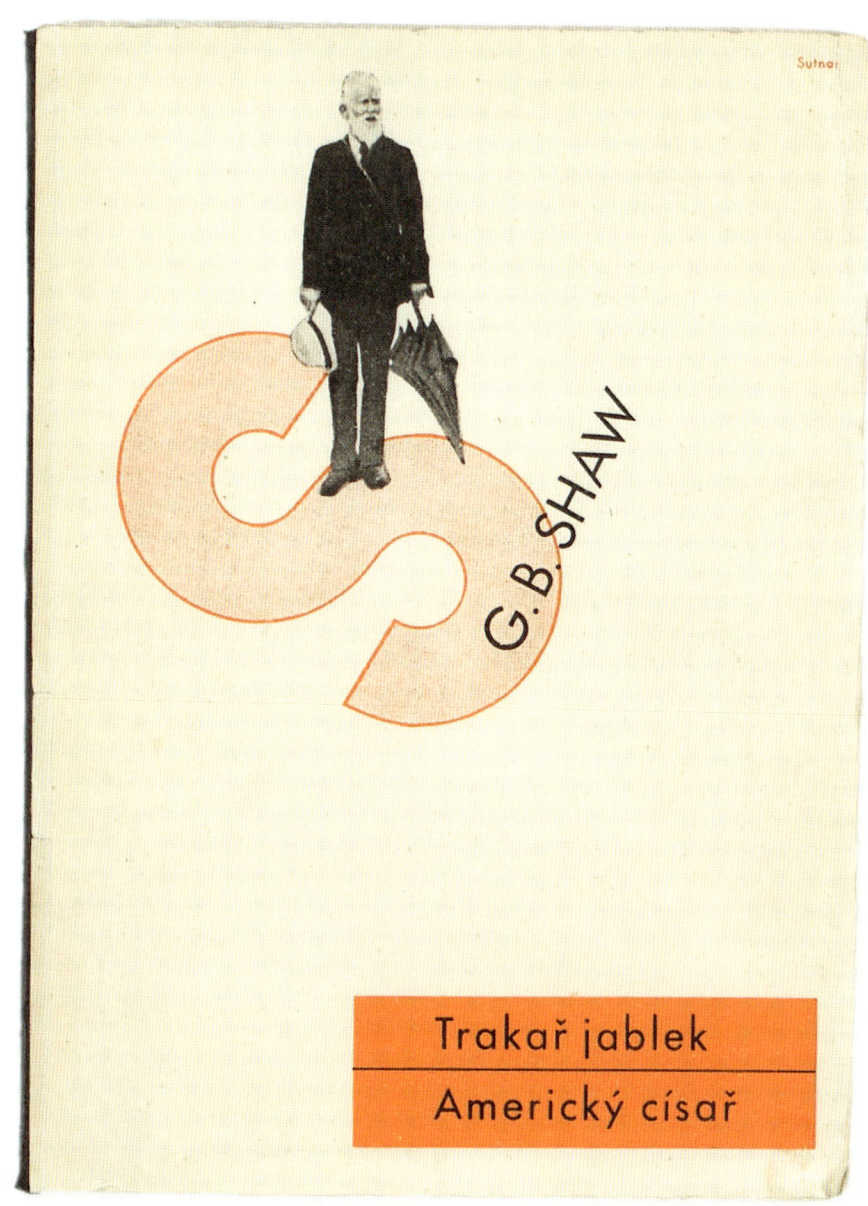

Ladislav Sutnar, cover for *Trakař jablek*, 1932.
19.2 x 14 cm
Private collection

Ladislav Sutnar, cover for *Drobnosti*, 1933.
19.3 x 14 cm
Private collection

Ladislav Sutnar, cover for *Muž budoucnosti*, 1933.
19.2 x 14 cm
Private collection

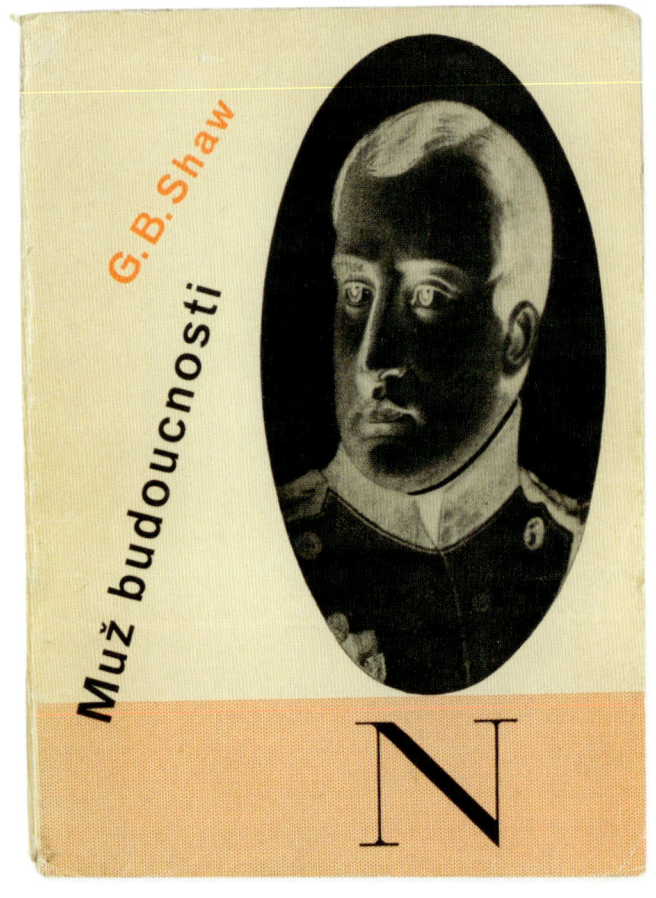

Ladislav Sutnar, cover and spread for *Svět nic neví*, 1934.
18.6 x 13.1 cm
Private collection

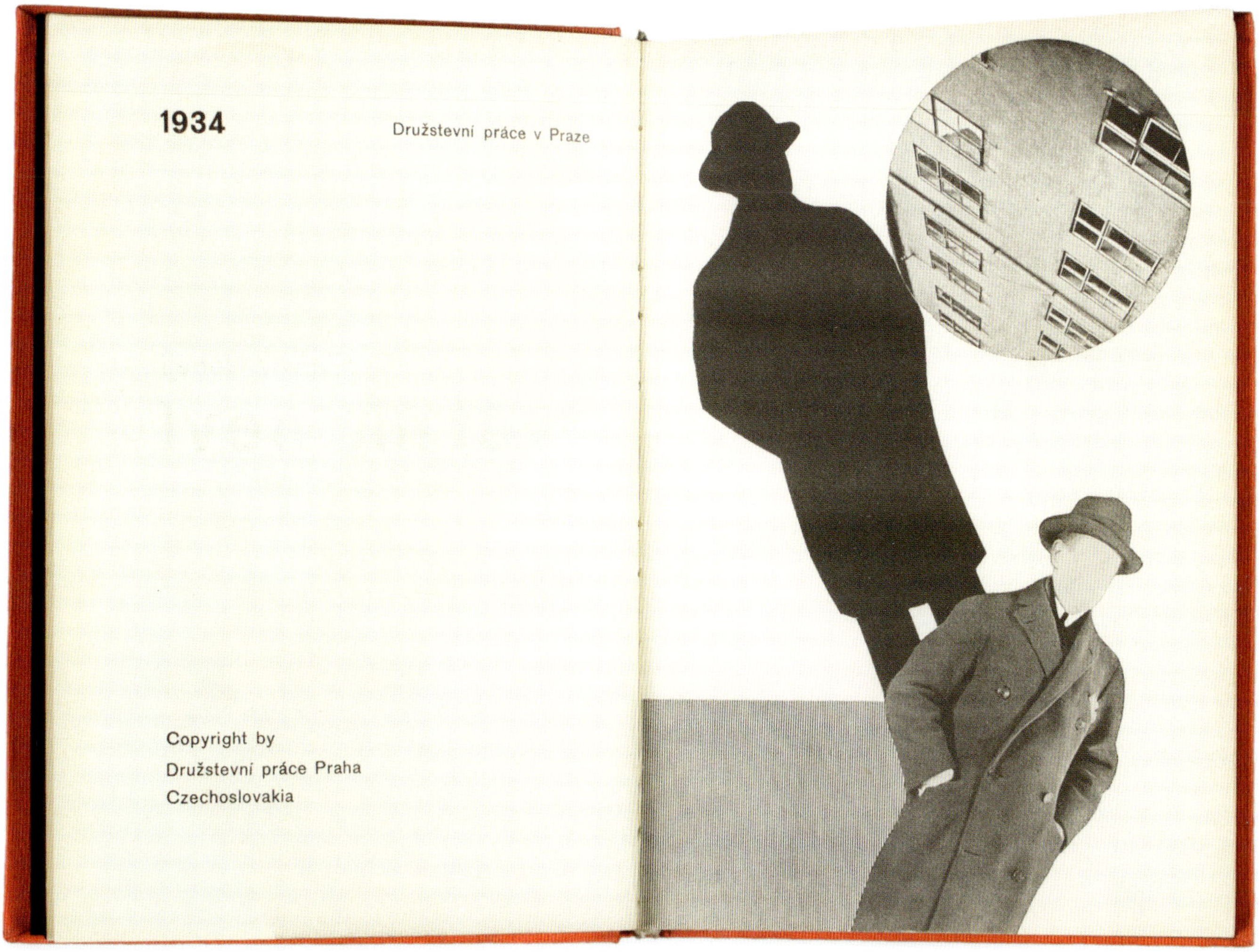

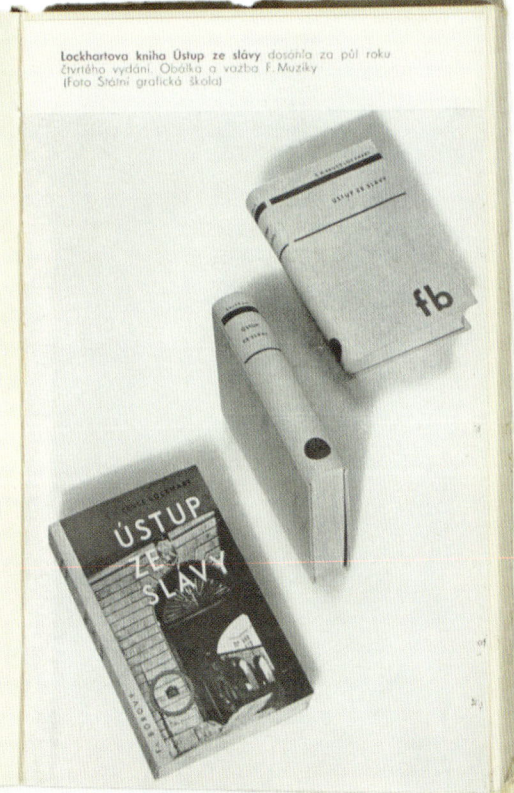

Ladislav Sutnar, cover for *Almanach kmene*, no. 35–36, 1935.
18.8 x 11.8 cm
Private collection

Ladislav Sutnar, cover for
Kniha vzpomínek, 1935.
20.3 x13.5 cm
Private collection

1931

Gerard Kiljan
1891–1968

Gerard Kiljan, leaflet for
Koopt weldadigheids postzegels en briefkaarten,
P.T.T., 1931.
21.6 x 16 cm
Private collection

Gerard Kiljan, cover for
Rijks-serie toestellen,
P.T.T., 1932.
14.9 x 20.9 cm
Private collection

1931

Anton Stankowski
1906–1998

Anton Stankowski, "Studio Max Dalang (Founded in 1916)", cover for *Injecta S. A.*, 1931.
20.8 x 15.1 cm
Private collection

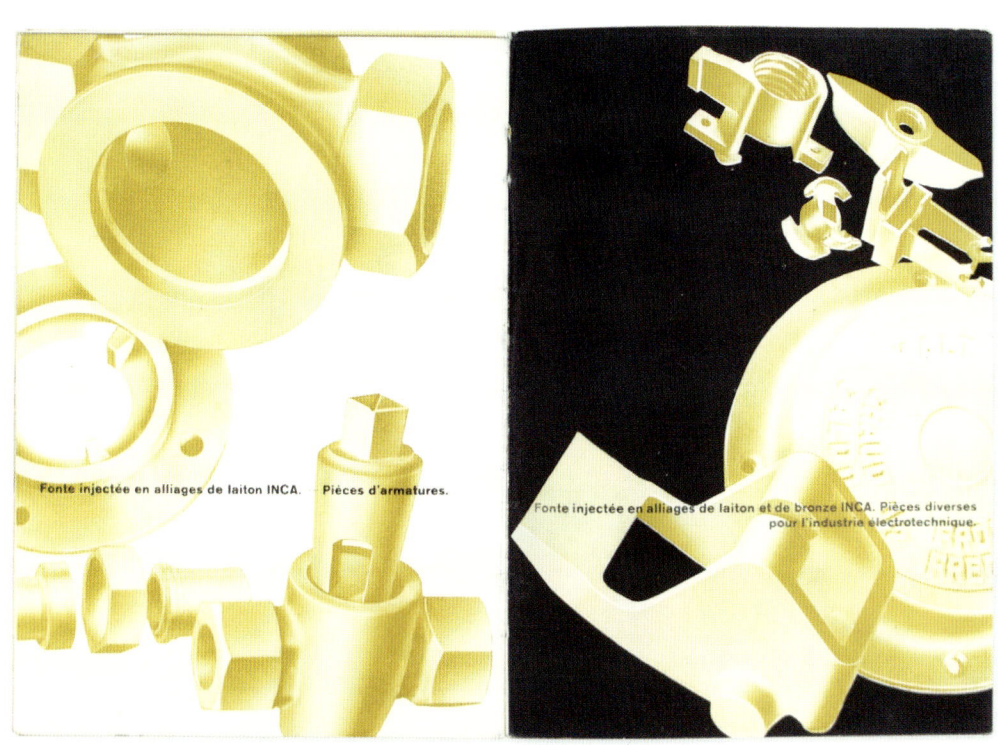

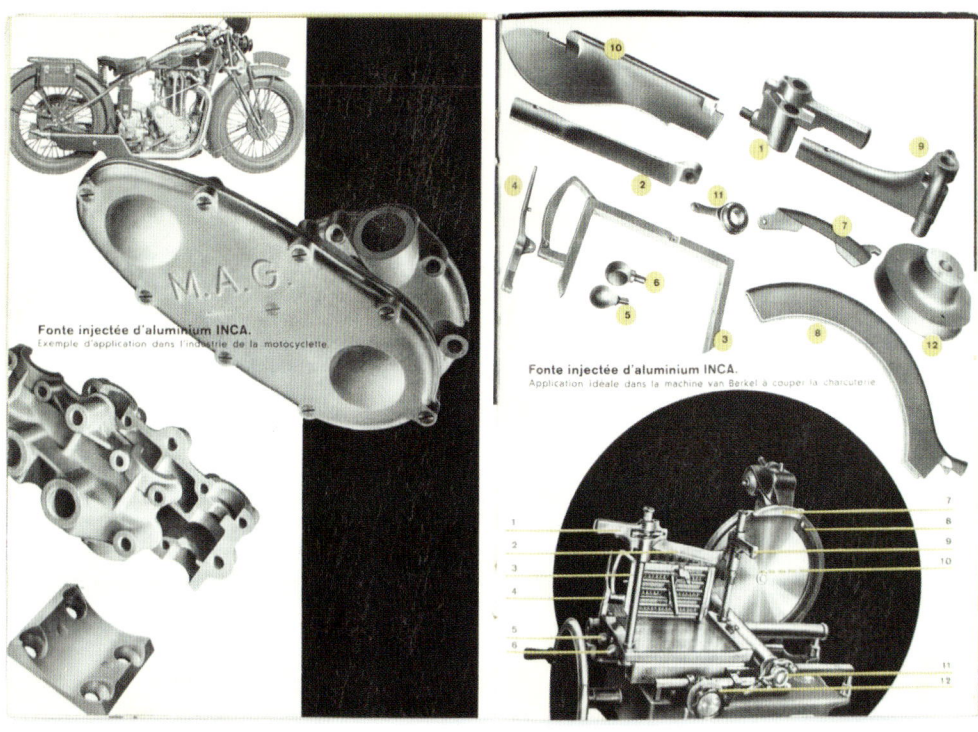

Solomon Telingater
1903–1969

Solomon Telingater, *Literature World Revolution*, no. 2, 1931.
24.8 x 17.6 cm
Private collection

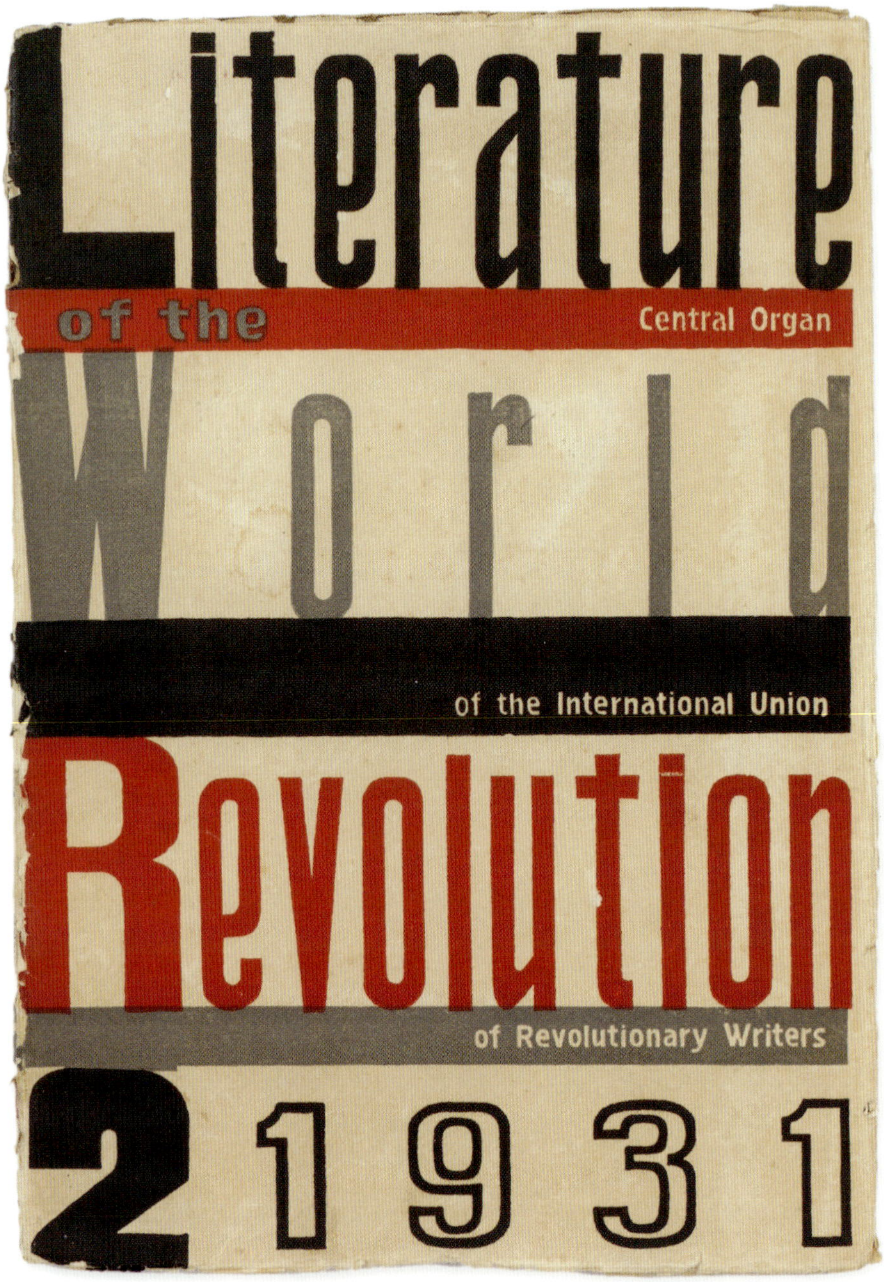

1931

Paul Urban
1901–1937

Paul Urban, cover for
Der rote Handel droht, 1931.
20.8 x 13.5 cm
Private collection

1932

Max Bill
1908–1994

Max Bill, covers for *Magazine Information* nos. 1, 2, 3, 5, 11, 1932–1933.
21.1 x 14.8 cm
Private collection

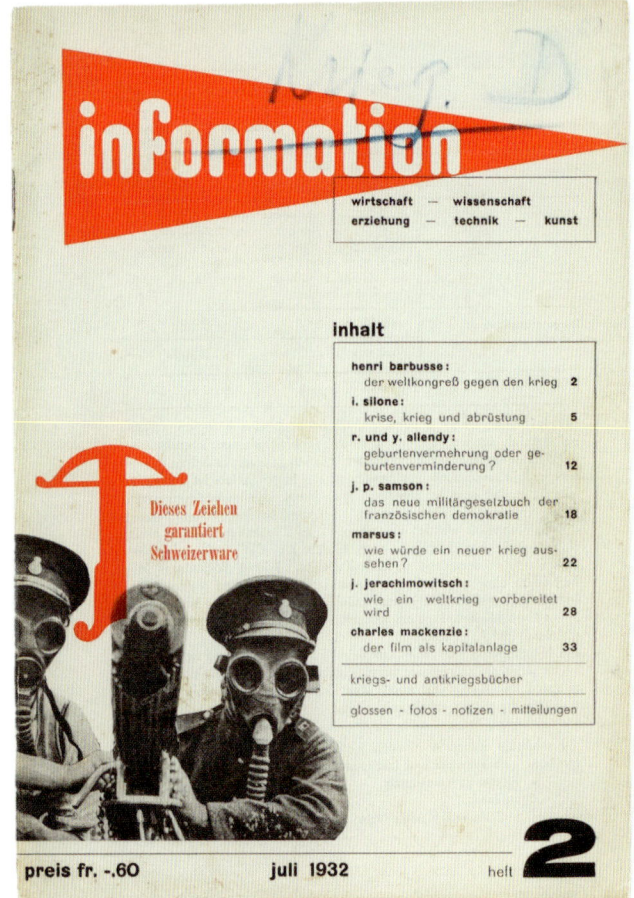

Max Bill, poster for
Tanzstudio Wulff, 1932.
63.9 x 89.9 cm
Private collection
Courtesy www.iaddb.org

1932

Jacob Jongert
1883–1942

Jacob Jongert, design for van Nelle's *Cirkel*, 1932.
4.7 x 8.7 cm
Private collection

Jacob Jongert, cover for
*Raucht van Nelle's Shag Tabak:
The Rising Hope*, 1932.
13.2 x 22.1 cm
Private collection

Alfred Willimann, poster for
*Ausstellung Kunstgewerbe-
museum Zürich*, 1932.
129 x 90.6 cm
Private collection
Courtesy www.iaddb.org

Alfred Willimann
1900–1957

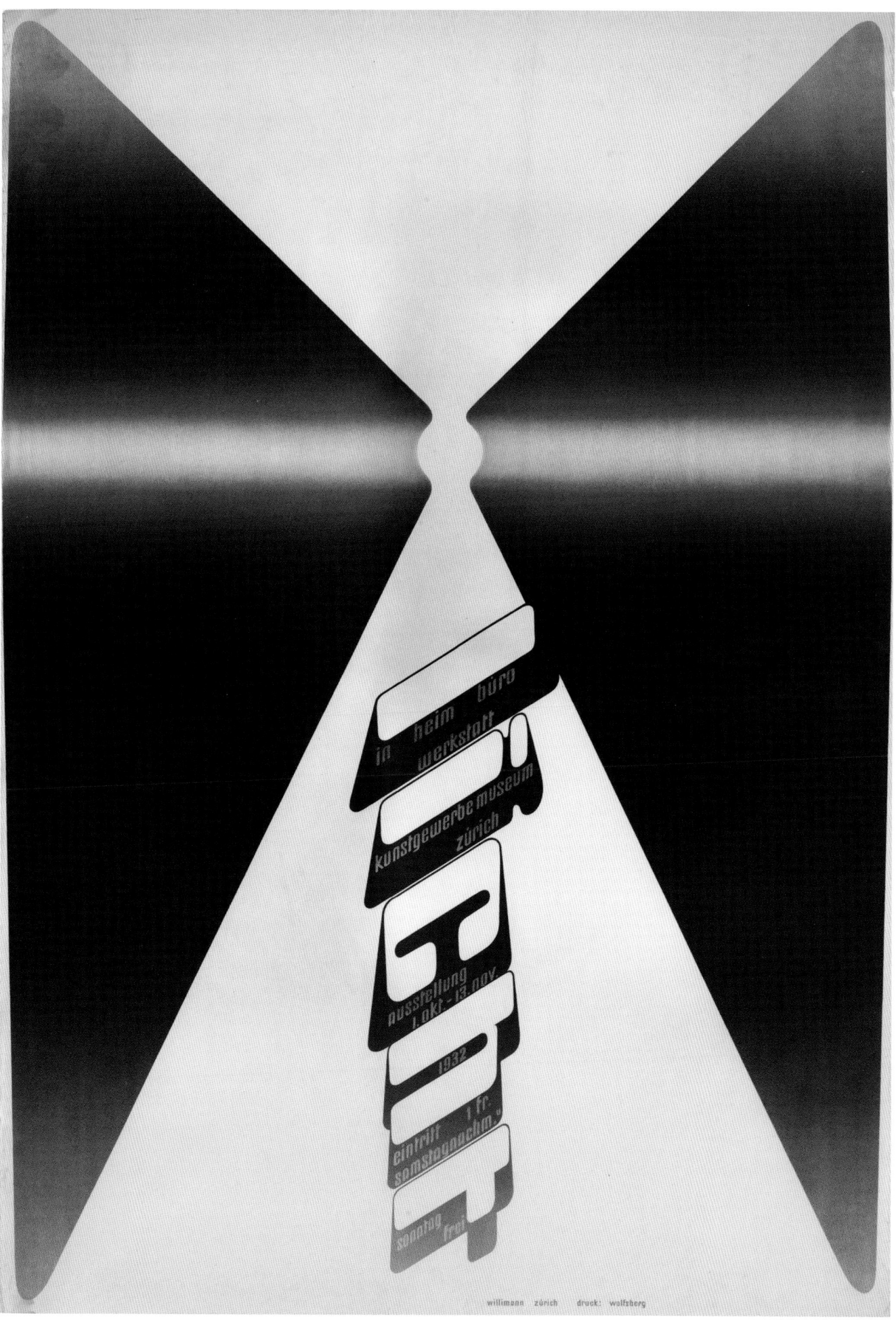

Max Gebhard (Gebs), election poster *Arbeiterkinder! Werdet junge Pioniere*, c. 1932.
72.5 x 49.5 cm
Private collection
Courtesy www.iaddb.org

Max Gebhard
1906-1990

1933

Herbert Matter
1907–1984

Herbert Matter, magazine cover for *Gebrauchsgraphik*, 1933.
30.9 x 23.4 cm
Private collection

Herbert Matter, cover and spreads for *Foto*, no. 5, 1933.
31.2 x 23 cm
Private collection

Steiner

Gotthard Schuh: Negativ

Widder

Steiner

353

Herbert Matter, travel poster for *Engelberg*, Switzerland, 1934.
102 x 64 cm
Private collection
Courtesy www.iaddb.org

Herbert Matter, travel poster
for Switzerland, *Svizzera*, 1934.
102 x 64 cm
Private collection
Courtesy www.iaddb.org

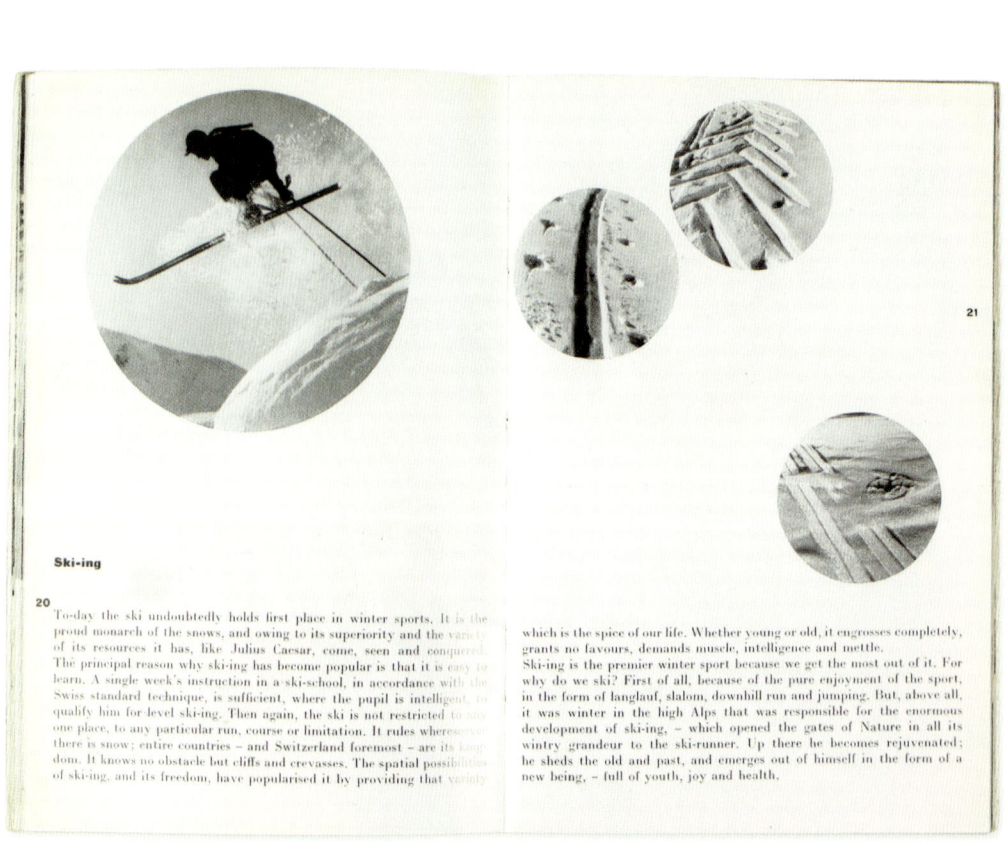

Herbert Matter, brochure cover and spreads for *Die Schweiz im Schnee*, 1935.
18 x 12.1 cm
Private collection

Swiss Ski-School

23

Standardized Technique everywhere

Herbert Matter, travel poster for *All Roads Lead to Switzerland*, 1935.
101 x 63.5 cm
Private collection
Courtesy www.iaddb.org

Herbert Matter, travel poster for *Pontresina*, Switzerland, 1936.
102 x 63.5 cm
Private collection
Courtesy www.iaddb.org

Andreas K. Hemberger,
poster for *BMW,* 1933.
102.5 x 74.5 cm
Private collection
Courtesy www.iaddb.org

Andreas K. Hemberger
1901-1978

František Muzika
1900–1974

František Muzika,
cover for *Povětroň*, 1934.
19.2 x 12.5 cm
Private collection

František Muzika, cover
for *Obyčejný život*, 1935.
19.2 x 12.5 cm
Private collection

1934

Pizzi & Pizio
Design grafico Anonimo

Pizzi & Pizio,
cover for *Milan*, 1934.
16.5 x 11.8 cm
Private collection

Pizzi & Pizio, cover for
L'Italie vue du ciel, 1936.
22.4 x 29.8 cm
Private collection

1934

Xanti Schawinsky
1904–1979

Xanti Schawinsky, cover for *S. A. Cervo Italia*, Princeps, 1934.
34.1 x 24.3 cm
Private collection

1934

Vojtěch Tittelbach
1900–1971

Vojtěch Tittelbach, cover for *Jaro 1934, Almanach Kmene*, 1934.
18.3 x 11.7 cm
Private collection

1935

Wim Brusse
1910–1978

Wim Brusse, book cover for *Mannen in leer*, 1935.
22 x 14.5 cm
Private collection

Wim Brusse, book cover for *Nieuwe mensen in Moskou*, 1935.
22.6 x 14.5 cm
Private collection

1935

Walter Herdeg
1908–1995

Walter Herdeg, cover and spread for *St. Moritz*, 1935.
22 × 11 cm
Private collection

Walter Herdeg, spread for
St. Moritz, 1935.
22 x 11 cm
Private collection

ST. MORITZ — «LE» centre des sports d'hiver! Tout le monde le sait: C'est à St. Moritz que se pratiquent tous les sports d'hiver. C'est à St. Moritz que se trouve la piste de bob la plus rapide du monde. C'est à St. Moritz que se disputent nombre de records. C'est à St. Moritz que la vie sportive rivalise d'éclat avec la vie mondaine. Pour n'importe quel sport, les conditions sont bonnes au possible – le décor naturel est incomparable. Le repos et le calme ne s'en offrent pas moins à qui les recherche. Le «promeneur» trouvera à sa disposition un vaste réseau de chemins soigneusement entretenus.

1935

Antonín Pelc
1895–1967

Antonín Pelc, cover and spreads for *Chléb domova*, 1935.
18.5 x 13.5 cm
Private collection

Antonín Pelc, cover for *Ve všech koutech světa*, 1935.
18.7 x 13.4 cm
Private collection

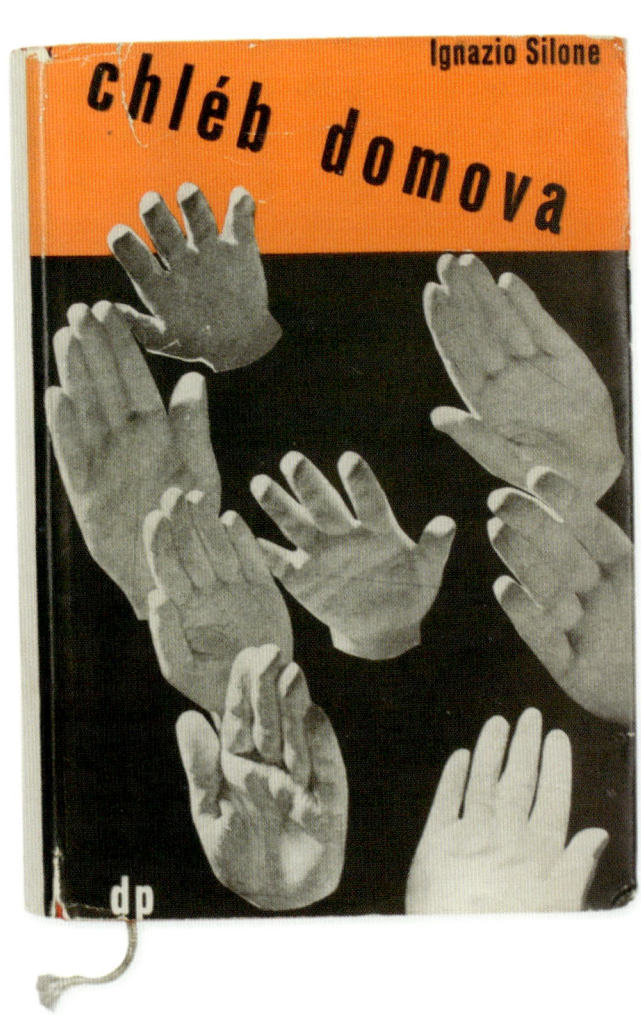

1935

Zdeněk Rossmann
1905–1984

Zdeněk Rossmann, cover and spreads for *Na shledanou*, 1935.
21.3 x 15 cm
Private collection

Hans Aeschbach
1911–1999

Hans Aeschbach, cover for a brochure *Die Schweiz*, 1936.
34.3 x 24.4 cm
Private collection

1936

Hermann Eidenbenz
1902–1993

Hermann Eidenbenz, brochure cover for *Grafa International*, 1936.
20.9 x 14.7 cm
Private collection

Hans Vitus Vierthaler, poster for Nazi exhibition of modern art in Munich, *Entartete Kunst*, 1936.
120 x 86 cm
Private collection
Courtesy www.iaddb.org

Hans Vitus Vierthaler
1910–1942

Geometric sans-serif alphabets, type specimen proofs, and other experiments with new type emerged after the late 1920s. An impression: the creative process of different designers for individual typefaces.

Sans-serif Typefaces

Herbert Bayer, design for
a universal alphabet, 1925.
22.5 x 30.5 cm
Private collection

Ferdinand Kramer,
Schablonenschrift (stencil font),
c. 1925.
28.5 x 19.8 cm
Collection Kramer Archiv,
Frankfurt am Main

Front page and pages of folder from the Bauersche Giesserei for the Futura typeface, c. 1927.
30.5 x 22.5 cm
Private collection

Rudolf Koch, typeface Kabel light, two ads from a series of ads that introduced Kabel's range of weights to German designers and printers, c. 1928.
28.5 x 20 cm
Private collection

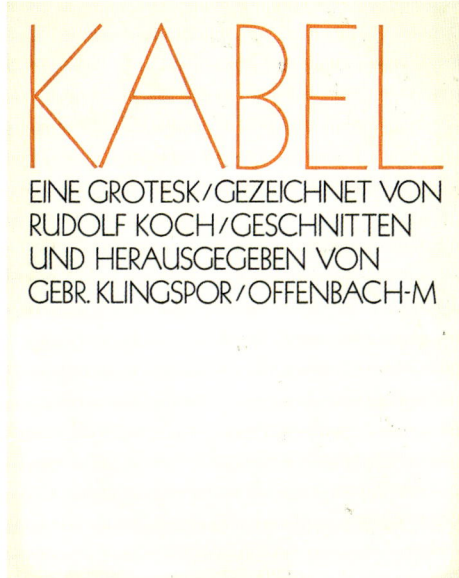

Jan Tschichold, type design 1928, from the magazine *Buch- und Werbekunst*, vol. 7, no. 7, p. 239, with the article "Das neue Plakat" by Jan Tschichold, 1930.
31.5 x 23.5 cm
Private collection

Jan Tschichold, front page and page from a type specimen of Transito, issued by Lettergieterij Amsterdam, 1931.
27.3 x 19.8 cm
Private collection

Paul Renner, Futura Type Specimen für Fotomontage, Bauersche Giesserei, Frankfurt am Main, c. 1930. 28.5 x 19.8 cm Collection Museum Angewandte Kunst, Frankfurt am Main. *Alles Neu!*, av edition, Stuttgart

Paul Renner, Futura Type Specimen 1, Bauersche Giesserei, c. 1930. 30.5 x 22.5 cm Collection Prof. Friedrich Friedl, Frankfurt am Main

Jan Tschichold, front-page advertisement folder for *Uhertype*, 1933.
29.7 x 21 cm
Private collection

Jan Tschichold, two pages of advertisement folder for *Uhertype*, the pioneering photo typesetting system, 1933.
29.7 x 21 cm
Private collection

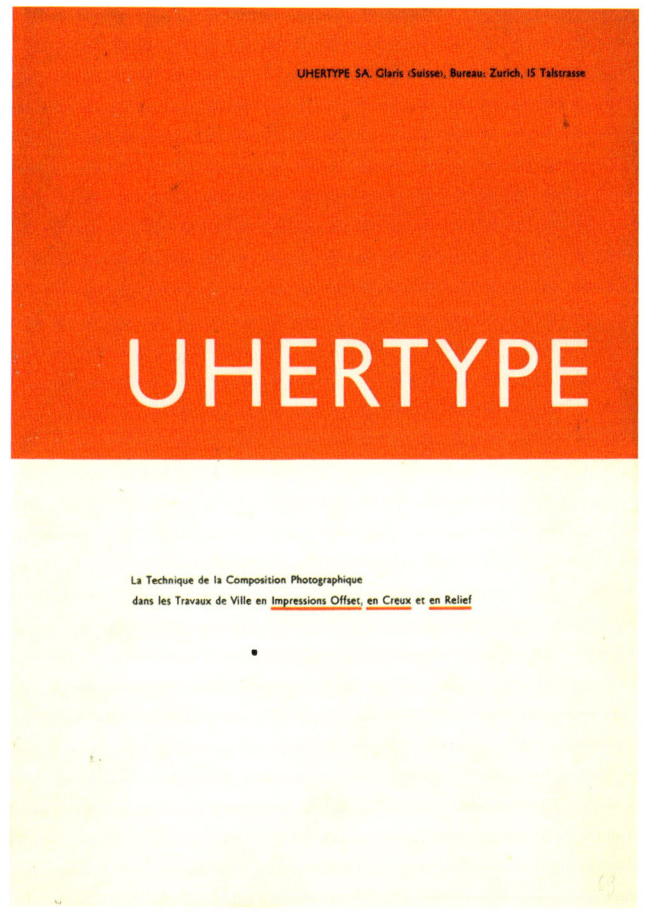

Previous page, a detail of:
Nikolai Prusakov & Grigori
Ilyich, poster, 1927.

Bibliography

A

Ades, Dawn. *The 20th-Century Poster: Design of the Avant-Garde*. New York: Abbeville Press, 1984.

Ades, Dawn. *Photomontage*. London: Thames & Hudson, 1976.

Ades, Dawn. *Dada and Surrealism Reviewed*. London: The Arts Council of Great Britain, 1978.

Ades, Dawn. *The Dada Reader: A Critical Anthology*. Chicago: University of Chicago, 2006.

Adkins, Helen. *Erwin Blumenfeld: Dada Montages 1916–1933: I was Nothing but a Berliner*. Berlin: Hatje Cantz, 2009.

Andel, Jaroslav. *Avant-Garde Page Design 1900–1950*. New York: Delano Greenidge Editions, 2002.

Andersen, Troels. *Malevich*. Amsterdam: Stedelijk Museum, 1970.

Arendt, Hannah. *Illuminations: Walter Benjamin*. New York: Schocken Books, 1969.

B

Barron, Stephanie and Sabine Eckmann. *New Objectivity: Modern German Art in the Weimar Republic 1919–1933*. Munich/London/New York: Delmonico Books/Prestel, 2015.

Bartram, Alan. *Bauhaus, Modernism and the Illustrated Book*. London: British Library, 2004.

Beek, Willem van. "El Lissitzky 1890–1941." *Kunstbeeld*. Volume 13, no. 12, December–January (1990–1991).

Bergdoll, Barry and Leah Dickerman. *Bauhaus, 1919–1933: Workshops for Modernity*. New York: Museum of Modern Art, 2009.

Blackwell, Lewis. *Twentieth-Century Type*. New York: Rizzoli International Publications, 1992.

Bookbinder, Paul. *Weimar Germany: The Republic of the Reasonable*. New York: Manchester University Press, 1996.

Borchardt-Hume, Achim (editor). *Albers and Moholy-Nagy: From the Bauhaus to the New World*. New Haven, CT: Yale University Press, 2006.

Bullivant, Keith (editor). *Culture and Society in the Weimar Republic*. Manchester: Manchester University Press, 1977.

Burke, Christopher. *Paul Renner: The Art of Typography*. London: Hyphen Press, 1998.

Bury, Stephen (editor). *Breaking the Rules: The Printed Face of the European Avant Garde 1900–1937*. London: British Library, 2007.

C

Cardinal, Roger and Gwendolen Webster. *Kurt Schwitters*. Berlin: Hatje Cantz, 2011.

Professor Childers, Thomas. *A History of Hitler's Empire, Second Edition*. Course guidebook. Chantilly, VA: The Great Courses, 2001.

Churton, Tobias. *Aleister Crowley: The Beast in Berlin; Art, Sex, and Magick in the Weimar Republic*. Rochester, VT/Toronto: Inner Traditions, 2014.

Cinamon, Gerald. *Rudolf Koch: Letterer, Type Designer, Teacher*. New Castle, DE: Oak Knoll Press, 2000.

Citroen, Paul, Kurt Löb, and Jan Bons. *Paul Citroen en het Bauhaus*. Utrecht/Antwerpen: A. W. Bruna & Zoon, 1974.

Cohen, Arthur A. *Herbert Bayer: The Complete Work*. Cambridge, MA: MIT Press, 1984.

Cohen, Elaine Lustig and Ellen Lupton. *Letters from the Avant Garde: Modern Graphic Design*. New York: Princeton Architectural Press, 1996.

Coutts-Smith, Kenneth. *Dada*. New York: E. P. Dutton and Co., Inc, 1970.

D

Dachy, Marc. *Dada: The Revolt of Art*. Translated by Liz Nash. London: Thames & Hudson, 2006.

Demetz, Peter. *Reflections: Walter Benjamin*. New York: Schocken Books, 1986.

Dluhosch, Eric and Rostislav Svácha (editors). *Karel Teige / 1900-1951*. Cambridge, MA: MIT Press, 1999.

Dooijes, Dick. *Over Typografie en Grafische Kunst*. Amsterdam, 1966.

Droste, Magdalena. *Bauhaus, 1919-1933*, Cologne: Benedikt Taschen Verlag GmbH & Co., 1990.

Drucker, Joanna. *The Visible Word: Experimental Typography and Modern Art, 1909 – 1923*. Chicago: The University of Chicago Press, 1994.

E

Evans, Richard J. *The Coming of the Third Reich*. New York: Penguin Group, 2003.

F

Friedrich, Otto. *Before the Deluge: A Portrait of Berlin in the 1920s*. New York: HarperCollins, 1995.

Friedman, Mildred. *De Stijl: 1917-1931: Visions of Utopia* New York: Abbeville Press, 1982.

G

Gay, Peter. *Modernism: The Lure of Heresy*. New York/London: W. W. Norton & Company, Inc., 2008.

Gay, Peter. *Weimar Culture: The Outsider as Insider*. New York/London: W. W. Norton and Company, 2001.

Girard, Xavier. *Bauhaus*. New York: Assouline, 2003.

Gordon, Mel. *Voluptuous Panic: The Erotic World of Weimar Berlin, Expanded Edition*. Port Townsend, WA: Feral House, 2000, 2006.

Gordon, Peter E. and John P. McCormick (editors). *Weimar Thought: A Contested Legacy*. Princeton and Oxford: Princeton University Press, 2013.

Grosz, George. *Ecco Homo*. Berlin: Malik-Verlag, 1923.

Gray, Camilla. *The Russian Experiment in Art 1863-1922*. London: Thames & Hudson, 1962.

Gualdoni, Flaminio. *Bauhaus*. Italy: Skira Editore, 2009.

H

Hansen, Thomas S. *Classic Book Jackets: The Design Legacy of George Salter*. New York: Princeton Architectural Press, 2005.

Holstein, Jürgen (editor). *The Book Cover in the Weimar Republic (Buchumschläge in der Weimarer Republik)*. Köln: Taschen, 2015.

Hopkins, David. *Dada and Surrealism: A Very Short Introduction*. Oxford: Oxford University Press, 2004.

Hubert, Renée Riese. *Surrealism and the Book*. Berkeley: University of California, 1988.

Hughes, Robert. *The Shock of the New: Art and the Century of Change*. London: British Broadcasting Corporation, 1980.

J

Jaffé, H. L. C. *De Stijl: 1917-1931*, Amsterdam: Meulenhoff/Landshoff, 1956, reprinted 1986.

James, Howard. *The Czech Avant-Garde and Czech Book Design: The 1920s and 1930s*. Madison, New Jersey: Fairleigh Dickinson University, 1995.

Janssen, Hans and Michael White. *The Story of De Stijl: Mondrian to Van Doesburg*. New York: Abrams, 2011.

Jong, Cees W. de, Alston W. Purvis, Martijn F. Le Coultre, Richard B. Doubleday, and Hans Reichardt. *Jan Tschichold, Master Typographer: His Life, Work and Legacy*. Laren, Netherlands: VK Projects; London: Thames & Hudson, 2008.

K

Kaes, Anton, Martin Jay, and Edward Dimendberg (editors). *The Weimar Republic Sourcebook*. Berkeley/Los Angeles/London: University of California Press, 1995.

Kahn-Magomedov, Selim O. *Rodchenko: The Complete Work*. Cambridge, MA: MIT Press, 1987.

Kater, Michael H. *Weimar: From Enlightenment to the Present*. New Haven, CT: Yale University Press, 2014.

Kepes, György. *Language of Vision: Painting, Photography, Advertising-Design*. Paul Theobald and Company: Chicago, 1944.

Kolb, Eberhard. *The Weimar Republic*. Translated by P. S. Falla and R. J. Park. New York: Routledge, 2005.

Kostelanetz, Richard. *Moholy-Nagy: An Anthology*. New York: Da Capo, 1991.

Kramer, Hilton. *The Triumph of Modernism: The Art World, 1985–2005*. Chicago: Ivan R. Dee, 2006.

L

Lavin, Maud. *Cut with the Kitchen Knife: The Weimar Photomontages of Hannah Höch*. New Haven, CT: Yale University Press, 1993.

Lewis, Beth Irwin. *George Grosz: Art and Politics in the Weimar Republic*. Madison, WI: The University of Wisconsin Press, 1971.

Le Coultre, Martjin F. and Alston W. Purvis. *Jan Tschichold: Posters of the Avantgarde*. Laren, Netherlands: VK Projects, 2007.

Lewis, Michael J. "The Bauhaus Restored." Review. *The New Criterion,* December 2009.

Lissitzky-Kuppers, Sophie and Herbert Read. *El Lissitzky: Life, Letters, Texts*. London: Thames & Hudson, 1968.

Löb, Kurt, Paul Roelof Citroen, and Jan Bons. *Paul Citroen en het Bauhaus*. Tschichold, Gualdoni, Flaminio. *Bauhaus*. Milan: Skira, 2009.

Lucie-Smith, Edward. *Lives of the Great 20th Century Artists*. London: Thames & Hudson, 1999.

M

Margolin, Victor. *The Struggle for Utopia: Rodchenko, Lissitzky, Moholy-Nagy, 1917–1946*. Chicago and London: The University of Chicago Press, 1997.

McLean, Ruari. *Jan Tschichold: Typographer*. Boston: David Massachusetts: David R. Godine, Publisher, Inc., 1975.

Mommsen, Hans. *The Rise and Fall of Weimar Democracy*. Chapel Hill and London: The University of North Carolina Press, 1996.

Moorsel, L. Leering-van. "The Typography of El Lissitzky." *The Journal of Typographic Research. Vol. II, no. 4, 1968, pp. 323–340.*

O

Orwell, George. *Homage to Catalonia*. London: Martin Secker & Warburg, reprint, 2008.

Overy, Paul. *De Stijl*. New York: Thames & Hudson, 1991.

P

Paret, Peter, Beth Irwin Lewis, and Paul Paret. *Persuasive Images: Posters of War and Revolution*. Princeton, NJ: Princeton University Press, 1992.

Peters, Olaf (editor). Preface by Ronald S. Lauder. Foreword by Renée Price. *Berlin Metropolis, 1918–1933*. Munich/London/New York: Prestel, 2015.

Peukert, Detlev K. *The Weimar Republic*. New York: Hill and Wang, 1987.

R

Richter, Hans. *Dada: Art and Anti-Art*. Translated by David Britt. London: Thames & Hudson, 1965.

Rodchenko, Aleksandr M. and Varvara F. Stepanova. *The Future Is Our Only Goal*. Munich: Prestel, 1991.

Roman, Harrison and Virginia Hagelstein Maquardt. *The Avant-Garde Frontier: Russia Meets the West*, 1910–1930. Gainesville, FL: University Press of Florida, 1992.

Rose, Jonathan. *The Holocaust and the Book*. Amherst: University of Massachusetts Press, 2001.

Roth, Joseph. *What I Saw*. Translated with an introduction by Michael Hofmann. Cologne: Kiepenheuer & Witsch; Amsterdam: Verlag de Lange, 1996.

Rothschild, Deborah, Ellen Lupton, and Darra Goldstein. *Graphic Design in the Mechanical Age: Selections from the Merrill C. Berman Collection*. New Haven, CT: Yale University Press, 1998.

Rubin, William S. *Dada, Surrealism, and Their Heritage*. New York: Museum of Modern Art, 1967.

S

Schrader, Bärbel and Jürgen Schebera. *The Golden Twenties: Art and Architecture in the Weimar Republic*. New Haven, CT and London: Yale University Press, 1990.